TAMING THE

TAMING THE PHOENIX

Cirencester and the Quakers
1642-1686

Brian Hawkins

William Sessions Limited
York, England

ISBN 1 85072 205 6

Printed in 11 on 12½ point Plantin typeface
from Author's disk
by Sessions of York
The Ebor Press
York, England

Contents

List of Illustrations

List of Tables

Abbreviations

Notes are to be found at the end of each chapter. The following abbreviations have been used in the text.

CSPD   H.M. Public Record Office: *Calendar of State Papers Domestic.*

GBS   *Great Book of Sufferings*, held in Friends House Library, London.

GRO   Gloucestershire Record Office.

Memoir –   *Memoir of John Roberts, by His Son, Daniel Roberts, verbatim as from the original manuscript* as given in E.T. Lawrence (1898): *A Quaker of Olden Time*, Headley, London.

MMfS   Minutes of the Meeting for Sufferings, London Yearly Meeting of the Religious Society of Friends.

MSS Memoir a manuscript copy of the Memoir of John Roberts held in the Gloucestershire Record Office, D 1829.

OR   *Some memoirs of the life of JOHN ROBERTS by his son DANIEL ROBERTS*, facsimile reproduction of a New Edition by Oade Roberts 1859, Friends Home Service Committee, London, 1973.

PRO   Public Record Office, Kew, London.

Preface

THE PHOENIX, RISING FROM its ashes to greet a new dawn, was adopted by the town of Cirencester as its emblem long before the outbreak of the English Civil War. As a sign of optimism and new beginnings, it must have held special significance at points of resurgence and new hope in the town's history. I believe that one such point was in the year 1642 when it seemed that the nation as a whole was about to shake off the trammels of feudalism and launch itself into the modern age. This book is about the shape that phoenix took and the methods by which it was eventually tamed.

The book is essentially about people and how they lived. Using the unique opportunity of a graphic contemporary biography to transform the historical record, we can enter the life-world of seventeenth century Gloucestershire, explore its priorities and understand more clearly why people behaved as they did. Its main characters are people like ourselves, bringing up children and making a living, though we do encounter some of the professionals and the gentry. There is much here for both the local and the family historian; and for the more general reader there is a good story with its excitement and humour, as well as some sadness.

A number have explored parts of our route before us, and I am grateful to them for the waymarkers that they have left behind. I think, for Gloucestershire history, of Sir Robert Atkyns, K. Beecham, R. Bigland, T. Fosbrooke, F. Hockaday, S. Rudder, and, for Quaker records, of W. Braithwaite, E. Lawrence and N. Penny. Then, there are the countless unnamed local historians and archivists who have helped to marshal and calendar the wealth of material now made available to us from the seventeenth century. And more immediately, my thanks must be expressed for the patient and efficient manner in which the staff of our county and public record offices, of the county local history collections, and of Friends House library have dealt with my demands and offered helpful advice.

I wish to acknowledge my debt to Joyce Barker and Linda Viner and other palaeographers of Cirencester who taught me to read and interpret seventeenth century manuscripts; to Russell Howe for his infectious enthusiasm and encyclopedic knowledge of Gloucestershire history; and to Trish for her forbearance, support and constant encouragement in this enterprise.

I am particularly pleased that it has been possible to include a number of illustrations to support the text. My thanks go to the Corinium Museum for permission to use the Kips engravings of Cirencester and Lipiatt Manor; to the Bingham Library for the prints of the Ram Inn, the Market Place and John Beecham's *Wrecking of Lord Chandos' coach*; to the Gloucestershire local history collection for the print of Dr. George Bull and that of the county gaol in Gloucester Castle; to Friends House Library for the print of John Roberts' house; to Brian Cater for his generosity in providing me with maps of Cirencester and Siddington; and to Trish for nobly filling in the gaps in the art work with the remaining illustrations.

Finally, I acknowledge the generous funding from the Sessions Book Trust which has helped to price this book within, I hope, the range of most readers.

Foreword

MOST OF US LEAVE FOOTPRINTS in the wet sands of this life, to be smoothed away, inexorably, within a short space, by the tides of time. Our persons and doings live on in the memory of family and acquaintances, perhaps for a generation or two, and then are forgotten. But occasionally who we are or what we have done inspires the observer to take up the pen and compose a record for posterity. Such an observer was Daniel Roberts, who, in his old age, felt that he could not leave this world without committing to paper the story of his father, John Roberts. Not that he thought it would invite a general audience or command wide interest, but at least the enterprise would justify the effort if later generations of his own family were able to admire their ancestor's courage, breathe his faith, smile at his wit and be thankful for his life.

In the event, his manuscript, since it was first published in 1746, has run to a further 34 editions or reprintings and gained for his father honourable mention in such standard Gloucestershire histories as Rudder's *A New History of Gloucestershire*, or Beecham's *History of Cirencester*, or Stratford's *Good and Great Men of Gloucestershire*, or, more recently, Rollison's *Local Origins of Modern Society, Gloucester 1500-1800*.

Daniel Roberts was born in 1658 and lived at a time when people felt a strong sense of family. Not only surnames, but often first names as well, were passed on, to be kept alive in their children. Heritage, heirlooms and family homes were prized, preserved and bequeathed. For those who possessed one and could read it, the family bible had become the symbol of continuity and time-lessness, of inspiration and comfort amid the changing fortunes of an uncertain existence. It was there, on blank pages that the births, deaths and marriages of family members were carefully and solemnly written, as memorials to be contemplated within the intimate circle of descendants. Undoubtedly there was a Roberts family bible, but Daniel, who had a gift for words, wanted to say a great deal more than could be fitted into so small a space. And so, in the last year of his life, Daniel, with the help of his unmarried daughter Elizabeth, composed *Some Memoirs of John Roberts*. His purposes were neither literary nor academic. This was to be a private document to be kept within the family.

Thus, major events on the public stage of history find little mention: it is not a chronicle of its age. Even local happenings, which the historian would identify as significant milestones in the development of Cirencester or frames to the life of its inhabitants, attract scant interest. The scene of action centres around the fireside of a farmhouse in Siddington Peter, or in the parlour of a town house in Chesham, Bucks., or even within the drab walls of the bridewell in Gloucester Castle, where the tales were told and re-told. Characters who make up the web of local daily life – whether the squire, or the priest, or treasured friends and family – appear on cue and re-enact events which hold great meaning for the teller and his circle. But it is not dumb-show. They have lines to speak as well as attitudes to strike: questions to ask, replies to make, threats to utter and beliefs to proclaim. Such is the liveliness of this family story-telling which wiles away most pleasantly and instructively the long hours of a winter evening or dreary years of unjust imprisonment.

These are the strong merits of Daniel's tale. The door is opened on the inner thought world of a family group in the second half of the seventeenth century. The contours of their priorities and values, of their aspirations and fears, can be picked out. They speak their mind unashamedly and without reserve, for they speak in confidence before kin and close friends. Personal uncertainties, inner conflicts, moments of religious experience, normally kept hidden from public gaze and guarded against censure or mockery, are fully revealed. The family is of middle rank, industrious, respected, compassionate, but locked in an ideological struggle with a social establishment which is bent on its destruction. Thus, in its revealings, Daniel's account has much to contribute to an understanding of the social and religious conflicts of the age.

His story stands in its own right, as its many editions witness, but for modern readers, possessing a more developed sense of historicity, the events it relates lack precision as to historical time and political circumstance. Daniel saw his world in terms of local personalties, friendly or hostile, and his time-scale was that of his own life. It is to amplify the account in the *Memoirs* that I attempt this study – to locate it in the ebb and flow of events in Gloucestershire and on the wider national stage.

Using the *Memoirs* as a biographical framework, my purpose is to take the modern reader back to the busy seventeenth century market town of Cirencester and view the scene through the eyes of a local yeoman farmer. One of the richnesses of the *Memoirs* is the frequent use of dialogue, and this I shall draw upon freely, so that we can hear authentic voices, often with a Gloucestershire burr. To this will be added other voices of the period, drawn from letters, reports, journals, narratives or pamphlets, from Gloucestershire as far as possible, but from further afield when necessary. Factual material, as to dates, persons and places, and summaries of events will be derived from the many contemporary church, legal and Quaker records still available to us. To create a 'feel' for the period, I shall retain the spelling, punctuation and syntax of the originals; such features say much about the education and social background of the writer. But dates I shall modernize, ignoring the seventeenth century practice of beginning the year on Lady Day in March. I also override earlier Quaker sensitivities at naming days and months after pagan deities. Notes will be provided to amplify points, but principally to indicate where to explore the subject further.

The text of the *Memoirs* to be used is that contained in E.T. Lawrence's *A Quaker of Olden Time*. This well-researched edition of the *Memoirs* can be found in public libraries, and is much to be preferred to the more readily available Victorian version, abridged and partly re-written by Oade Roberts. Page references to both editions are given in the notes. Readers who consult Lawrence will find that he embarked on this enterprise 100 years before us, and his preparatory work will make our journey the smoother. He was, however, addressing a different age and relied principally on a collection of Roberts family papers and the work of Joseph Besse. Today not only do we have the benefit of the work of William

Braithwaite and Norman Penny and the transformation of seventeenth century studies pioneered by Christopher Hill, but there is also more readily accessible to us a wealth of primary source material in our county and public record offices and in the library of Friends House, London.

John Roberts, known in his day as John Hayward or Roberts *alias* Hayward, was born in the early 1620s and was old enough to serve in the Civil War; he was also idealist enough to feel quite betrayed by its outcomes. He lived on through the period of the Restoration and died in 1684. We shall begin our exploration by considering the town of Cirencester itself, where he was educated and which he often visited, then the village of Siddington where his family lived. His near encounter with death in the Civil War leads to his re-assessment of his own life and the beginning of a determined spiritual search. This will take us into the turbulent waters of the later Commonwealth and the Restoration, where the growth of a group of like-minded people in the Cirencester area presents a serious challenge to the church and civil establishments. It is through the bitter conflict that this engenders that we shall be able to penetrate the opaqueness of everyday life and glimpse a little more clearly the values, motivation and relationships of ordinary folk in the town more than 300 years ago. I hope that the reader will find the experience both enjoyable and instructive.

CHAPTER 1

The Seventeenth Century Town

> Cirencester has been distinguished from the remotest Period
> of this Kingdom, in Time of our Subjection to the Roman
> Empire, as a large and magnificent City; and since the
> Conquest by the Normans, as a principal Vill or Borough, of
> which Description it still remains.
>
> Ralph Bigland: *Historical, Monumental*
> *and Genealogical Collections*

M ODERN CIRENCESTER STANDS AT the gateway to the
southern Cotswolds. Administratively the chief town of the
Cotswold District, and commercially a thriving centre of busy
shops, light industry and a livestock market, it provides for a
medium-sized population. Its attractiveness to the growing
numbers of those who choose to make it their place of retirement,
or to the many groups of tourists and school children who visit, lies
not so much in these features as in its quaintness and the strong
sense of history it exudes. Its parish church, a prominent landmark
for miles around, is a mini-cathedral from the fifteenth century, set
centrally in a confusing pattern of narrow mediaeval streets lined
with buildings in Cotswold limestone. And earlier than these,
vestiges of Roman occupation can be found in an impressive
amphitheatre, sections of the city wall and in the many artefacts
unearthed from under its streets and buildings and now preserved
in a celebrated specialist museum.

Roman Corinium had been the second largest town of the
Province of Britannia, covering a 240 acre site, and located at the

1

hub of a wheel of major highways radiating from it. Following the withdrawal of Roman power from Britain during the fifth century this prominent political and economic centre fell into general decay, and its ruins were eventually re-occupied by Saxon settlers who established themselves more modestly within its ramparts, selecting the slightly higher ground to the north of the forum. Saxon 'Cyrencaestre' was traversed from north to south by the still important Ermine Street, while the east-west line of the Fosse (Lewis Lane) formed its southern boundary. The southern sector of the Roman town was not occupied and eventually reverted to grazing land.

The rigidity of the Roman grid system of streets, implying dense occupation of the site, was abandoned by the less numerous Saxons in favour of straggling ribbon development along a more elementary street pattern, adopted to suit a smaller and less organized population. The establishment of an abbey in Norman times perpetuated this pattern since its endowment with lands to the east and west of Ermine Street, and to the north of the market place, had the effect of strangling housing development and permitted little modification to the existing streets. At the dissolution of the abbey in 1539 its estates were divided into two large holdings which became, in the seventeenth century, the extensive estates associated with the early Jacobean manor houses of Oakley Grove to the west and Cirencester Abbey centrally and stretching towards the east. These large estates maintained the constricting pressures, so that the mediaeval street pattern has continued largely unchanged to the present day, apart from a widening of the market place in the nineteenth century. Expansion south of the Fosse (Lewis Lane) into the Watermoor Common area and Pitacre Estate did not take place until the 1850s.

The eleven streets and associated lanes described by Rudder in 1779[1] as composing the town are quite recognizable to us, and most appear again in the list of the Lady Chapel Register of 1460:[2] Dyer-strete, Cricklade-strete, New-strete, Fosse, Shoter-strete, Gosditch-strete, Cecily-strete, Battle-strete, Raton-rewe, St. Lawrence-strete and Abbot-strete. Tomkins proposes that among a less literate populace of the mediaeval or early modern period the naming of streets would have depended less on written signs and

Cirencester Abbey, seat of the Master family.

Cirencester with Oakley Grove, seat of Viscount Newburgh.

more on custom and word of mouth.[3] Thus, street names could become more readily corrupted with usage, as in the case of Dollar (Dolehall) Street or Sheep (Shoter) Street, or a given street may have been known by more than one name. In local wills and deeds of the period we find St. Thomas alias Battle Street, or Black Jack Street and St. John Street, or Dyer Street and Chepying Street being used concurrently. Fig. 1.1 is a putative outline of the seventeenth century town, based on the researches of Reece and Catling.[4]

These mediaeval street names re-appear in an important source document of 1608.[5] This is a compilation of those men capable of bearing arms. The entries for the hundred of Cirencester are arranged under the headings of seven streets: Dyer, Castle, Dollar, St. Lawrence, Criclet, Instrope, and Gosditch. These are perhaps better conceived as wards of the town: the street in question with its associated side lanes and courts. The sequencing of the entries of men's names for each 'street' is not alphabetical, nor by occupation, nor by their assessed utility to the militia. If one accepts that it is not random sequencing, then a possible explanation could be that the lists follow the order of the houses along each street, probably beginning from the 'better' end, for example leading off the market place. Thus, John Robert's father, also a John Roberts *alias* Hayward, appears as John Hayward, a chandler, living at the far end of Cricklade Street, the main road leading south, next to the inn kept by Henry Powle. In addition to each man's name and residence, details of occupation, height and approximate age are given, with some assessment as to his potential as a soldier. John Hayward was aged about 20, and classified as 'of middle stature fitt to make a musketyer'.

By using the data of residents' occupations, we can reach some assessment of the character of particular areas of the town.

Dyer Street (formerly Chepying Street) appears to be one of the smarter streets, containing the houses of several gentlemen and a large wine merchant. At the top end, where it widens to form the marketplace, are the two barber-surgeons and an apothecary, and the establishments of two mercers, a hatter, a draper and a brazier. Further down is a baker, a butcher and a victualler. Possibly in the side lanes are the houses of the seven weavers, the workshops of

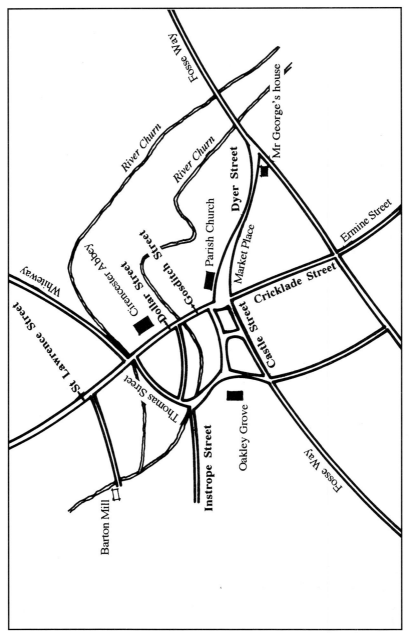

Fig. 1.1: *Map of seventeenth century Cirencester.*

ten shearers, and a boarding house for three labourers. Well down the street are a farrier, two saddlers, a plumber and a cutler.

Castle Street[6] has quite a different character, occupied almost entirely by artisans: four smiths, three joiners, two masons, two butchers, two weavers, two tailors, a bookbinder, a young musician and, on the marketplace, the scrivener.

The Dollar Street area is one of contrasts. Some distance down, next to a well-to-do clothier, lives a gentleman, with another gentleman living at the far end. However, two tanners have their yards there, supplying five shoemakers. There are two smaller clothiers and the homes of nine weavers, some certainly in Coxwell Street, five glovers, a hatter and a tailor. Two butchers and a baker serve the 'street'.

St. Lawrence Street (now Gloucester Street) has the largest grouping of weavers, fourteen in all, some large enough to employ a living-in assistant. At the top end is the establishment of a large clothier. Six shoemakers have their businesses there. In the side courts, or possibly lodging with some of the weavers, are fourteen labourers. Other houses are occupied by two tailors, a glover, a pavier and a tiler.

Cricklade Street is different again. It has an inn on the marketplace and another at the far end. Five butchers live next to one another, which suggests the 'shambles',[7] with two further down the street, or living adjacent in side lanes. There are also the establishments of a large saddler and a large clothier. At the further end the character is agricultural, with the farms of two yeoman farmers, and cottages of two husbandmen, a shepherd and a gardener. Eight labourers, even a loiterer, reside there. Living in the side lanes, perhaps, are two weavers and two card-makers, together with two slaters and a mason.

Instrope Street (afterwards St. Cecyly Street, and now Cecily Hill) belongs to the poorer area. A short street of 22 entries, there are nine labourers, a wood yard with two sawyers and a carpenter, a carrier, a pedlar, a shepherd, one weaver and one tailor, and at the top end a brewer.

Gosditch Street is the most populous division in the town.[8] At the 'better' end, it has six mercers, a collar-maker and a card-maker.

But then come the ale-house, a transport business with two carters and two ostlers, a coaching inn with inn-keeper and tapster, two chamberlains and two ostlers. Lower down, or round the corner, there are another carter, another ostler and a smith, and at the further end two wheelwrights and a sixth ostler, all drawing their trade from the travellers on Ermine Street, Akeman Street and the Fosse, which intersect in the town. Busy with this traffic, it would also see the livestock or carcasses supplied to six butchers, and possibly the flock of the shepherd living there. Three husbandmen and a hivemaker also contribute to an agricultural character, but there are the building tradespeople as well – carpenter, mason, joiner, glazier and smith – and, perhaps in side lanes, six weavers, two glovers, a draper and a tailor.

The distinctive character of the town wards receives confirmation from the hearth tax returns of some sixty years later (Fig. 1.2). Between 1662 and 1689 a yearly tax of two shillings per hearth was levied on all dwellings with an annual value of more than twenty shillings. Those living in houses worth less than this figure were discharged by legal certificate; also exempt were all who were in receipt of poor relief. Not all the entries for Cirencester are any longer decipherable, but sufficient are legible for general conclusions to be drawn. The poorer areas are strung principally along the north-south axis of Ermine Street in the Lawrence (Gloucester Street) and Cricklade wards, where the paupers are housed and householders too poor to pay the tax outnumber taxpayers. There is a further area of poorer housing in the Instrope ward. The Dollar ward maintains its contrasts, with a higher preponderance of larger houses, set against a sizable number of humble dwellings. Clearly, the better and middling sort have gravitated towards the Dyer and Gosditch wards, where more than 70% of the householders are classed as taxpayers. Dyer ward has seen considerable expansion since the beginning of the century.

Among Washbourn's collection of documents relating to the Civil War in Gloucestershire is a Royalist account of Prince Rupert's capture of Cirencester in February 1643, which provides further insight into the physical features of mid-seventeenth century Cirencester:

Figure 1.2: *Hearth Tax Returns* (GRO D 383)

A Survey of Firehearths and Stoves within the County of Gloucester and Citty and County of Gloucester for a whole yeare. Viz from Michelmas 1671 (thereafter) to Michelmas 1672 Exclusive. Viewed and surveyed by me Charles Smyth Gent. Receiver.

CIRENCESTER

Taxpaying households

ward	no. of hearths	no. of houses	av. no. of hearths	% total no. of houses for ward
Castle	112	47	2.4	57
Cricklade	?	52	?	46
Dollar	182	61	3.0	61
Dyer	282	105	2.7	74
Gosditch	*212	70	*3.0	72
Instrope	?	17	?	46
Lawrence	65	28	2.3	37

* this figure is distorted by three large houses occupied by Lady Poole (21 hearths), Thomas Master (18), and Mr. B. (14). Excluding these, the number of hearths would read 159, with an average of 2.4 hearths per house.

Non-taxpaying households

ward	no. of hearths	no. of paupers	no. of houses	% total no. of houses for ward
Castle	38	–	36	43
Cricklade	54	12	61	54
Dollar	44	–	40	40
Dyer	38	–	37	26
Gosditch	31	–	27	28
Instrope	25	–	20	54
Lawrence	42	9	48	63

a town of many streets and 2,000 communicants .... It is more
than half incompassed with water, a great part with a high wall
.... The gardens and backsides [yards] be divided by many dry
stone walls.[9]

Interest turns on the defences of the town, and the valour of
the Royalists in penetrating them. The Spittalgate, to the east, was
particularly impregnable, 'defended by high walls and works, and
houses whose eaves were lined with musquetiers'. Gun batteries
were set up in the gardens of large houses, 'on Mr. Poole's mount
at the SW corner, another in George's backside [rear of the house]
at the SE corner'; and in the centre, at Cirencester Abbey, the
residence of Sir Thomas Master, was mounted a brass sacker. At
the western approaches to the town, down the lane from
Minchinhampton to Cecily Hill (the route of Prince Rupert's main
force), there was a high garden wall, extending from the lane up to
the mount in Mr. Poole's garden. On the other side of the lane was
Giffard's house (Barton House) and a square high garden wall with
farm buildings. To the north of the town, at Gloucester street end,
was 'voyd ground' with two water mills. 'By this runns the river
and other waters'; this area is still often water-logged in winter.

The action to capture the town lasted 90 minutes, suggesting
that there was minimal damage to the fabric of the buildings, other
than the known firing of Barton House, though a Parliamentary
account[10] does to refer to the deliberate firing of some houses after
the town had been taken. Nevertheless, there appears to have been
a steady re-building following the Civil War, with a change in
building style from the timber frames of the Tudor period to a
preference for stone and mullioned windows with drip moulds.
Dated stone buildings can be found in Coxwell Street for 1658
(No.1), 1676 (No.2), 1674 (No.25); in Gloucester Street for 1679
(No.105) and 1694 (No.7); with the keystone arch of the Unitarian
chapel in a court off Gosditch Street inscribed 1672. The original
part of the Friends' Meeting House dates from 1673. Undated
buildings of this period have been identified by Reece and Catling[4]
and include further houses in Coxwell and Gloucester Streets, and
Beeches Grove. The earlier half-timbered style predominates in
early prints of the town, which also depict Butter Row, Butcher
Row and Shoe Lane, demolished in 1826 to widen the market-

place. Beecham (1887) recalls the overhanging picturesque Tudor buildings in Cricklade Street which had been pulled down only 20 years earlier at a dangerous angle in the street.[11]

Contained in Atkyns' survey,[12] published in 1712, are engravings of some of the county's notable stately homes by the Dutch artist, Kips. These include for Cirencester: firstly, the Jacobean mansion of Cirencester Abbey, residence of Sir William Master, standing in formal gardens stretching down to the Churn and the former Abbey fishponds, its Park lying beyond, lost in the distance; and secondly, Oakley Grove, in 1712 the residence of Allen Bathurst, Esq., but retaining its Jacobean E-shape before being later remodelled by this new owner.[13] Both engravings convey a general, if optimistic, impression of Cirencester at the end of the seventeenth century: its ribbon development along the main thoroughfares, comprising mainly two and three storey houses with lengthy gardens; Gloucester House, residence of William George, and the succession of inns along Dyer Street, with the former Ram Inn at the head of the market place; the plain-fronted Monmouth House in Thomas Street; and the extensive gardens of the three main residences. Atkyns, whose own seat was at Pimbury Park, five miles away at Sapperton, comments of his neighbours:

> Master hath a very pleasant large House in this Town, with beautiful Gardens, and a large Enclosure of Rich Pasture, near the Church on the site of the Abbey. ... Another handsome house and gardens in the Town, late the possession of William George of Baunton.[14]

The latter house stands in the left foreground, the 'backside' at the southeast corner of the town which figured prominently in the defences during the Civil War.

A visitor to the town at the end of 1682, Thomas Baskerville, comments on the 'fair streets, good houses and inns, of which the 'King's Head' is chief'. Staying at the latter inn, he was particularly taken with the church tower and its 'eight very tunable bells, with which the young men are much delighted, as also with the art of singing, for lying at the 'King's Head in the Christmas holidays, in the morning before day, as I lay in my bed I heard them sing some Christmas carols very musically'.[15]

The bells must have been something of a special attraction; as early as 1615 a vestry meeting was instructing the churchwardens: 'yf anie Strainger be desirous to heare the Bells for pleasure that he geve three shillings for every peele ... and every Townsman two shillings and six pence for every peele'.[16] By 1614 the church tower had already been fitted with a chiming clock, for which the sexton was responsible.[17] In 1683 there is record of an organ being erected in the church by contributions of the town and neighbourhood, and Charles Badham was appointed organist on 16 July 1684.[18] The church was also the repository for three great church ladders, 74 fire buckets, the town crook (for pulling down burning thatch) and, by the end of the century, the 'large Engine for extinguishing Fire', donated by Sir Benjamin Bathurst; a sober reminder of the ever-present danger in the seventeenth century of fire rapidly engulfing a whole town.[19]

*   *   *

Atkyns[20] computes the number of houses as 800 with 4,000 inhabitants at the end of the century. There are 103 births and 87 burials annually, which would suggest a steady increase in population. But the population figure of 4,000 is confirmed by the later Diocesan survey of 1735. Atkyns describes the parish:

> It consists of Arable Land, with a good Share of Meadow, Pasture and Woods; the River Churn runs thro' it, and is there divided for the Benefit of the Town and for the Use of several Mills.[14]

Water from the Churn, in fact, flowed down St. Lawrence Street (Gloucester Street) in an open channel, five feet deep in parts, as far as the second bridge at the end of Dollar Street, where it re-entered the river.[21] The channel was later filled in 1780 . At the bottom of Cecily Hill was Gumstool Bridge over one of the arms of the river, the site of the ducking-stool and a watering place for horses. Park Street and Park Lane were formerly known as Lawditch, which took its name from the stream which flowed through it, and between Coxwell Street and Black Jack Street ran an open sewer, not arched over until 1854. It is unlikely, however, that many of the inhabitants drew their drinking water from these supplies: Rudder comments that 'the water is sufficiently pure and pleasant, rising in a fine gravel fourteen or fifteen feet below the surface, and almost every house has a pump.'[1]

Rudder, a Cirencester bookseller and printer, is at pains to demonstrate the more healthy climate of the Cotswolds in comparison with that of the Severn Vale, quoting in support the case of a Cirencester doctor at the beginning of the eighteenth century:

> The air is so remarkably pure and salubrious that a physician who settled here about forty years since, after staying a time sufficient, as he thought, to make his success, pronounced it impossible for one of his profession to subsist on the practice the town and the neighbourhood afforded.[1]

Despite the substantial rebuilding in stone of the houses and businesses of the affluent middle class during the eighteenth century, Beecham points out, however, that poorer people were forced to live in dwellings in courts, in many cases unfit for human habitation, which remained until the Victorian era.

Centred on the parish church were a number of charities established by local benefactors to relieve the sufferings of these people. The charities were administered by the churchwardens, who were supported in this work by a 'Biddle of the Beggars', a kind of moral guardian of the poor. The office had been created in 1618 and by 1641 was paying the beadle £8 per annum; it may have lapsed during the Commonwealth period but was revived in 1666. The beadle's task was to exercise a careful scrutiny: keeping 'strange' [from elsewhere] beggars out of the town; preventing charity money being paid to the 'wicked' poor; ensuring that those 'honest' poor in receipt of charity did not offend by idleness, drunkenness or theft; 'travaylling up and downe the streetes to make enquiry what honest poore by sickness or any other ympotency are fallen into great wante'; giving 'knowledge to such Alehouse keepers as entertayne in theire houses such poore as in theire drunkenes spende theire Evenyngs without all care of wyfe and children at home'; preventing any poor begging in the streets, and ensuring 'that no children or younge people above the age of seaven yeares be suffered to wander or go idlye about the streetes'; and giving 'warning to the poore they be of good behaviour that with their noyse of chydinge and stryvinge amongst themselves they give no offence'. He had the additional duties of impounding roaming pigs, making householders clear any rubbish from in front of their doors and 'to take specyall care for the restrayning and punishing of such as in a rude and brutish manner do fowle and defyle the streetes to the great annoyance of the Inhabytants and other pasingers [passers-by]'.[23]

Three ancient charitable institutions existed during our period: St. Lawrence's Church, converted into a hospital at the corner of Barton Lane for two poor women who each received 12d weekly; St. John's hospital for three poor men and three poor women given 20d weekly; and St. Thomas' hospital or Weavers Hall 'for the Benefit of four decayed Weavers' at 8d each weekly.

Individuals made their legacies to charity in the form of gifts of money, but frequently in bequests of houses or farm land. An annual sum of £67 derived from the rents of houses in the town was used to repair the parish church and also to provide £8 towards the salary of the schoolmaster at the grammar school. The latter received, in addition, £20 from the Exchequer. The work of the school will be explored more fully in our next chapter.

★   ★   ★

There were three fairs held annually, the first on Easter Monday, a second on the Feast of St. Simon and St. Jude (28 October) and the third on the Feast of Thomas à Beckett (29 December). In addition, two Cloth Fairs were held, one in the week before Palm Sunday and the other in the week before the Feast of St. Bartholemew (24 August).

As nowadays, Mondays and Fridays were market days. The Monday market was for Corn, Cattle and Provisions, of which Leland writes in 1535: 'Cirencester hath the most celebrate market in al that quarter on a Monday', listing besides it only Bristol, Gloucester and Tewkesbury as the other market towns in the county.[23] Atkyns describes the Friday market as being 'chiefly for Wooll, for which Commodity it is the greatest Market in England'.[14] Atkyns' assessment is confirmed by Defoe who visited the town at the turn of the seventeenth century:

> Cirencester is still a very good town, populous and rich, full of clothiers, and driving a great trade in wool – which is brought from Leicester, Northampton and Lincoln where the largest

sheep in England are found and where are few manufactures. The vast quantities sold here are almost incredible. The wool is bought up here chiefly by the clothiers of Wilts and Gloucestershire for the supply of that great clothing trade I have mentioned already. They talk of 5000 packs a year.[24]

The growth of this wool market had coincided with a decline in wool production in the downland areas of Wiltshire, Hampshire and Dorset, where Defoe observes a change to arable farming, particularly wheat production. Wool was now being transported from the north-east to meet the increasing deficiency in the south and, in particular, to satisfy the needs of a flourishing cloth industry which had developed around Trowbridge and Bradford along the Avon valley.

The wool market was held in the Boothall which, until 1812, stood on the site of the present Corn Market building in the market place. Writing in the middle of the eighteenth century, Rudder[1] records the collapse of this market, undermined by wool dealers travelling the country and buying wool direct at the farmhouse door; yet within living memory of his contemporaries, 'vast quantities out of Bucks, Berks, Northampton and Oxfordshire were brought weekly, and the principal street so thronged with wool waggons that it was difficult for other carriages to pass'.

Some of Rudder's waggons would have used new turnpike roads established during the eighteenth century, hence supplies of wool being drawn from a sector located to the east of the town. In 1700, however, and earlier, supplies of wool were being brought south down a corridor running north-east along the line of the Fosse Way. Defoe praises this 'common road' (i.e. free of tolls) as a 'grand highway', a principal arterial road into which a series of other ancient routes fed: Akeman Street from Buckinghamshire joining the Fosse a few miles to the east of Cirencester, Grimms Dike and Aves Ditch from Oxfordshire, and the Wold Way (Ermine Street) from Gloucester. He is astounded at the good state of repair of the Roman roads after 1200 years, discusses in some detail Roman road building techniques, contrasts these with the deplorable state of the English roads, particularly those from the north to London passing through the clay districts of the Midlands, and regrets that now at the end of the seventeenth century it would be impossible to emulate ever again the glory that was Rome, the price of labour being what it is.

Such enthusiasm for travelling the Fosse was not shared by Shakespeare at the beginning of the seventeenth century, who has the Duke of Northumberland complain of 'the tediousness and process of my travel' from the Yorkshire coast to Berkeley Castle, describing the Cotswolds as:

> These high wild hills and rough uneven ways
> Draws out our miles and makes them wearisome.[25]

One of the principal problems facing road-builders is the availability of suitable material. Marshall, in his study of the rural economy of Gloucestershire, points out:

> Roads are made across these [Cotswold] hills with singular facility – pits are dug by the sides of them and stones wheeled on, in barrows. The materials are more plentiful than durable, presently grinding down under heavy carriage. But the repairs are equally easy as the forming.[26]

Nevertheless, there were times when the state of the roads was far from satisfactory. At the Quarter Sessions of Easter 1682 the justices of the peace found it necessary to fine Cirencester £50, the village of Siddington £12 and the hamlet of Chesterton £10 to enforce the repair of the local roads.[27]

By the middle of the century these roads were being used by a regular postal service, established under the Commonwealth and continued at the Restoration. In 1666 the post for the 'Gloucester road' was leaving London at 2.00 a.m. at usually weekly intervals, and arriving in Gloucester two days later at 5.00 or 6.00 a.m. There were complaints that the post boys, who were on horse-back, were only averaging 3 mph, and attempts were made to achieve an average of 5 mph during the winter months, and 7 mph between March and September.[28]

The roads were also the haunt of highwaymen. In 1677 John Hodges, imprisoned in Hertford jail, confessed his involvement in attacks on travellers in the vicinity of Cirencester:

> Thomas at the *Plow* at Cirencester did set [set up to be robbed] a pedlar woman of Burford to Moore and others [his confederates] for £200. They had Hodges' horses but took only £5

and 20 black hoods. The said person and Harry, an idle fellow of the town, robbed a Welsh drover of £100 near Cirencester. Bowsier and they have often said that they used to knock the woolmen down and take their money.[29]

★   ★   ★

Not only wool but other goods would have been transported down the Fosse Way and thus passed through the town. Defoe mentions Gloucester cheese which 'Gloucestershire men carry all by land carriage to Cricklade and Lechlade on the Thames, and so carry it down the river to London. ... [At Lechlade] you see very large barges at the key, taking in goods for London, which makes Lechlade a very populous place'.[30] It was during the early part of the seventeenth century that the Thames had been made navigable, the first barge reaching Oxford in 1635. Older inhabitants of Lechlade in 1719 could remember the wharves and warehouses being built in the 1650s.[31] Thomas Baskerville, in 1682, describes the river at Lechlade as 'thick set with boats full of provisions brought from Oxford'.

> Here is yearly kept on the 29th of August in a meadow by St. John's Bridge a very great fair for cattle, cheese and other commodities, more especially sage cheese, in various shapes and colours which I have scarce seen anywhere else to be sold.[15]

In 1664 Charles II had confirmed to Sir Edward Bathurst the right to hold a fair and market at Lechlade, and to have a free wharf there, prohibiting all others from holding fairs.[32]

According to Defoe, the principal area of cheese production was the lowland area stretching south from Cirencester to the Wiltshire ridgeway. This district was 'full of large feeding farms, called dairies' which made a cheese 'excellent good of its kind ... being soft and thin [it] is eaten newer than the Cheshire'. In spring the farms produced 'a vast quantity of what we call green cheese, resembling cream cheese, only thicker and very rich', so popular that they were unable to supply the demands of the London market. In conjunction with cheese manufacture there developed extensive pig-farming, producing high quality bacon for, again, the London market; 'the hogs being fed with the vast quantity of whey and skimm'd milk which so many farmers have to spare, and which must otherwise be thrown away'.[30]

*   *   *

The presence of a thriving wool market at Cirencester fostered the growth of cloth manufacture in the town, despite its uncertain and limited water supply to drive the fulling mills. In the 1608 account[4] of the occupations of men in the town weaving is by far the principal form of employment, giving rise to the associated male trades of card-maker, tucker, yarnmaker and, for the women, carding and spinning. All of these obtained their employment from clothiers, who were the wealthy entrepreneurial organisers and co-ordinators of a complex cottage industry. Initially purchasing the fleeces, they then dispersed them across a network of specialist operatives working at home. As each particular process was completed the material would be collected and passed on to the next worker. Thus the wool would be successively washed, beaten, carded, oiled, spun, woven, dyed, fulled, teazled and pressed.

To the west, in the narrow valleys which cut into the scarp of the Cotswolds, clothiers imported Spanish wool and specialised in the manufacture of high quality fabric. Stroudwater, Defoe comments, was:

> famous not only for the finest cloths, but also for dyeing those cloths of the beautifulest scarlets and other grand colours that are anywhere in England, perhaps in any Part of the World. The clothiers lie all along the banks of this river for nearly 20 miles and in the town of Stroud which lies in the middle of it, as also at Painswick.[33]

Clothiers had established themselves elsewhere in the southern Cotswolds and also in Wiltshire. The gossip and commentator of the 1670s, John Aubrey of Malmesbury, has little good to say of them: 'Our clothiers combine against the wool-masters, and keep their spinners just alive: they steal hedges, spoil coppices, and are trained up as nurseries of sedition and rebellion'.[34] It must be said that his views may well have been coloured by an earlier, and unfortunate, attachment to Joan Sumner, a Wiltshire clothier's daughter. Himself an impoverished gentleman, Aubrey considers the clothiers social upstarts and climbers, and takes delight in telling how John Sumner, Joan's brother, styling himself as 'gent.', had placed over his door a stone escutcheon 'with a coat of arms to which the family pretended'. The coat of arms was not recognized by the

College of Arms, the family being described as 'ignobiles omnes' [none of the nobility] at the Visitation of 1623.[35]

The imposing mansions of the clothiers, still to be seen in Cirencester in Thomas Street and Dyer Street, do not boast a coat of arms over their doors, but it is not difficult to draw parallels between the social aspirations of the Wiltshire Sumners and those of the Cirencester Coxwells, for example, who, in addition to their considerable holdings of property in the town itself, and their acquisition of the former Langley lands in the adjoining parish of Chesterton and the right of tithes in Siddington just outside, held estates at Turkdean and the manor of Ablington.

★   ★   ★

This chapter forms the backdrop against which our story will unfold. Using eye-witness accounts and records from contemporary sources as far as they are available to us, an attempt has been made to sketch in the salient features of the seventeenth century town – its physical characteristics, its location at the intersection of important national routes, and its trade and industry.

The impact of improved water transport on local agriculture and trade is already discernible, drawing closer the links between Cirencester tradesfolk and the capital. The institution of a regular postal service between the town and London has made communication easier and life a touch more predictable, and therefore capable of tighter organisation. The time schedules of the post-boys, and the commerce which depends on them, have a ring of modernity about them.

Reference has been made to the presence of a powerful local landed gentry, whose wealth and influence are countered by the entrepreneurial activities of rich clothiers from outside; significant also in number and influence is a disparate group of tradespeople, shopkeepers, inn-keepers and craftsmen; and at the bottom of the pile, badly housed and with little say in the town's affairs, the broad mass of the common sort. Such contrasts in wealth and power create structural tensions which surface at times of crisis in politics and religion. It is they that will enable us to penetrate the more placid surface of the everyday and probe the private worlds of some of the citizens. Here lie rich rewards for the student of social history as the emotional springs of belief and motivation become revealed.

We now sharpen our focus as attention is turned to the activities of a particular inhabitant who, at the beginning of the century, attempts to cross a social divide. He is introduced in the next chapter, and we shall consider the dynasty he attempted to found. His social move demanded a physical one, translating our scene from Cirencester to Siddington, a village one mile to the south, then, as now, largely an appendage to the town.

NOTES

[1] S. Rudder, *op. cit.*, p.344.

[2] K.J. Beecham, *op. cit.*, p.181.

[3] R. Tomkins, *op. cit.*

[4] R. Reece and C. Catling: 'Cirencester, the Development of Buildings of a Cotswold Town'. *British Archaeological Report* No. 12. From observable structures in the town and data contained in Atkyns' survey of the county,[12] they argue that the street plan and location of the houses remained virtually unchanged for a hundred years until the drawing of the first known town map in 1795.

[5] J. Smith, *op. cit.*

[6] Castle Street connected the marketplace with a Norman castle built at the western approaches to the town. The castle, the marketplace and the abbey are characteristic of methods used by the Normans to consolidate their conquest: by force of arms, if necessary, but, more lastingly, through a prospering economy and the unifying cultural and spiritual influence of the Christian Church.

[7] The shambles are traditionally accepted as being in Butcher Row at the top of the market place. Did the butchers have their shops in the market place and a second establishment close by for slaughtering the animals? Or, did Butcher Row belong to Cricklade ward, rather than to Dyer ward? By 1887 houses in Dyer Street, opposite the Waterloo, were known as the shambles (K.J. Beecham, *op. cit.*).

[8] K.J. Beecham (*op. cit.*) suggests that this area included Butter Row, Butcher Row, and Shoe Lane at the west end of the market place, demolished in the nineteenth century, Black Jack Street, Park Street, parts of Silver Street and Park Lane.

[9] *A Particular Relation of the Action taken before Cyrencester*, p.161, in J. Washbourn: *Bibliotheca Gloucestrensis*.

[10] *A Relation of the Taking of Cicester in the County of Glocester on Tuesday, Febru. 2, 1642, by Seven Thousand Cavaliers under the command of Prince Rupert* in J. Washbourn, *op. cit.*

[11] K.J. Beecham, *op.cit.*

[12] Sir Richard Atkyns: *The Ancient and Present State of Glostershire*. A substantial part of the survey is the work of Dr. Richard Parsons, Chancellor of the Diocese of Gloucester from 1677, whom we shall meet later. His material was assembled during the second half of the seventeenth century, using returns made by the incumbents of the parishes for data of the number of dwellings, births and deaths. Poor health and the infirmities of age prevented Parsons from finishing his work, and his friend, Sir Robert, saw it to its conclusion.

[13] The house was built by Henry Danvers, Earl of Danby, who made the famous physic garden for the public use of the university of Oxford (S. Rudder, *op. cit.*). It was later sold to Henry Poole, whose son William in 1645 assigned it firstly to his mother, Lady Poole, and then on her death to his daughter Anne. Anne married James, Earl of Newburgh, and it was their son Charles who sold Oakley Grove to Sir Benjamin Bathurst in 1695. Allen Bathurst, Sir Benjamin's nephew, inherited the estate in 1704 and was raised to the peerage in 1712. It was in 1715 that work was started to re-shape Oakley Grove into the present Cirencester House.

It must be recognized that Kips has used considerable licence to enhance the prospect of Oakley Grove, as Reece and Catling show.[4] To provide it with a dominating position, Kips positions the parish church tower centrally and omits the old town hall in front of the church.

[14] Sir Robert Atkyns, *op. cit.*, p.347.

[15] T. Baskerville: *Travels in Gloucestershire*, Historical Manuscripts Commission 13th Report, Appendix Part II, p.299.

[16] Cirencester Parish Book, GRO P86 IN 6/3, f.30.

[17] *Ibid*, f.37.

[18] *Ibid*, f.41.

[19] *Ibid*, ff.4v and 5.

[20] Sir Robert Atkyns, *op. cit.*, p.349.

[21] S. Rudder (*op. cit.*, p.344) believes that this water course ran the length of the town, continuing down Cricklade Street, and emptying itself into the Churn beyond Watermoor. In support, he refers to excavations at the west end of the marketplace, where workmen uncovered a line of parallel upright stones with what appeared to be stepping stones crossing them.

22 Cirencester Parish Book GRO P86 IN 6/3, f.30v.
23 Quoted in K.J. Beecham *op. cit.*, p.201.
24 D. Defoe, *op. cit.*, Vol.2, p.33.
25 W. Shakespeare: *Richard II*, Act 2, scene 3.
26 W. Marshall, *op. cit.*, Vol.2, pp.8, 9.
27 GRO Q/SO2 ff.5, 5v, 11.
28 *CSPD* 1666-7, p.388, 1666.
29 *CSPD* 1677-8, 21 July 1677.
30 D. Defoe, *op. cit.*, Vol.2, p.131.
31 D. Rollison, *op. cit.*, p.50
32 *CSPD* 1663-4, p.641, 14 July 1664.
33 D. Defoe, *op. cit.*, Vol.1, p.281.
34 A. Powell, *op. cit.*, p.116.
35 *Ibid,* p 117.

CHAPTER 2

The Roberts *alias* Haywards
of Siddington

THIS CHAPTER MARKS THE opening of our story. It has as its
background the period of the early Stuarts when, on the
national stage, attempts were being made by both king and parliament to define and re-define kingship. Within the national church
forms of government and issues of control were also the subjects
of challenge and controversy, finding particular expression in a
confrontation between episcopacy and presbyterianism, and in a
tentative radicalism among the growing sectaries. Our concern with
these issues, however, is limited to the extent to which they intrude
upon the life of a rural community in south Gloucestershire. But
intrude they did, both in fiscal affairs and in the worship of the
village church, as we shall see, until matters came to a head and
the villagers were called to arms in 1642.

Moving from the general to the particular, we have to do with
one John Roberts *alias* Hayward, born in the 1590s and living in
Cirencester. This John was father to the John who is the subject of
our study; and he, in turn, had an eldest son John, and also a son
Daniel, the youngest and author of the *Memoir*. Undoubtedly
already confused, the reader is referred to the family tree given in
Appendix 1.[1]

Daniel Roberts' grandfather, John Roberts *alias* Hayward, is
listed by Smith[2] in 1608 as John Hayward, a chandler,[3] living in
Cricklade Street. He is of medium height and in his teens or early
twenties. Evidence presented in Chapter 4 suggests that his family

23

has become prosperous and respected in the town, sufficiently so for John's own father, Daniel's great grandfather, to marry late in life into a well-to-do family of Roberts, where his new wife later insists that her family name is preserved in the double family name.[4] Still known locally as Hayward, Daniel's great grandfather is proud of his social connections and wishes now for his family to be known as Roberts *alias* Hayward. In 1608 he is well over 60, or even dead, for he does not appear in Smith's listing, and his son John (from now called John the elder) is managing the family business.

A few years later John the elder inherits a small estate,[5] most probably from the Roberts' side, which enables him to re-assess his life-style and prospects. He decides to establish himself as a yeoman, a gentleman farmer, purchasing a property in Siddington from William Welden on 7 November 1617.[6] Administratively, Siddington was a unit of 80 communicants in 1603;[7] but in church affairs it was divided into the parishes of Siddington Mary and Siddington Peter.[8] John's newly acquired farmhouse lay in Siddington Peter.

Welden has been living away most of the time from the village, and his first name is not known to Smith,[2] who enters him as '--- Welden, gent.' among the other land-owning gentry of the parish: Henry Lord Danvers, John Coxwell and Thomas Nicholas. John is now approaching their circle, but still a step removed. Welden sells off the rest of his holding in Siddington during the next two years: 1 March 1618 one messuage, one garden, one orchard, 74 acres of arable, 12 acres of meadow and 4 acres of pasture and common to Robert Plummer of Wyddhill, in parish of Cricklade, Wilts;[9] and 6 November 1619 the Old Parke (45 acres) to the rector of Siddington Mary, George Spurrett.[9] He thus creates a small but significant social echelon of freeholding farmers in the village community, one step above the husbandmen, who were tenant farmers, but one below the gentry themselves.

John is now an eligible young man, and he is allowed to court and win the affections of Mary Solace, daughter to a well-to-do Cirencester family. Mary's mother, Joan, a widow, dies and is buried on 3 December 1618, leaving Mary £300, a considerable sum, but all her lands and tenements pass to Mary's brother, Andrew.[10] Trained as a lawyer, Andrew is to become, as we shall see, one of

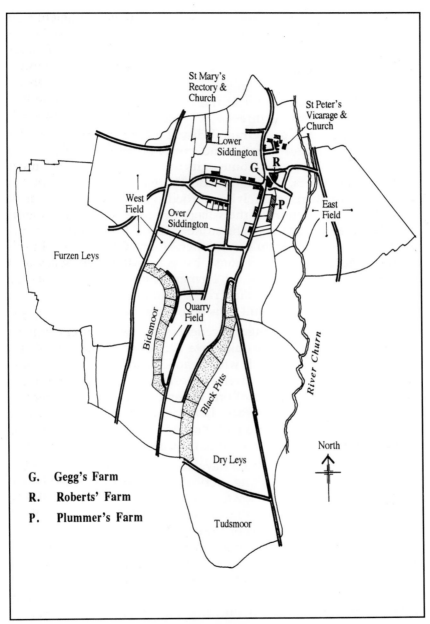

Map of Siddington: enclosure and common fields c.1624.

the leading citizens of the town and a justice of the peace. In 1619 John the elder and Mary Solace marry.

Welden has probably neglected the house, or perhaps it is too old-fashioned for Mary's taste. Whatever the reason, there is evidence that, while the older and adjoining malt-house was retained, the house itself was rebuilt at the beginning of the seventeenth century. The imposing three-storey, stone-built farmhouse still stands in Siddington as a Grade II listed building, now flanked by a red-brick Victorian terrace, and backs on to a small estate of modern semis.[11] It retains some of its original stone-flagged floors and stone fireplaces, oak doors and beams, but otherwise it has been substantially restored. It has six bedrooms, and there are large gardens, well-hidden from the village by stone walls and a newly planted screen of conifers. The stone gateway opens out on to the junction of the roads from Cirencester, South Cerney and Ashton Keynes. Facing north, the house looks across a large field to a complex of stone buildings: the former vicarage, Church Farm, a mediaeval stone tithe-barn and, rising behind them, the church. A footpath from the house still runs across the field to the church.

In 1617 a line of cottages, predecessors of the estate of semis at the rear of the house, would have flanked the same side road, Siddington Common Road, which ran down to a small common and the meadows along the river. Opposite the Roberts' farm stood another farm house, home of one branch of the Geggs, and forerunner of the Victorian terrace. Living there were Thomas Gegg and his wife Elizabeth, who had married on 25 September 1617, starting a family at about the same time as John and Mary.

With the farm John would have acquired not so much land as rights to using land: to tilling sections of the common fields and also grazing rights on the waste or commons of Siddington. The earliest extant field map of the village is one drawn to accompany the text of the Enclosure Act of 1780.[12] This Act is concerned with the enclosure of the remaining unenclosed land of the village, mainly the two common fields of Westfield and Quarry Field, and shows the Roberts family already holding a close called Black Pitts, Seven Acre Close adjoining Bidsmoor, and a consolidated area of fields to the north-west on Furzen Leys, in all 70 acres. At the beginning of the seventeenth century, however, it is unlikely that

John Roberts' house.

the Furzen Leys had been enclosed, and one should imagine a more open landscape of sweeps of grass land, gorse and moor to the west and south, meadow land along the river and, centrally and to the east, three large tracts of arable land, marked off from one another and the waste by a line of hedge. The farms would be concentrated in the centre of the village, each with its associated outbuildings, yard, garden and close.

Village wills for the period give indications of agricultural practices. Cash does not seem to have been a readily available commodity, and apart from items of household furniture legacies are often expressed in terms of small quantities of livestock, frequently a ewe and a lamb, or in bushels of wheat or barley. An iron-bound cart and the ploughing team seem to be precious possessions to bequeath,[13] or the moulding board.[14] John Cooper bequeathes his wain, sullo [plough] and harness.[15] Thomas Gegg the elder leaves to his fourth son, Richard, 'my whole teeme or plough of four oxen and four horses, with my plowes, waines, carts, harnesse and all other chaines and tacklings belonging to my teeme'. He also gives him 'all the crop of corne and grasse which shall be growing upon my tenement upon the the death of his mother'. His eldest son Thomas is given the two year old mare colt; his son John has returned to him 'the heifer of a year old which I bought of him'; and other beneficiaries are left varying quantities of ewes and lambs.[16] Philip Breache leaves Joan, his wife, 'the 32 bushels of barley already sent to Cirencester' and 12 bushels of wheat.[17]

The parish register for Siddington Peter prior to 1687 has been lost, with only the bishop's transcripts now available, and these are by no means complete. They do tell us, however, that by 1623 John Roberts *alias* Hayward the elder was established enough and sufficiently prominent in church and village affairs to become churchwarden, and continued in that office for at least another year. In May 1623 John and Mary have their son Samuel baptised, but a few weeks later the baby dies and is buried on 4 June. Records for preceding years are missing, but it can be argued with some certainty that John the younger, Daniel's father, and the subject of our study, in bearing the dynastic name, would have been their first son and must, therefore, have been born in the period 1620-22. A sister, Mary, is baptised on 29 March 1624 and a brother, who is again given the name of Samuel, on 26 July 1629. We learn later of a sister Alice and there could well have been other siblings since the records for 1625, 1627, 1630, 1632-36 are also missing.

John the elder did not remain long as churchwarden. Although the office, then as now, conveyed status on its holder, it was not always so readily sought since it carried wider responsibilities. The Siddington churchwardens, in addition to their present duties relating to church services or the fabric of the building, were also required to act as the long arm of the ecclesiastical courts. At the triennial visitation of the bishop to the deanery they would have been given the charge to concern themselves with the moral and spiritual welfare of their neighbours, in particular with sexual irregularities, lapses in church attendance or heretical beliefs. Further, they were to see to it that offenders were shamed or brought to book and punished. Many found such duties irksome and relinquished the office with relief. John was churchwarden in 1623 and 1624 together with his neighbour Thomas Gegg; he serves again with him in 1640.

It was during his first period of office that John Roberts and Thomas Gegg would have been involved in the vestry meeting at which it was decided to enclose three plots of common land, Old Laines, Common Leys and Common Furzes (remembered in the glebe terriers of 1677 and 1698).[18] This was part of a process of enclosure by local agreement which, undoubtedly, had already begun by 1624 and subsequently gathered pace until by 1780 1460 of the 2018 acres of the village had been enclosed. Further examples of the process can be seen in Black Pitts and Bidsmoor where the segmented pattern of ten small closes reflects a local decision to establish corrals on the edge of then open grazing land: nine farmers, of which the Roberts and the Geggs were two, were the beneficiaries, with the tenth close going to the parson in lieu of the tithes payable on the others. In the course of time Bidsmoor itself, Dry Leys, Furzen Leys and the arable land of Eastfields were parcelled out, until by 1780 only the waste of Tudsmoor and the arable of Quarry Fields and Westfields remained to be allocated.

The newly created fields were given unimaginative names which registered the owners – Geggs New Ground, Pollards New Ground, Pages New Ground or Roberts Meadow – or, more basically, the owner's share of the cake – Four Acres, Six Acres, or Sixteen Acres. From references in the *Memoir* it would seem that the Roberts' holding on the Furzen Leys was already established by 1670, even if it had not been all cleared of scrub.[19]

*   *   *

John the elder remained a deeply religious man until his death. Daniel records the family tradition of his grandfather's last conversation:

> After some time my father perceived him [grandfather] to shake very much, insomuch that the bed shook on which he lay; my father asked him, 'How is it with you?' He replied – 'I am well and feel no pain, but it is the mighty power of God that shakes me'; and after lying still sometime, he broke forth into sweet melody of spirit, and said, 'In the Lord only have I righteousness and strength. In God have I salvation!' And I do not remember to have heard that he said anything more before his departure.[20]

He was buried, with his wife Mary later beside him, in the central aisle of the church in front of the chancel arch. Alongside lay the grave of his fellow churchwarden, Thomas Gegg, and Rebecca his wife. All trace of these burials has been effaced in the renovation work of the nineteenth century when the flooring of the aisles was uniformly tiled. The tombstones, however, do feature in litigation of November 1726[21] when Jonathan Gegg, churchwarden, complains to the Chancellor of the Diocese that his predecessor, Thomas Fewster, has reduced the churchyard by six feet to the north and to the south in rebuilding the wall. Further, Fewster has overcharged for the stone and 'without calling a vestry meeting and without the consent of the parishioners ... pulled down severall seates in the said Church that did not want repairation and rebuilt them narrower ... and altered to the dissatisfaction of the said parishioners and inhabitants and to the prejudice of the persons whose grave stones and inscriptions thereon were in part covered thereby and without any Absolute Necessity for the Ornament Beauty or Uniformity of the said Church'. Gegg's claims are supported by a dozen depositions from other incensed parishioners, in particular by Henry Brunsdon, the parish clerk, who accuses Fewster of 'putting the same seats further forward in the Body of the Church and thereby covering part of the Inscription belonging to the Family of the Geggs and the other to the Family of the Haywards [Roberts]'. Stephen Cowper maintained that the pews now covered 'one third or more of each Stone and not to be read'.

Encapsulated in this local storm is the parishioners' sense of outrage that Fewster's high-handedness had disturbed the almost divinely ordained order within the village church. Sunday by Sunday, most probably at 9.30 a.m., by desire, custom or statute, the whole population of Siddington Peter would assemble for worship. Each house had its allotted space within the nave: the grander granted the privacy and superiority of imposing oak box pews at the front, and the more humble dwellings the plain benches at the rear. This arrangement, finely regulated by the parish meeting or, in the case of dispute, as here, by the ecclesiastical courts, reflected, confirmed and maintained the social gradations within the village at large.[22] Fewster had been so presumptuous as to interfere with these, repositioning and reducing the size of some of the pews. He had also impugned the dignity of two worthy families, the Geggs and the Roberts *alias* Hayward, by partially obliterating the inscriptions on their forbears' tombs.

The hearth tax returns of 1671/72[23] also reflect this social gradation. The Fewsters do not appear as such in the returns and will have been relative newcomers to the village; a Richard Fuster signed the parish register as churchwarden in 1684 and in 1689 was the miller of the Siddington water grist mill.[24] The vicar, who after 1663 doubled as rector of Siddington Mary, has seven hearths to pay for. Edward Simmonds has four. The Curtices, Pollards and Roberts *alias* Haywards have three each; while the Geggs – Robert, Thomas and William – together with Mr. Stone, Thomas Allen and Widow Ranell each have only two. The Geggs, a long established and extensive family, though only of the middling sort, were sensitive as to their social position.

The present day church, with its added broach spire, was restored in Victorian times and little remains of the Norman original. Several significant vestiges, however, have survived. The font with its Norman chevron patterning, where John the elder and his wife, Mary Solace, took their children to be baptised, stands centrally in the church. The oak pulpit bearing the date 1610, from

which Edward Allaway and then George Bull preached, in the
south-east corner of the nave, is to be found now only in the guide-
book of 1890 and has been replaced by Victorian neo-gothic. The
shell of the Langley chapel, added to the north side of the nave in
1470 'in Salutation of the Virgin' and built in the perpendicular
style, is all that remains. A bold Norman arch still leads into the
chancel, whose roof rests on stone supports of the mediaeval period,
carved into a flight of angels. But most striking of all is the well preserved Norman entrance to the church. A tympanum surmounts
this doorway: Christ seated in majesty, presenting a key to Peter
who kneels, holding his bishop's crook, and balanced by another
kneeling figure to the left of Christ, possibly representing Paul.
Enclosing this proclamation of authority and power in earth and
heaven is a bizarre semi-circle of fifteen staring beak-heads, comic
and yet fiendish; and located centrally and prominently above these
is their master, a goat-headed devil – a chill and disturbing message
to the worshippers each Sunday. Church door-way, font, chapel
and chancel – these major features of Christian worship are of
sufficient individuality to evoke the ambiance in which John and
Mary with their growing family crossed the field to attend divine
service in the 1620s and 1630s.

In 1712 Atkyns records Siddington Mary as 'intermixt with the
other Siddington (St. Peter or Lower) and has the same Patron,
Incumbent and Lord of the Manor'. Both were in the deanery of
Cirencester. The joint parish 'consists of good Meadow, Pasture
and Arable. The river Churn runs thro' it down into the Isis
[Thames] at Cricklade.' It contains 14 houses with 60 inhabitants,
10 being freeholders. There are 5 births and 4 burials annually.[25]

The rectory of Siddington Mary was worth £80 per annum
and the vicarage of Siddington Peter £25 per annum. At St. Mary's
'there was a steeple designed for Bells, but unfinished, being of
equal height with the Body of the Church, having but one Bell'.
On the north side there was a chapel dedicated to the Virgin Mary,
but in ruins. St. Peter's also had an unfinished tower at the west
end. 'A fair chapel' [the Langley chapel] stood on the north side
of St. Peter's. St. Mary's was subsequently demolished under the
Enclosure Act of 1778.[12]

An earlier record, before the amalgamation of the two parishes which took place under Dr. George Bull in 1663, describes the living of Siddington Peter in 1650: 'Wee find there a viccaridge worth thirty pounds per annum. That Rev. Edward Allaway hath it and taketh the profits thereof. It consists of 26 families.'[26] A century earlier, at the time of Bishop Hooper's visitation in 1551, there were about 24 communicants.

★   ★   ★

It was in classes held by this Edward Allaway that the formal education of John Roberts the younger began, at the age of five or six. Many years later, in the second of his lengthy confrontational debates with Bishop Nicholson, John recalls the time:

> I was bred up under a Common Prayer Priest; and a poor, drunken old man he was. Sometimes he was so drunk he could not say his prayers; and at best he could *but* say them. But I think he was by far a better man than he who is Priest there now.[27]

Under the tutelage of this Anglican priest, for whom he clearly holds some affection, the boy learnt to read and was proficient enough to manage the English Testament, a requirement for passing to the next stage of his education.

This was the Free School along Lawditch Lane [Park Lane] in Cirencester, which he would have entered at the age of seven or eight in 1627/8. The building still stands, but the original was extensively repaired and renovated towards 1640, when the whole school room frontage was re-built and mullion windows added.[28] The school was a much earlier foundation, endowed as an all boys school by John Chedworth, Bishop of Lincoln, in the fifteenth century.

Under articles of government revised in 1620 it was conceived as 'a semynarie and seed plott for the education of youth in virtue and learneinge and for the trayninge them upp to doe some service in the Church or Commonwealth to the Honor of God and the publike good'. The admission fee was twelve pence for the sons of Cirencester inhabitants. John Roberts, as 'an Owt dweller', would have paid three shillings. This money was used by the school governors to 'buy and provide such bookes as shal bee most necessarye for the publike use of the said schollers to be tyed fast by little chaynes of iron for that purpose in some convenyent place of the said schoole'. Fees thereafter were one shilling per annum, to be paid quarterly, and waived in cases of hardship.

At school John would have made new friends from among families of the middling and the better sort, even of the local gentry. One of these was Thomas Master of Cirencester Abbey, the Jacobean mansion which stood in extensive grounds to the rear of the parish church; we shall meet Thomas again in a later chapter.

John's teacher was Henry Topp who came to teach in Cirencester in 1616 and took over control of the school in 1621. Each day there was 'publike prayer by the schoole mayster and schollers', and on Monday and Friday evenings before going home they sang a psalm. Each Sunday and on holy days the boys were required to attend the Cirencester parish church with their teacher and 'decently and orderlye quietlie and soberlie to beehave themselves to their own commendacions and to the good example of others'. A further requirement was that they should learn either the shorter or larger catechism, depending on their ability.

There is no record of their curriculum but, based on contemporary practice at the grammar school in Ashby-de-la-Zouch, Ireland proposes a narrow classical education:

> Year 1 – elementary Latin grammar; Year 2 – learning to speak and write true Latin; Year 3 – introduction of rhetoric, intensive study of Latin grammar; Year 4 – rhetoric, elementary Greek; Year 5 – set books of Roman authors; Year 6 – ideally elementary Hebrew, but in practice further Latin, with Greek only for the ablest who were aiming at university entrance.[28]

John would then have left school in 1635/6 at the age of thirteen or fourteen, to join his father and learn the business of managing the Siddington farm. This occupied him until the outbreak of war in 1642.

*   *   *

The life of Edward Allaway, John the younger's first tutor, must have contained a number of disappointments. He did not take holy orders until he was 24, suggesting an unusual and unexpected change in occupation. He matriculated at Magdallen Hall, Oxford in 1608 but failed to continue with his studies, leaving to become vicar of Chipping Norton the same year. Here all could not have been well for in May 1616 he moved to the much smaller and poorly paid living of Siddington Peter. This was to fill an unexpected vacancy caused by the sudden death of George Bailey, who had been appointed only in the previous month.

The suspicion that Edward Allaway arrived in the village under a cloud is confirmed by the outburst of one Thomas Robins *alias* Roberts on Christmas Day 1618. The Robins were a family of labourers, William working on Walter Hone's farm in 1608, and Andrew without a steady job.[29] Thomas was Andrew's father, possibly in his late fifties, too old to be listed by Smith. Thomas and Andrew were liked enough to be left a bushel of barley in the will of Thomas Coulston, one of the respected husbandmen in the village, in 1611.[30] Clearly, something happened during the Christmas festivities of 1618 to make Thomas throw all caution to the winds and to confront his vicar outside the church, in front of his congregation, with the words: 'Thou Art A Base, Beggarly, Scurvey whoremaster Preist And thou hast Lyen with other mens wives, meaning hereby that the said Edward Allaway was a whoremaster And had the Carnal Knowledge of divers womens bodyes being mens wives. And so in common understanding is the sense and meaning of the said scandalous words'.[31] Allaway brought an action for defamation of character in the consistory court in February 1619, and managed to ride out the scandal.

Allaway died in 1663 at the age of 79. Because of the incompleteness of the bishop's transcripts of the parish registers, it is difficult to piece together the details of his family. From his will dated 10 September 1662[32] it emerges that his wife Jane predeceased him. His married son John was living in the village in 1636 and was churchwarden in Siddington Mary. His daughter Jozian was also in the village, having married into the family of the Boydens, but dead by 1662. He also lost his daughter Mary, who was buried 10 December 1626. A third daughter Jane married Thomas Berry and moved away. Alice Allaway, possibly John's wife, was buried 29 March 1638. He had three grandchildren.

★   ★   ★

At first sight the parish suggests a picture of a small, quiet, close-knit Gloucestershire farming community, largely untouched by the ebb and flow of national politics. In 1599 Marion Jones, a widow, appears before the ecclesiastical court for not coming to church and for working on the Sabbath.[33] In 1616 Alice Urget is in trouble with the church authorities for 'not receiving the communion at Easter nor since': her behaviour gives rise to suspicions that she is a papist.[34] But for these two isolated incidents, however, it is to be assumed that the parishioners regularly and dutifully attended St. Peter's Church Sunday by Sunday, year in, year out, and conformed to the 39 Articles of Faith of the Church of England, as required by statute.

In 1631 the parish attracts the attention of the church authorities once more. The churchwarden, Richard Plummer, is presented to the consistory court 'for that the bell frame and wheeles are out of repair. The surplesse [surplices] are not sufficient.'[35] A common method of fund-raising was to hold a church-ale on a Sunday afternoon, and that year Thomas Horton is presented 'for keeping churchale being noe churchwarden and refusing to give the parish any accompte hereof'. He protests 'that he did not sell any ale nor made any benefitt hereof'.[35] Three years later, in 1634, Frank Liddell is reported to the bishop and publicly shamed 'for begetting his wife with child before marriage'.[35]

That same year the churchwardens, Roger Boydon and Robert Rogers, are in more serious trouble: they are presented to the consistory court for not bringing in a certificate that the Book of Sports has been read out in church, presumably by the vicar, Edward Allaway.[35] The Book or Declaration of Sports had originally been issued by James I in 1618 for clergy to read to their congregations. Its purpose was to regulate public behaviour on Sundays, permitting such activities as 'dancing, archery, leaping, vaulting or other harmless recreations', but banning others, for example, bull and bear baiting or bowling. Intended as a moderate measure to placate extremes of opinion, it steered a mid-course between the complete abstention from work and amusements of all kinds urged by Puritans and the demand for freedom to enjoy traditional Sunday sports by others. In the event the Book of Sports satisfied few people, too restrictive for many, but for the Puritans an open encouragement of frivolous behaviour on a day they wished kept in quietness and solemnity. After the initial outcry had subsided, the parish of Siddington Peter no doubt patched up a *modus vivendi*, tending towards the Puritan position. But now the measure had been re-issued the previous year, in 1633, under Charles I. Clearly, strong feelings had been aroused, with the vicar and his church-wardens adopting a provocatively Puritan stance of choosing not to read the Declaration in church. They were not alone in this, for the churchwardens in a number of other parishes in the deanery, including Siddington Mary, were also presented for the same reason.

More trouble followed two years later in 1636, when again the churchwardens were presented to the consistory court. This time the complaint was that the communion table, unrailed, still stood centrally in the chancel.[36] Reformed practice for the past eighty years had been for the congregation to celebrate the Lord's Supper seated on benches around a long communion table standing east to west in the chancel. Now all were to adjust to the high church preferences of Charles I's archbishop, William Laud, who required the communion table to be re-positioned on a raised area against the east wall of the chancel, standing north to south, thus becoming a high altar; it was to be railed off as a holy of holies and entered only by the priest and his acolyte. Further, the priest was to wear a white surplice over his black gown.

The location of the communion table and the re-institution of the 'popish' practice of kneeling at the rail to receive the elements became the focus of Puritan discontent with the Laudian reforms. In Essex there was widespread rioting and demonstrations, and in a number of parishes the rails around the communion table were torn away.[37] In Shropshire Gough relates the experience of the village of Myddle:

> At that time there was a new Communion Table made, a very good one, and alsoe new Communion Railes, which were placed on three sides of the Communion Table. The old Communion Table was brought into the School-house for the boys to write on. ... When Parliament gott the upper hand of the King, they made an ordinance, that the Communion Railes should be pulled downe in every place; and these att Myddle

were taken downe and the Chancell floore made levell, and the Communion Table place in the middle of itt ... Francis Watkins, when hee was warden, bought a new Communion Table which was a long one and two jointed formes for the communicants to sitt att the table.[38]

Of a Puritan persuasion, Edward Allaway rode out the controversies which dragged on and eventually burst in the Civil War, no doubt making the required adjustments to the furniture of the chancel by the following Candlemas as demanded. Under the Commonwealth he should have found the Presbyterian arrangements of church order more congenial, and he died before being required to subscribe to the Act of Uniformity after the Restoration. His Puritan counterpart in Cirencester, Alexander Gregory, was not so fortunate in the timing of his career: he refused to take the Oath of Uniformity in August 1662 and was deprived of his living.

*   *   *

Tracing the social advance of the Roberts *alias* Haywards has taken us into the microcosm of a Gloucestershire village under the early Stuarts. Sufficient data are available to suggest how its established social structure was experiencing modification, as part of the already fragmented holdings of the early manor of the Langleys was sold off, and economic pressures or opportunities were lending weight to the introduction of agricultural practices based on enclosure and more intensive land utilisation. Our imagination, however, must fill the gaps in our data to construct the daily round and yearly cycle for its inhabitants, but documentation of personalities and prominent families is sufficient to give some shape to the drama of social interaction.

It is not difficult to conceive the rate at which national news and opinion would reach the commercial circles of Cirencester, but ripples from the larger political sphere have been seen to penetrate the quieter waters of Siddington. Issues of central control versus local freedom, and the clash of high church practices with Puritan principles find their way to the heart of the village, its weekly gathering for Sunday worship. Episcopal pressure on the churchwardens to conform appears innocuous enough, but masks the currents of feeling which would eventually erupt in civil war.

How this should ever happen is the subject of our next chapter.

NOTES

1   I have deliberately brought to the fore the difficulties of family dynas-
    ties which confront the student of local history. In Siddington, for
    example, three generations of John Roberts *alias* Hayward or Thomas
    Gegg occur in records during the seventeenth century. Similar diffi-
    culties are faced in Quaker records over the generations of such names
    as Richard Bowly, Elizabeth Hewlings or Richard Townsend. I have
    avoided the modern dynastic practice of distinguishing generations by
    Roman numerals and preferred to use 'the elder' or 'the younger', less
    precise but more familiar to the period.

2   J. Smith, *op.cit.*, p.242.

3   'Chandler' is found used in the restricted sense of one whose trade it
    is to make candles, though to avoid ambiguity it is often prefixed with
    'tallow' or 'wax'. It was also used to describe, often somewhat con-
    temptuously, the proprietor of a general store:
    1583: 'Be there any chandlers here? ... What do they sell for the most
          part?'
          'Almost all things, as namelie butter, cheese, fagots, pots,
          pannes, candles, and a thousand other trinkets beside.'
          (*A New English Dictionary on Historical Principles*).

4   '*alias* was frequently used from the fourteenth to the seventeenth
    century to indicate a change of surname connected with the inheri-
    tance of property, particularly with the inheritance of land in the female
    line or the desire to perpetuate the ancestral name on the female side.
    A complete name change [as was the case with the Haywards family]
    might take place if there were a marriage into an important family.'
    (D.J. Steel, *op.cit.*, Vol.1, p.89ff) Thus, Oliver Cromwell appears in
    some documents as '*alias* Williams', the Cromwells having sometimes
    used this form. Oliver's great-grandfather, Richard Williams, assumed
    the surname of Cromwell from his maternal uncle, Thomas Cromwell.

5   *Memoir*, p.65 (*OR* p.1).

6   The present existence of the deed for this sale is uncertain, but it had
    been seen by Lawrence (E.T. Lawrence, *op.cit.*, p.243). It is also quoted
    in a schedule of property transactions in a mortgage agreement of a
    later Daniel Roberts dated 11 April 1804 (GRO D2525 Box 23
    North Furzen Leaze). Here the sale is described as being between
    William Welden of London, gent., and John Roberts *alias* Hayward of
    Cirencester, chandler.

7   GRO EN Dr. A.Percival.

8   I follow the seventeenth century Puritan practice of omitting 'Saint'
    from the village names. Siddington Mary was also known as Over
    Siddington, and Siddington Peter as Lower Siddington or Siddington
    Langley.

9 GRO D 2525 Box 22.

10 GRO Solace 1618/111.

11 In 1993 the property was placed for sale. The house itself was offered at £450,000. The market value of one of the neighbouring semis was £85,000. This modern price differential may indicate something of the social divide that John Roberts the elder crossed in 1617.

12 GRO Q/RI 127 Siddington.

13 GRO Mason 1546/237.

14 GRO Haule 1570/81.

15 GRO Cooper 1599/70.

16 GRO Gegg 1629/157.

17 GRO Breache 1621/99.

18 GRO P293 IN 3/1 and 3/2.

19 *Memoir*, pp.114 and 157ff (*OR* pp.33 and 61ff).

20 *Ibid*, p.69.

21 GRO GDR B4/1/2198.

22 Gough, who, in fact, chooses to arrange his village history according to the church pews, gives an account of one such parish meeting:
1. Know all men whom it may concerne; that on the 7th day of February 1658, the Minister, Churchwardens, and a considerable part of the parish of Myddle, beeing mett togeather, for the settling of severall inhabitants within the said parish in vacant seates, have ordered and appointed John More of Myddle, for his tenement there, and Thomas Mather for his liveing in Balderton, to enter into and take possession of the seate beneath Captain Watkins' seate ....(Gough, *op.cit.*, p.117).

23 GRO D383.

24 GRO D2525 Box 9.

25 Sir Richard Atkyns, *op.cit.*, pp.650-652.

26 Hockaday Abstracts: *Siddington*, Gloucester Reference Library.

27 *Memoir*, p.125 (*OR* p.40). John's reference to Edward Allaway as the drunken priest of Siddington St. Peter can be understood in two ways. The more obvious is that Allaway was poor, old and drunk when young John Roberts attended his classes. He was, however, only 42 in 1626 when John was 5 or 6. But Allaway was still the incumbent and already in his seventies when John eventually broke with the parish church to become a Quaker. It is to this latter phase that John is more likely to be referring. The passage would then read: firstly, John is emphasizing the orthodox instruction he received as a boy from a priest of the Church of England; secondly, when he was an old man, this priest lived in straitened circumstances, had taken to drink and was to be pitied.

28 For this section I am indebted to J. Ireland: *History of Cirencester Grammar School.*
29 J. Smith, *op.cit.*, p.245.
30 GRO Coulston 1611/170.
31 GRO GDR B4/1/2197.
32 GRO Allaway 1662/24.
33 GRO GDR 87.
34 GRO GDR 125.
35 GRO GDR 175.
36 GRO GDR 191. On 24 November 1550 an instruction had been sent in the king's name to every bishop 'to give substantial order' that 'with all diligence all the altars in every church or chapel ... within your said diocese to be taken down, and instead of them a table to be set up in some convenient part of the chancel within every such church or chapel, to serve for the ministration of the blessed communion.' (J.R. Tanner, *op.cit.*, p.116). Now, under Archbishop Laud, high altars were in favour again.
37 J.A. Sharpe, *op.cit.*, p.105.
38 R. Gough, *op.cit.*, p.79.

CHAPTER 3

Going to the Warres

'Liberty of Conscience is a natural Right. ... All the Money in
the Nation would not have tempted Men to fight on such an
account as they have engaged, if they had not Hopes of
Liberty better than they had from Episcopacy or than would
have been afforded them from a Scottish Presbytery or an
English either.' – Oliver Cromwell in a speech before
Parliament, 12 September 1654.

IT IS DIFFICULT TO over-estimate the disturbing effect of civil
war on the structure of seventeenth century society and the train
of social change set in motion at the time. That a nation or a local
area or even a family should divide itself over such matters as
suzerainty and religious belief and *take up arms*, was to the participants almost beyond belief, and yet they found themselves so
embroiled. Two generations later, in Gough's collection of obser-
vation and village gossip[1] the allegiances of individuals and
accounts of local skirmishes are still the talk of the Shropshire
village. In similar vein, Daniel Roberts, in 1725, finds it important
to begin his biography with tales of the civil war, in particular,
damage to his grandfather's farm and his father's war experiences.
It is almost as if this is the baseline from which all subsequent
developments in personal history are to grow. No doubt, with the
passage of time and the frequency of the telling, to later generations of hearers these stories lost something of their horror and
anguish, but to the original willing or unwilling combatants vivid
memories of hatred, mistrust, deception, ruthlessness, as well as
of valour, compassion and sacrifice, must have remained.

In this chapter we attempt to experience, through the eyes of contemporary Gloucestershire folk, the mounting tension and the events which, in the end, triggered open hostility. We then focus on the involvement of John Roberts the younger of Siddington Peter.

That times were bad, there was little doubt. Hill[2] describes the period 1620-1650 as among the most terrible economically in English history. Blame was attributed to the mismanagement of the economy by early Stuart governments, particularly to their policy of creating monopolies and using other fiscal devices to raise revenue, which then served to increase the cost of living. This was particularly felt in the clothing trade where Gloucestershire cloth-iers blamed falling sales abroad on the monopolistic control of the Merchant Venturers in London.

In 1614 government policy to ban the export of unfinished broadcloth, and to insist that finishing and dyeing be completed in England, created a boycott in Holland. Further, the outbreak of the Thirty Years War on the Continent four years later disrupted normal channels of trade and adversely affected sales. A slump is recorded in 1622, with poverty among local weavers who held unsold stocks. Attempts to boost foreign sales through enforcing regulations as to quality were met with mistrust and hostility from the clothiers who favoured price reductions at the expense of quality. In the popular view, their misfortunes were to be placed at the door of the the king and his government. When the time for decision came, the clothing towns of Gloucestershire sided with Parliament, and clothiers were willing to lend money to prosecute the war and maintain soldiers at their own charge against the king.

But a depressed economy seems scarcely a sufficient reason for going to the extreme of unleashing what Clarendon called the 'Great Rebellion'. Did Cirencester people, in fact, really want to rebel and be embroiled in war? In Gloucestershire Sir Robert Poyntz complained:

> The Gentry come in apace, but the commons not so heartily, not in any considerable number. The true reason is .... my countrymen love their pudding at home better than musket and pike abroad, and if they could have peace, care not what side had the better.[3]

Corbet also notes a reluctance on the part of 'the common sort' to commit themselves and defend the county against the king's forces:

> The business chiefly rested on Sir Robert Cooke, Sir John Seamore, Master Nathaniel Stephens, Master Edward Stephens, Master Thomas Hodges with the rest of the deputy lieutenants; and setting aside these men with some gleanings from the gentry, the yeomen, farmers, cloathiers and the whole middle ranke of the people were the only active men.[4]

Some of the gentry had greatly resented the attempts of Charles I to raise revenues without consulting parliament, indeed, for eleven years without even calling parliament. Was not parliament the ultimate safeguard of the nation's liberties and supremacy of the law? In 1626/7 the king ordered the collection of a Forced Loan from those deemed able to pay and deputed justices of the peace to carry this out. John Dutton, Nathaniel Stephens, Sir Robert Poyntz and Henry Poole of Sapperton refused to levy or collect it, while John Georges in Cirencester paid his own contribution but was slow in making demands on others. Ship Money was another contentious issue in 1635/7, over which justices refused to co-operate with the sheriff. Edward Stephens lost his shrievalty, and Nathaniel Stephens and Henry Poole were removed from office as justices.

When a financial crisis over his war against the Scots ultimately forced Charles I to call parliament in 1640, known opponents and critics of the king's policies were returned for the Gloucestershire constituencies. John Georges, who had taken exception to the king's irregular fiscal measures, was returned for Cirencester;[5] and it was he, together with other prominent citizens, who persuaded the town to declare for parliament against the king, when, in 1642, Charles I raised his standard at Nottingham. The gentry of the county, however, became a class divided against itself over the issue of taking up arms against their sovereign.[6]

But were these matters of practical politics and self-interest or questions of principle? John Corbet's view was that many people of influence did see the conflict in terms of principle:

> But some higher cause had a greater influence on the endeavours of many for a well-bounded freedome and regular priviledges; a knowledge of things pertaining to divine worship according to the main principles of the Christian profession.[7]

Corbet, a radical Puritan divine, had been appointed incumbent of St. Mary de Crypt, Gloucester in 1639 and was to serve as Colonel Massey's chaplain throughout the siege in 1643. 'The Christian profession hath moreover an irreconcilable enmity against arbitrary government and will worke its selfe out of bondage when the felicity of the times shall give power and lawful call.' These times had now come. A choice lay between striving for liberty of a Christian conscience or accepting unquestioning subservience to a temporal lord. He saw social classes dividing over this issue. He makes little attempt to conceal his scorn for 'the powerfull gentry who for the most part care not [do not object] to render themselves the slaves of princes, that they also might rule over their neighbours as vassals'. They it is who despise stability and hard work, and 'eate their bread in the sweate of other men'. They are self-seeking opportunists: 'neglecting a secure estate, [they] rejoice rather in the height of fortune though inconstant and dangerous. Such is the predominant humour of gentlemen in this corrupted age.'

In contrast to these, he holds up the virtues of those of middle rank, 'yeomen, farmers, petty free-holders, and such as use manufactures that enrich the country and passe through the hands of a multitude, a generation of men truly laborious, jealous of their properties, whose principall ayme is liberty and plenty.' These 'did undoubtedly foresee greater hopes of liberty from the parliament than from the king's party.'

Such ideals and values, he claims, have been fostered by a style of Christian teaching to be found among the congregations of the city and county of Gloucester: this encouraged individual questioning and debate of both faith and ethics and led to personally held belief. It was 'a practicall ministry which hath not only its powerfull working in divine things, but also inables vulgar capacities more fitly to apply themselves to such things as concerne the life of a morall man. We have found that the common people addicted to the king's service have come out of blinde Wales and other dark corners of the land; but the more knowing are apt to contradict and question.'[7]

As a practised social observer, Corbet is under little delusion as to the interplay of principle and self-interest in human motivation, or as to the construction of events as much from happenstance, half-ignorance or fear as from assiduous planning and rationality. He locates the critical moment of mounting tensions in the arrival of Lord Chandos in Cirencester in August 1642 to execute the commission of array in the name of the king.

In February 1641 Chandos had been appointed lord lieutenant of the county by the king on the recommendation of parliament. In this office he was supported by 25 deputy lieutenants in the county and 7 in the city of Gloucester, though Corbet claims they 'shunned this imployment'. Their particular work, under parliament, in the summer of 1642 was to draw together the trained bands and to suppress all who should levy troops by any commission from his majesty. They were directed to seize upon all horses, arms, ammunition, plate or other provisions whatsoever, raised or provided for his majesty's service; to be ready to assist the Earl of Essex with horse and foot, and fight with, kill and slay all as should by force oppose them. They were ordered to disarm all papists and ill-affected clergy, to take possession of the magazine in Gloucester and raise what fortifications should be thought fit.

The decision of Lord Chandos to waive such instructions and attempt to raise troops for the king was, therefore, seen as a treasonable act against his office.

In some way word got out as to the lord's intentions. A thousand armed men from other parts of the county came into Cirencester to assist the townsfolk who had fortified the streets with posts and chains. When Chandos arrived on 23 August 1642, he was only admitted when it was seen that his retinue comprised no more than 30 horsemen, armed only with swords. His coach drove into the grounds of Cirencester Abbey, the home of Sir William Master, where he took conference with other local gentry. This meeting was, however, rudely interrupted by a group of armed men who burst into the house and required the lord to surrender his commission of array. Some even wanted to bring him before parliament. After the intruders had eventually been persuaded to leave, Sir William Master conveyed his guest privately through the house and let him out a back way. 'The souldiers coming to look for him the next morning were extreamly enraged and had like to have pulled down the house.' Instead they took the Chandos coach

John Beecham: The wrecking of Lord Chandos' coach.

and drew it themselves into the market place, where a gathered mob cut it and tore it to pieces.

This outpouring of anger and hate against the luckless lord's coach became the symbol and focus for wider feelings of frustration, resentment and discontent of the populace, which surprised their literary contemporaries and possibly the participants themselves. More surprising still was that this blatant attack on the otherwise respected representatives of traditional authority, Chandos and Master, expressed in open civil disorder and defiance, went apparently unchecked and certainly unpunished. Other local justices were standing back and allowing it to happen. This Corbet describes as 'the inexplicable self-ingagement of the common people which prudent men promote and maintain, yet no further than themselves can over-rule and moderate.'[8] He sees this subtle management of general unrest as the critical factor in gaining popular support for parliament. 'Hereupon the full streame of the country [district] runs for the ordinance of the militia and against the king's declarations and commission of array.' Now was the moment of euphoria when members of parliament for the county, rather than the dilatory deputy lieutenants, were able to raise bands of volunteers for the parliamentary cause.

In the absence of a standing army in early Stuart times, the local militia, the trained bands, was the principal line of defence in the time of national crisis. Reference has been made in Chapter 1 to Smith's compilation, some 30 years earlier, of the muster rolls of able-bodied men in Gloucestershire, aged between 16 and 60. From this reservoir volunteers were sought in the autumn of 1642, though it is apparent from the Cirencester pamphleteers that pressure from either landowner or employer was put on many to enlist. In many areas the social undesirables and misfits were conscripted, and it could well be that the Cirencester constables drummed up recruits from the local lay-abouts and trouble-makers or even emptied the bridewell.[9] One colonel complained, 'Most counties press the Scum of their Inhabitants, men taken out of prison, Tinkers, Peddlers and Vagrants that have no dwelling and such as no account can be given; it is no marvel if such run away'.[10]

Most probably among the willing volunteers, rather than the reluctant, would have been John Roberts the younger, aged 19, and his friend John Gegg, aged 17, who came from the farm next door in Siddington.[11] In Gloucester one company of volunteers was added to the trained band, while in Cirencester the trained band and volunteers were combined to form a regiment under the command of Colonel Fettiplace of Coln Aldwyns, and a few horse and dragoons were also raised. It was in this contingent of dragoons that the two Johns were placed. Professional soldiers, usually mercenaries who had seen service in the Thirty Years War on the continent, were sent down from London by parliament to train these forces.

The local regiment in Cirencester, in the main, would have been a kind of homeguard, to be called out at the first sign of danger. Living at home and pursuing their usual trade or occupation, they would have reported at intervals for training through the autumn. In a similar situation, in March 1640, when 1500 recruits were required from the county to fight the king's war against the Scots, the Earl of Northumberland wrote to the mayor of Gloucester and the deputy lieutenants, instructing them to exercise the men weekly in companies of a hundred, 'with false Fire or noe Fire', under 'inferior' officers. Colonel Fettiplace and other officers drawn from the local gentry would also have turned out to review their troops. When at this period the veteran Skippon was appointed to the command of the London trained bands, he harangued them:

> Come, my boys, my brave boys, let us pray heartily and fight heartily. I will run the same fortunes and hazards as you. Remember the cause is for God, and for the defence of your-selves, your wives and children. Come, my honest brave boys, pray heartily and fight heartily, and God will bless us.[12]

We can be sure that Cirencester men heard the like sentiments expressed to them that autumn, probably in the Querns fields adjoining Sheep Street Lane.

Success in turning these civilians into soldiers, however, was only relative. Corbet comments: 'The trained bands .... were effem-inate in courage and uncapable of discipline, because their whole course of life was alienated from warlike employment, insomuch that young and active spirits were more perfect by two daies service'.[13] But the regular drilling and arms practice under the supervision of the few professional soldiers available did convey some sense of corporate purpose, 'which disposition might fit them for a suddaine service, and the very posture conferre something of a warlike spirit.'

In the September of 1642 there was local alarm at the news that 500 of the king's horse under Prince Rupert had arrived in Worcester, and on 23rd the first skirmish of the war took place on the fields across the Severn at Powick Bridge. Corbet remembers: 'The noyse of the neare enemie raised the volunteers of the country [the Gloucestershire area] who marched under the conduct of some gentlemen towards Worcester'.[14] The royalists withdrew and the Earl of Essex occupied Worcester for parliament.

A month later, on the northern scarp of the Cotswolds, the first major engagement of the war was fought at Edgehill. Its inconclusive result dashed all hopes for a quick victory for parliament and an early end to the war. The initial euphoria now gave way to gloom and even fears that the king might win after all. Corbet again: 'And because the meere pompe of military preparations, and the hopes of a sudden victory now past, the warre hath put on a blacker visage, and the sad effects thereof come home to these parts'.[15]

From Edgehill both armies moved away to take up winter quarters. Colonel Thomas Essex marched into Gloucester with two parliamentary regiments of foot and was appointed governor. Within four weeks he and his troops had been transferred to Bristol, leaving Gloucester undefended. The Earl of Stamford hurriedly brought his regiment of foot and two troops of horse to cover the city, but he, in turn, was transferred to the West Country. Behind him he left Lieutenant Colonel Massey as governor to organize the city's defence.

Massey also assumed responsibility for co-ordinating the defence of the county. Cirencester's strategic importance was early recognized, both as a frontier town abutting the sphere of royalist control centred on Oxford, but also as the gateway to a hinterland rich in supplies of food, provender, cloth and leather, urgently needed by the royalist forces. Corbet records: 'The strength of the county was drawne to Cirencester, ... then made a garrison to prevent incursions of the enemy, as well as to preserve the country from ruine'.[16] Four great iron pieces of artillery were sent from

Bristol and two brass pieces from Gloucester. A magazine was established, containing 2,000 weapons, while two companies from Lord Stamford's Blue Coats were despatched to support the local regiment composed of the trained band augmented by volunteers.

As the autumn wore on, drilling and training continued. Defences were thrown up around the town, with turnpikes built at the main entrances, boosting public morale. Corbet, however, had no illusions about the quality of these defenders: 'And if the country must be preserved, it must be done by volunteers, which were yet as a cake not turned, a kinde of souldiers not wholly drawn off from the plow or domesticke imployments, having neither resolution nor support suitable to service: but the greatest defect was the want of able and experienced officers'.[16]

On 7 January 1643, to the horror of the townsfolk, the main strength of the king's army, 6,000 horse and foot under the command of Prince Rupert and Prince Maurice, 'came against Cirencester, prepared and resolved to storm it'. The town was summoned but stood firm, and John Georges sent back a haughty reply. The royalist forces then withdrew to their night quarters in surrounding villages, where, according to a contemporary pamphlet, 'they soon eat up all provision of victuall and consumed and made great waste of hay and corn'.[17] After two days they had gone, possibly because of the extreme cold on the hills.

Encouraged by this 'success', Massey decided to attack Sudely Castle, the home of the ill-fated Lord Chandos, near Winchcombe. A force of 300 musketeers, with two sackers [small canon], set out from Gloucester, assisted by a troop of 80 horse. Four companies of dragoons rode over from Cirencester, among whom would have been John Roberts and his friend John Gegg. The castle was summoned but refused to render on quarter. The attack came next day. The musketeers established themselves behind barricades of beds and wool-packs obtained from the neighbourhood, while the Johns' group of dragoons took possession of a small garden and set fire to some hay and straw. Under cover of this smoke the ordnance was brought up, facing the weakest point of the castle. Dismayed, the defenders surrendered on conditions and the castle was occupied for parliament.

In the meantime, on 26 January, Prince Rupert's forces had set off north from Oxford to relieve the besieged castle at Ashby de la Zouch, but while they were still moving through Warwickshire news came that the castle had fallen. The prince took the decision to veer south-west to relieve Sudeley Castle, having learnt that it also was under attack, but arrived on 30 January with 4,000 horse and foot, two days too late to prevent its capitulation. Feinting that the royalists, in turn, would lay siege to Sudeley, he made rendezvous with reinforcements from Oxford at Bradwell Grove, south of Burford on Akeman Street, and moved the bulk of his forces overnight to mass in Oakley Wood, appearing before Cirencester the following morning. Straightaway the royalists launched a surprise attack, and within an hour and a half the town was taken.

Corbet describes the pandemonium. The defenders 'were at their wits end, and stood like men amazed; feare bereft them of understanding and memory, begat confusion in the minde within, and thronging thoughts did oppresse and stop the course of action, that they were busied in everything, but could bring forth nothing. Few were slaine in the fight, but many murthered after the taking of the towne'.[18] The houses were pillaged for three days, while, for the 1,160 prisoners, there began an ordeal of intimidation and humiliation.

One of them recalls how they were first paraded in front of the royalist commanders in a field on the outskirts of the town. There they were threatened with execution and stripped by the common soldiers. Many were beaten up. After this, for two days and nights, they were kept herded together in the parish church without food or water. Then, roped together into a procession, which included John Georges, Colonel Fettiplace and Alexander Gregory, the vicar, they began their march to Oxford. Their captors 'bound us all with match and so drove us along without stockings on our legs, or shoes on our feet, or hats on our heads, many having no Dublets and some Gentlemen of good quality without Breeches.' A halt was made on Burford Hill to receive some meagre refreshments: 'we waited a long time upon the hill, the wind blowing very cold, and we standing barefoot and bare-legge'd in the snow'. Finally, on their reaching Oxford, 'a Mile from the City His Majestie with the Prince and the Duke of Yorke came thither to see us drove along more like dogs and Horses then men, up to the knees in mire and dirt along the horse-way, and aboundance of the Scollers much rejoycing at our misery.'[17]

News of the disaster quickly spread. Anger at the presumed cowardice or incompetence of the parliamentary officers in Cirencester produced a ground-swell of popular feeling. Corbet records that 'thousands of men armed and unarmed flocked together and resolved to take the enemy', urging an unnamed but 'grave and well-minded patriot' to take command. But he 'refused to engage himselfe and them upon a certaine destruction, nevertheless the people bitterly railed against him and curst him as a traitor to his country'.[19] In the meantime the army commanders manoeuvred their troops. Colonel Massey decided to concentrate his efforts on the defence of Gloucester, abandoning Sudeley and Berkeley castles and even withdrawing the garrison and ordnance from Tewkesbury. In turn, Prince Rupert, leaving Prince Maurice as governor of Cirencester, advanced to Gloucester and summoned the city, but, when it would not yield, retired with his forces to Oxford.

A weekly newsbook for 13-20 February 1642 records: 'the Cirencester men have submitted to the king and inlisted themselves for his soldiers; whereupon they are released out of restraint, have their arms restored unto them and march out daily to be examined and trained; only 50 of them stood out and refused to comply, and thereupon are forced to work in the trenches that are raising about the city'.[20] Such confident reporting hides the anguish and despair of the defeated. An alternative account provided by Edmund Chillenden, who was already a prisoner in Oxford Castle, gives the figure of 15 for those who refused to submit; these joined him in the castle and suffered barbarous treatment at the hands of the prison-keeper, Captain Smith.[21] Also not accounted for in the newsbook report were the 46 Cirencester men who did not enlist but petitioned the king to be allowed to return home and resume their normal employment;[22] this was granted on 25 February. The leading name among these petitioners, and probably the principal author of the petition itself, was John Roberts' uncle, Andrew Solace. So abject and obsequious was the phrasing of the petition that the king had it printed on 28 February and circulated nationally for propaganda purposes.

It is before Andrew Solace's release and return to Cirencester that we next hear of John Roberts.[23]

Rumours of the events in Cirencester and Oxford would have been rife; fears and distress would have mounted among the young and bewildered dragoons now relinquishing Sudeley castle for Gloucester. It is some comment on the military discipline of the time that around 12 February[24] John and his friend decided to risk a visit to Siddington to reassure themselves as to the well-being of their families and farms. Perhaps others before them had slipped over to Cirencester and returned to the garrison safely. The two young men rode down the Whiteway from Winchcombe and hoped to skirt the town, taking bridle ways and tracks to their village. But before they had reached the river they were observed by two mounted cavaliers who gave chase. When the lads saw that escape was impossible, they dismounted and took to their heels: they had little stomach for fighting. Whether they hoped their pursuers would be satisfied with their horses as booty, or whether they thought they could take a path where horses could not follow, is not clear. The ruse did not work. Impeded by their riding cloaks and top boots, they soon fell prey to the cavaliers.

The first to be attacked was John Roberts, who dropped to his knees and begged for quarter, but to no avail. With his arms he tried to protect his head from the slashing swords. He collapsed to the ground. There were stabbing thrusts to his jaws and neck, and he was left for dead. His friend John Gegg was then pursued and killed. Not waiting for the cavaliers to return, John Roberts struggled to his feet and tottered down a steep bank to the river, then in spate. He discarded his cloak and attempted to cross, his boots filling with water. Half wading, half swimming with the current, and bleeding profusely, he reached the other bank. The cavaliers reined in their horses. They were not willing to risk them in such a river to pursue a dying man, and they abandoned the chase.

His uncle's house was only half a mile distant[25] and he managed to reach it undetected by other royalist soldiers. Uncle Andrew had, of course, been taken prisoner and was being held in Oxford. John realised that it would be only be a matter of time before he was discovered, and he needed medical help desperately. He sent a servant to fetch a friend of the family from Cirencester, a woman of means and influence. She had, in fact, senior army officers billeted on her and was able not only to persuade them to give John quarter but also to secure the services of their own surgeon to attend to his wounds. Very grudgingly, the surgeon attended to him and John's life was saved.

This story must have been a favourite with Daniel Roberts, for he tells it in the *Memoir* with such detail. He had seen the scars on his father's arms and jaws and neck and had been taken to the spot along the river where John made his escape. He would have seen, too, the grave in Siddington Mary churchyard where the body of John Gegg was taken to be buried. To Daniel and the Roberts family it was nothing short of a miracle, for at this early part of the war the royalist generals looked on their enemy as rebels rather than as soldiers and treated them as traitors, showing no mercy. Then Daniel recalls the two points at which his father always said he had sensed God speaking to him: in his despair when the swords were slashing at his head, he had felt told to fall on his face; and later, after he had been left for dead, he had heard the words 'Arise and fly for your life'. John Roberts always acknowledged his preservation as due to the hand of God.

Once he had recovered sufficiently, John was moved across to Siddington to convalesce. There he found his father very ill in bed. 'Greeting each other with many tears intermix'd with joy and sorrow, they told each other what they had met with since they parted'.[26] But he dared not stay and take charge of the farm: he would not be safe there while he remained committed to the parliamentary cause. So he left to rejoin his comrades in Gloucester.

This is, perhaps, the clearest indication we have of where John's allegiances lay. Most of the original Cirencester garrison had lost heart and enlisted with the king. A group of influential citizens, led by his uncle, had successfully petitioned the king in Oxford to be allowed to return home and resume their occupations. John, however, his resolve hardened by his experiences, rejected both these options and made his way to rejoin the parliamentary forces

under Colonel Massey, determined to see the war through to
victory.

★   ★   ★

This was a young man's war: Prince Rupert and Colonel
Massey were only 23, just three years John's senior. It could well
be, therefore, that John obtained a commission. Gough records
similar situations around Myddle in Shropshire: 'there were
severall Gentlemen in our neighbourhood that were forced to fly
from theire houses in the warres, and to shelter themselves in
Garrisons; and because they could have butt little benefit from
theire lands towards maintaining them, therefore they had com-
missions to bee captaines, to the end they might receive a captain's
pay to maintaine them'.[27] John was, in all probability, among the
defenders of Gloucester during the siege in August 1643, which
was eventually raised by the arrival of the London trained bands
under the Earl of Essex. He would have taken part in other cam-
paigns as the war dragged on, but he is silent on these, preferring
to efface the memory, if possible, of horror and bloodshed, the
death of comrades, and meaningless suffering and destruction – as
those returning from war so often do.

What was at the forefront of his mind, and this he is willing to
share, was his own terror at the first face-to-face combat with the
enemy, his nearness to death at the hands of merciless royalists,
and his sense of being miraculously spared by the grace of God.
Undoubtedly, his early terror bred fearlessness, his encounter with
an implacable enemy developed the determination to defeat it, and
his religious experience in being spared led to a sense of mission.

★   ★   ★

While John was recovering from his brush with death, there
would have been bitter heart-searching and recriminations among
the defeated Cirencester men following their incarceration in the
parish church and the gruelling march to Oxford. They felt humiliated and deceived, and at great personal cost. These feelings
surface in the pamphlet *A Warning-Peice to all his Majestie's Subjects
of England* which a group of them wrote in Oxford, and which the
royalists were only too pleased to publish before the end of March
1643. The writers feel out of their depth, embroiled in a political

power struggle beyond their understanding: 'Nor was it to be imagined that we, who for the most part were bred at the plough, should be able to discusse the Rights of a Scepter'. Trying to explain their sorry state to themselves in retrospect, they believe that they have been caught up in a programme of manipulation and intrigue which they can trace back to the parliamentary elections of 1640 where 'wee were told that Popery was favoured and by all means we must chuse men as were opposite to that Religion .... Either threaten'd or bought we chose such as were not knowne to us by any Vertue, but only that of Crossnesse to Superiours'. Once elected, the parliament men 'did sweeten us with good Lawes, for the taking away of Monopolies, ship-Money and other grievances' and used 'men continually imployed for that purpose' to bring parliament's declarations, explain its privileges and justify deposing the king. Then the parliament men 'coyned inventions': there were 'strangely found letters of Papists, strange assurances beyond Seas, now of this Nation, then of that, which came to invade us at the Kings invitation'. Lecturers were sent 'who at first persuade us with many faire words the huge and unwearied endeavours of the Parliament for our Goods ... these firebrands of Sedition, our Lecturers, are to tell us in all their Sermons, or rather pratings, the happy condition of the low-Countries and ... give us to understand they meant to bring our Government to theirs.' Another ploy was to suggest that 'the King is pretended to be abused by ill Counsell, and must by our assistance be brought up to His Parliament, out of the hands of Cavaliers'. Finally, after the Battle of Edgehill 'they begin like the Divell to thrust Vs into the last act of despaire, telling Vs 'tis now too late to goe backe ... and that we must now at the least defend ourselves from Prince Rupert's Plundering'. These men, John Robert's earlier comrades, sum up: 'abused by theire damnable Flattery and Lyes ... have we made known our misfortunes and greivous sufferings under the Treacherous Government of those we took for friends.'[28]

How long did it take John to reach similar conclusions?

Disillusionment and despair became commonplace. This was someone else's war. People wanted to regain the fundamentals of life: home, family, employment, and, above all, peace. In their view too high a price in human suffering was being asked for the chimera of liberty. When Colonel Massey withdrew the garrison from Tewkesbury as part of the defence of Gloucester and left the town to negotiate its own surrender with royalist forces from Worcester, the townsfolk were relieved to be captured, almost regardless of the terms imposed:

> Thus the people entertained gladly those conditions, which though performed in part yet were a sufficient bondage, did impoverish their spirits, coole their zeal for religion, and lessen their former inclination to liberty; after which by frequent changes under many lords they became so feeble that they never durst confide in themselves to vindicate the towne into its former happinesse.[29]

As the First Civil War drew to a close, John Roberts returned to Siddington to his 'sorrowful family'. The royalists were finally defeated at Stow-in-the-Wold in 1646. There were few celebrations when the royalist garrison in Cirencester surrendered: people were only too keenly aware of the destruction that the war had brought in its train. A colonel with his men and horses had been billeted on the Roberts for a considerable time, who, as a consequence, 'suffer'd great Spoill',[30] with their hay and corn fields ruined.

Richard Baxter, vicar of Kidderminster and a staunch parliamentarian throughout the war, captures the mood of the moment:

> Look at England's four years blood, a flourishing land almost made ruined. Hear the common voice in most cities, towns and countries throughout the land .... Especially look but to the sad effects, and men's spirits more out of order; when most wonderful reformation by such wonderful means might have been well expected, and is this not cause of astonishing sorrow?

> Nothing appears to our sight but ruin. Families ruined; congregations ruined; sumptuous structures ruined; cities ruined; court ruined; kingdoms ruined. Who weeps not when all these bleed?[31]

The Cirencester experience of 'the warres' had started amid the impetuosity and euphoria surrounding the mobbing of Lord Chandos' coach. High spirits and bravado had been engendered by the novelty of military drill and building the town fortifications. Then came the creeping chill of fear at the first approach of the king's forces, followed by panic, anguish, then terror created by full-scale battle and subsequent defeat. After Prince Rupert's capture of Cirencester Corbet records: 'the country-men in generell were taken off, who in their jocund beginnings still concluded on victory, but never prepared for a blow, that the whole businesse was dashed at one clap'.[32]

But to return to the *status quo* was not an option. A train of events had been set in motion, for which few even of the political players could have foreseen the outcome or consequences. Their original cry for liberty had brought people into the modern age, but their social institutions and traditional assumptions over authority and control locked them in the middle ages. Whatever the immediate political solution, a foment of the spirit had begun, even if tinged with guilt and bewilderment. They were starting to move into unchartered territory.

Speaking for his generation, Richard Baxter again:

> Upon the most serious review of mine own and other men's proceedings I unfeignedly repent that we were not more zealous and studious for peace, and for the lenifying of exasperated and exulcerated minds and had not a deeper detestation of war. But who then knew what it was?[31]

NOTES

1 R. Gough, *op.cit.*
2 C. Hill: *The Word Turned Upside Down*, p.21ff.
3 C. Carlton, *op.cit.*, p.290.
4 J. Washbourn, *op.cit.*, p.16.
5 The only exception to this trend in the county was the other Cirencester member, Sir Theobald Gorges; he had married into the Poole family who, despite Henry Poole's protestation, remained staunchly royalist.
6 See J. Johnson: *The Gloucestershire Gentry.*
7 J. Corbet, *op.cit.*, p.9.
8 *Ibid*, p.8.
9 As we shall see in Chapter 5, George Fox gives a detailed account of attempts by the authorities in Derby to empty the jail and enlist the men to fight for parliament at Worcester Fight, 1651.
10 C. Carlton, *op.cit.*, p. 68.

11 The identity of John Roberts' friend can be established with some certainty. He is described in the *Memoir* (p.66) as John's 'next neighbour's son', which makes him a member of the Gegg family: their farm also fronted on to the Ashton Keynes Road, separated from the Roberts' farm by the side-road leading down to Siddington Common. An older brother, Thomas, contemporary with John Roberts, survives the Civil Wars and appears as a householder on the hearth tax returns of 1671/72. John Gegg, son of Thomas and Elizabeth, was baptised 25 April 1623; he was buried in Siddington Mary churchyard on 14 February 1643, some two weeks after the royalist capture of Cirencester.

12 J. Washbourn, *op.cit.*, p.cxxxix.

13 J. Corbet, *op.cit.*, p.11.

14 *Ibid*, p.12.

15 *Ibid*, p.15.

16 *Ibid*, p.16.

17 *A true relation of the late attempt made upon the town of Cicester on 7 January 1642/3.*

18 J. Corbet, *op.cit.*, p.21.

19 *Ibid*, p.22.

20 *Certaine informations No.5*, given in J. Washbourn, *op.cit.*, p.xxxii.

21 An anonymous pamphlet entitled *A true Relation of the taking of Cirencester and the cruell dealing of the merciless Cavaliers towards the Prisoners* contained as pages 13-15 in Edmund Chillenden's collection of pamphlets *Inhumanity of the King's Prison Keeper at Oxford*, 1643.

22 *The humble petition of the inhabitants of Cyrencester*, given in J. Washbourn, *op.cit.*, pp.189-191.

23 *Memoir*, p.66ff (*OR* p.2ff).

24 The burial of John Gegg in the parish register of Siddington Mary is dated 14 February 1642/3 (GRO PMF293/1).

25 The Solaces lived in the parish of Daglingworth, probably at Daglingworth Place.

26 *Memoir*, p.69 (*OR* p.3).

27 R. Gough, *op.cit.*, p.111.

28 *A Warning-Peice to all his Majesties Subjects of England.*

29 J. Corbet, *op.cit.*, p.24.

30 *Memoir*, p.66 (omitted in *OR*).

31 Quoted in J. Washbourn, *op.cit.*, p.cxv.

32 J. Corbet, *op.cit.*, p.25.

CHAPTER 4

Uncles and Cousins

THE FOLLOWING BRIEF SECTION, which deals with family history matters, has been interpolated into the main flow of events to enable the reader to locate particular individuals in the broader social context of the Roberts *alias* Hayward family. The data are summarized as family trees in Appendix 1.

John Roberts the younger met his wife, Lydia Tyndale, during the war when he was billeted on her uncle, Richard Cambridge, in Pudhill near Nailsworth.[1] Lydia and her brother Thomas were orphans and had taken refuge with their uncle after the family home, Melksham Court near Stinchcombe, had been fired by royalist troops at the beginning of the war. Lydia and John Roberts fell in love and married when the war was over in 1646.[2] The marriage settlement was drawn up by another of Lydia's uncles, Sir Matthew Hale, who was later to become Lord Chief Justice of England. Besides being wealthy and well-connected, the Tyndales were 'accounted a very religious Family and went by the name of the Puritan'.[3]

John and Lydia had six children: John (born 8 November 1647), Joseph (who died in infancy), Lydia (born 18 February 1651), Thomas (born 22 March 1653), Nathaniel (born 1 August 1655), and Daniel (born 12 April 1658).

The *Memoir* creates the impression that John the elder died in the 1640s during the First Civil War. This is not so. He was still alive on 20 October 1652 when he made his will in the presence of his son John and his brother-in-law, the magistrate and lawyer

Andrew Solace, and had died by 20 June 1654 when the will went to probate.[4]

In the will, after leaving 20 shillings to the poor of the two Siddingtons, ten shillings to Magdalen Bryan, his son's serving maid, twenty shillings and his 'wearing Apparell linnen and woollen' to his brother William, he confers the use of all his goods to his wife Mary during her life time.

The will then contains a number of surprises: firstly, a series of relatives, unknown to the *Memoir*, step from its pages; and secondly, there is the uneven manner in which John the elder wishes to dispose of his goods.

The only son mentioned is John, who is made an overseer of the will and is left nothing more than: the farm implements, the kitchen tableboard and frame, the iron jack, the furnace, the malt mill, and the 'ioyned [made with joints] Presse' in his father's bedroom. Nothing at all is left to John the younger's family with whom John the elder and his wife have been living: not to his daughter-in-law Lydia, nor to his grandchildren, John and Lydia, already born by 1652.

The only surviving daughter mentioned is Alice who has married into the well-to-do Clutterbuck family. Seven of her eight children are to receive ten shillings on the death of their grand-mother Mary. Deborah, Mary and Sarah are bequeathed a brass candlestick each, and the four boys, James, Giles, Daniel and Joseph are left the best chest, the best brass kettle, half a dozen pieces of pewter and the second bedstead and bed. The other young Clutterbuck, Hester, is in apparent disfavour, receiving no money and only her grandfather's 'least brasse pott'. Alice herself is bequeathed the brass warming pan, and her husband Samuel a brass pan.

All the rest of the household effects are left to a further grandson, Joseph Hamlett, who, in preference to John the elder's wife or son, is made sole executor. Joseph is an orphan and still a minor, and it is most likely for this reason that the will was referred to the Prerogative Court of Canterbury for probate. John the younger is confirmed as Joseph's natural and lawful uncle and lawful curator (i.e. as having the care of a minor aged more than 14) and is given letters of administration to carry out the terms of the will during Joseph's minority.

The choice of executor for the will is still quite unusual and must have stemmed from the grandfather's wish to see Joseph adequately provided for. Such a concern is reflected in a legal transaction a year earlier, on 1 July 1651, when John the elder and John the younger provide Joseph with a 99 year lease on a messuage [house] and a close of meadow land in Siddington Mary, with a trust to administer it: the trustees are John the elder's nephew, Andrew Solace the younger, and John Gibbes, mercer of Cirencester.[5]

But his choice of Joseph Hamlett as his executor is still puzzling, unless the grandfather believed he could live long enough for Joseph to reach his majority. And who is this orphaned grandson? Is this his daughter Mary's child? There is no mention of his Mary, nor of his second Samuel, born in 1629; have they both died? The will raises as many questions as it answers, inviting flights of poetic fantasy in search of explanations.

The farm itself had been settled on his wife Mary and his son John as part of the marriage settlement between the Tyndales and the Roberts *alias* Hayward in 1646; this becomes apparent in 1660 in the matter of the Quaker burial ground.[6]

Nothing is bequeathed to his brother-in-law, Andrew Solace, who in all probability drew up the will and is to act as one of its overseers.

Interesting is the reference to the grandfather's brother, William Roberts *alias* Hayward. Is he the William Hayward, working for the vintner in 1608 – or a brother who had left home and county by the time the muster rolls were prepared?[7] Could he be the William Roberts *alias* Hayward who is churchwarden in Down Ampney in 1634 and again in 1646? The Down Ampney parish register for this period is no longer available to us, and we have to make do with an incomplete set of bishop's transcripts. It would appear that this William's wife Alice was buried there 27 March 1634, and that he re-married almost immediately afterwards, with a son Walter being born to him the ensuing March. Other children follow – Mary (1637), Edward (1640) and Simon (1642). He himself is buried in Down Ampney 19 December 1661. Is it his son William Roberts *alias* Hayward who is living in the adjoining parish of Latton, Wilts. in the 1660s, who attends a Quaker meeting in Purton, Wilts., who subscribes to building the Quaker meeting house in Cirencester, and whose wife Mary and son Samuel lie buried in the Quaker burial ground in Siddington?[8]

William's son Edward, baptised 27 May 1640, dies and is buried the same day. A subsequent son must have also been given the name of Edward since it is he who begins to rear a family in Down Ampney in the 1670s. Is this the same Edward Roberts *alias* Hayward, described as a yeoman of South Cerney, who buys up the remainder of a lease of the parsonage house in South Cerney 27 September 1661?[9]

What is certain is that the double family name is not the sole prerogative of the newly established family in Siddington, since both John the elder and his brother William bear it, and we must look to an earlier generation to locate its origin.

A further complication to tracing the family tree is the record of a marriage on 8 May 1617 between Thomas Roberts *alias* Hayward and Elizabeth Batt in the Cirencester parish register. The only record of children being born to this marriage in Cirencester is that of the baptism of a daughter Elizabeth on 9 April 1631 and her burial the following day. This would suggest that the family initially lived elsewhere. A later Thomas Roberts *alias* Hayward becomes active in town's affairs in the 1660s. A daughter Mary is baptised in Cirencester 24 November 1650, providing a date for the return of this branch of the family to the town. This Thomas has legal training and is prosecuting counsel at the quarter sessions in 1662 and and sits on the petty jury in 1667.[10] He serves as churchwarden in 1665,[11] and is listed as the neighbour of Mr. Robert Morse, the attorney, living in Dyer Street in 1671.[12]

There are also a John Roberts *alias* Hayward and his wife Edith living in the village of Baunton, three miles from Cirencester, in the mid 1630s. They have born to them at least three children: Jane (1637), Richard (1641) and William (1643). This John Roberts *alias* Hayward was buried on 26 November 1645.[13] Is he the son of Thomas and Elizabeth?

These genealogical data suggest that John the elder had at least two brothers who subsequently moved away from the town: William who established himself at Down Ampney, and Thomas who married a Cirencester girl and then moved away. Contemporaneous with John the younger are at least three cousins living in the Cirencester area: William, a Quaker, who was a yeoman farmer in Latton, Wilts.; Edward, who had established himself in South Cerney; and Thomas, a member of the legal profession, and living in the better part of the town.

Among the Roberts family papers in the 1890s Lawrence saw a family tree, emblazoned with several coats of arms.[14] Such a family tree, possibly a copy, with the arms of the Roberts, Solers [Solaces] and Tyndales, is given in Fosbrooke (1807),[15] where the Roberts arms are described as: Az. three etoiles or, and a chief, wavy, or; and bearing the motto *Quae supra*. J. Burke *et al.* ascribe these arms to the Roberts family of Cornwall, which was granted them in 1614,[16] and Elvin gives this Cornish family as the origin for the motto.[17] Still preserved in Truro Cathedral are the recumbent early Stuart effigies of John Robartes [Roberts] and his wife Philippa, surmounted by this coat of arms.

The Robartes family papers were most probably lost in 1881 in a fire at their later country seat at Lanhydrock, so that little is known about the rise of this family. But according to a Royalist account written during the Civil War (the Robartes were Parliamentarians), a Richard Robartes (died 1593), coming from humble origins, established himself as a timber merchant in Truro and amassed a considerable fortune as a money lender.[18] His son John Robartes, whose memorial stands in the Cathedral, continued his father's business activities and was described as the greatest money lender in Cornwall. He built the Great House which stood in Boscawen Street (demolished in 1960), became Mayor and died in 1615 worth £300,000.

John Robartes' son, Richard, became High Sheriff of Cornwall and had a knighthood confirmed on him by James I in Whitehall in 1616 against a forced payment of £12,000, and was advanced to the peerage through the influence of the king's favourite, the Duke of Buckingham, in 1621.[19]

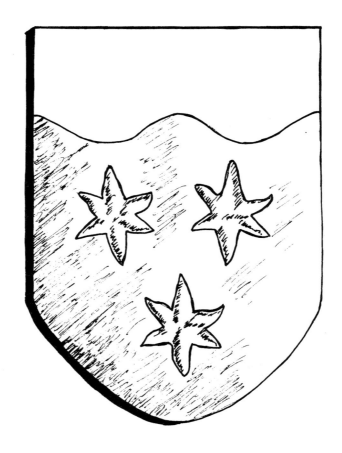

Roberts coat of arms.

It is in 1617 that we first find the use of the double name, Roberts *alias* Hayward, in Cirencester, and it is at this point that Thomas marries and John the elder buys his property in Siddington and then marries into the well-to-do Solace family. John Robartes of Truro had a sister Anne. Was the Anne Robarts, buried in the nave of St. Peter's, Siddington,[20] a daughter of Richard Robartes of Truro, and the mother of John the elder and his brother(s)? Had she married a Hayward, and, on the advancement of the family at court, did she receive financial support to enable her to live in a fitting style? Did she and her sons then adopt the name of Roberts, and John the elder use this money to purchase the farm in Siddington?

John the elder's brother-in-law, Andrew Solace, a lawyer, becomes a justice of the peace under the Commonwealth, is prosecuting counsel at the Trinity quarter sessions 1664 and a member of the grand jury at the Easter quarter sessions 1667.[21] He was buried at Cirencester 14 April 1669. Brasses in the parish church commemorating other members of his family describe him as gentleman. His son, Andrew, baptised 16 October 1625, became a yeoman farmer and was buried 23 August 1677. This branch of the family appears to die out, two of Andrew the younger's sons baptised Andrew dying in the 1660s, John in 1688 and finally Elinor in 1690. There is a further Andrew Solace who dies intestate in 1707,[22] possibly a son of Andrew the elder's son Richard.

Incomplete and disparate as the foregoing data may be, they coalesce to suggest a picture of the Roberts *alias* Haywards as a successful, upwardly mobile family, steadily establishing itself in the Cirencester area. John the elder, who cannot sign his name,[23] and his brothers are called upon to adopt, or seek for themselves, leading roles in local society and lay sound foundations for members of the next generation to improve their social standing still further. They have left trade behind,[24] aspire now to a certain independence as yeomen or in the legal profession, make well-connected marriages, and are drawn into the social establishment.

To what extent John the younger was to prove an embarrassment to them, the reader must now judge.

NOTES

1 *MSS Memoir*, p.3. The Stinchcombe parish register records the baptism of Lydia, daughter of Thomas Tyndale, on 17 October 1619 and of her brother, Thomas, on 31 March 1622.

2 An indenture dated 11 April 1804 was drawn between a later Daniel Roberts and William Wille to raise £2,000 on the Roberts' property in Siddington. The indenture, as is customary, contains a schedule of earlier legal transactions affecting the right to title. These are:

17 November 1617 indenture made between William Welden of London, gent., and John Roberts *alias* Hayward of Cirencester, chandler.

3 October 1646 counterpart of indenture of settlement between John Roberts *alias* Hayward the elder of Siddington Peter on the one part and Nathaniel Cambridge of Woodchester, clothier, and Thomas Tyndall of Stinchcombe, clothier on the other.

3 October 1646 counterpart of indenture of settlement between the same parties.

The last two entries refer to the settlement made on the marriage of John Roberts to Lydia Tyndale, by which the title to the Siddington property passed or would pass from John Roberts the elder to his son. (GRO D2525 Box 23).

3 *Memoir*, p.70 (*OR* p.4).

4 PRO PROB11/234. Bigland (R. Bigland, *op. cit.*, p.1080) says that his tombstone was in the nave of St. Peter's church, Siddington, inscribed:

Here lyeth the Body of
JOHN ROBERTS, deceased the
14 day of Sept. Anno Domi. 1658

Could '1658' have been a misreading for '1653', the figure possibly having been defaced by Thomas Fewster's alterations to the pews in 1726? (GRO GDR B4/1/2198).

5 Lincoln Record Office: Nelthorpe Papers VI/36/2.

6 See Chapter 9.

7 J. Smith, *op. cit.*

8 GRO D1340 A1/R1, GRO D1340 B3/Z2, GRO R96/1432 6401.

9 GRO D2957, p.236 68(3).

10 GRO Q/SIb1 f.139v, f.142.

11 GRO GDR 213, June 1665.

12 GRO D383 hearth tax returns 1671/2. Thomas Roberts [alias Hayward] occupies a house with three hearths.

13 GRO PFC39 IN 1/1.

14 E.T. Lawrence, *op. cit.*, p.245.

15 T.D. Fosbrooke, Vol.2, p.484. This family tree does not give any of the siblings of John the elder or younger. It does confirm 1646 as the year of John the younger's marriage to Lydia Tyndale, and 1653 as the year of John the elder's death.

16 J. Burke *et al.*: *Encyclopedia of Heraldry or General Armory*, London, 1844.

17 *Elvin's Handbook of Mottoes*, published by *Heraldry Today*, revised 1971, p.165.

18 'Lord Roberts ... his great-grandfather [Richard] was servant to a gentleman of this county, his hind. Afterwards lived in Truro and traded in wood and ferzen (for smelting); got an estate for 5 or £6,000: his son [John] was so bred and lived there too, put out his money and his debtors paid him in tin. He engrossed the sale of tin, grew to be worth many thousands. His son [Richard] was squeezed by the Court in King James his time of £20,000, so was made a baron and built the house at Lanhydrock, now the seat of Lord Roberts.' Quoted in C. Gill: *The Great Cornish Families*, Cornwall Books, Tiverton 1995.

19 B. Burke: *Genealogical History of the Dormant, Abeyant, Forfeited and Extinct Peerages of the British Empire*, London, 1883. One of the charges brought against the Duke of Buckingham in 1626 was, referring to the baronetcy, 'that knowing Roberts to be rich, he forced him to take that title of honour, and that in consideration thereof he [Richard Roberts] paid ten thousand pounds to the duke's use'. Although Richard's son John fought for parliament in the Civil War, he was favourably received by Charles II after the Restoration, appointed to the privy council, became Lord Privy Seal and then Lord Lieutenant of Ireland, being advanced to the dignities of Viscount Bodmin and Earl of Radnor.

20 A flat stone, recording her death on 13 October 1632, lay adjoining that of John the elder at the front of the nave. (Bigland, *op. cit.*, p.1080).

21 *CSPD* 1650, p.436, 13 November 1650; GRO Q/SIb1.

22 GRO wills, 1707.

23 Lincoln Record Office: Nelthorpe Papers VI/36/2.

24 This is not altogether certain. A John Roberts of Cirencester, born in 1712, ironmonger, married Susannah Dix, daughter of Thomas, also an ironmonger. This John was buried in the Presbyterian chapel burial ground in 1795. (L.G.H. Horton-Smith: 'The Hillier Family of Cirencester from 1635, together with the Family of Parry and Supplement', *Transactions of the Bristol and Gloucestershire Archaeological Society*, Vol. LXIV, 1943).

CHAPTER 5

Seekers and Finders

'she sees her own vanity and carnal mind; bewailing it, she
seeks after (as I hope also) what will satisfy. And thus to be a
Seeker is to be of the best sect next to a Finder, and such shall
every faithful, humble seeker be at the end.'

Oliver Cromwell writing in 1646 about his
favourite daughter, Lady Claypole.

THE PERIOD FOLLOWING THE surrender of the royalist forces
in Oxford in June 1646 was one of political turmoil.
Archbishop Laud had been executed by parliament the previous
year, and now, in the October, episcopacy was abolished and the
bishops' holdings of land put up for sale. But parliament had split
into two camps, the Presbyterians and the Independents. In the
New Model Army, too, there was division, principally between the
generals and the agitators, but with far-ranging reforms being
demanded by the unpaid and mutinous soldiery. The king, the
Scots and the Levellers also joined the political game as players,
each party with their own agenda of objectives, and each attempting
to negotiate, manoeuvre or impose political or religious solutions.
Further, by July 1648, when war broke out again, there was rebellion in Ireland and an invading Scottish army in England. In the
end, in 1648, the army generals imposed their will: London was
occupied, parliament purged of moderates or royalist sympathisers,
the king tried and executed, and the House of Lords abolished.

But there were no democratic reforms.

In 1647 two representatives, called Agitators, had been elected from each army regiment to meet with a council of officers. Their original purposes had been to voice the soldiers' grievances over pay, to demand indemnity against prosecution for acts committed during the First Civil War, and to resist parliament's plans for demobilization or the transfer of regiments to Ireland. To these immediate concerns, however, the Agitators now added the Levellers' radical programme for social and political reform. This included: the sole sovereignty of the House of Commons; the purge of the present parliament and a fixed term for its existence, followed by elections on a new basis (unspecified); a reform of the legal system with equal rights for the individual regardless of birth, wealth or influence; the abolition of monopolies, of excise tax and compulsory tithes; and protection for all dissenting Puritan sects against the intolerance of the Presbyterians. There followed the Putney debates with the generals and the Ware mutiny, with differences between the two camps reluctantly shelved in the face of the Second Civil War. That crisis over and the monarchy abolished, there were renewed demands for radical reform by mutinous troops.

On 1 May 1649 the Third Leveller Agreement was smuggled out of the Tower of London, where its authors lay incarcerated. It began:

> Having by wofull experience found the prevalence of corrupt interests powerfully inclining most men once entrusted with authority to pervert the same to their own domination, and to the prejudice of our Peace and Liberties, we therefore agree and declare ...

Their fear of the corrupting effects of power was only too quickly confirmed. That day eight troops of horse being transferred to Ireland mutinied in Salisbury and headed towards Oxford, perhaps with a view to gaining support from other regiments and then marching on London to have their grievances redressed. At Abingdon they found their way barred by soldiers loyal to parliament. Turning westward they reached Burford on 13 May, aware that parliamentary forces under Cromwell and Fairfax were in pursuit. Through intermediaries, however, they were reassured that the army was anxious to find a settlement by negotiation, and, unsuspectingly, they bedded down for the night in the Oxfordshire town. Cromwell and Fairfax attacked during the early hours, taking 350 prisoner and herding them into the church. After three days of imprisonment, on 17 May, three men were identified as ring-leaders and shot against the church-yard wall in the sight of their comrades.

News of these events would have quickly reached Cirencester, brought by some of 800 fleeing mutineers. One can only speculate on the reactions of the townsfolk, and particularly of young men like John Roberts who had served for more than three years with the parliamentary forces. Burford and Oxford held bitter memo-ries for Cirencester men, and three days of incarceration in the parish church was almost a re-run of their own experiences in 1643. But this now was not at the hands of the royalists but of their own generals, for whom, they had been led to believe, they had fought in God's cause to protect their liberties against the tyranny of royal power. Where were these liberties now? Where was protection against the tyranny of their new masters? Seven years earlier anger at the abuse of power had spilled over into the wrecking of Lord Chandos' coach in Cirencester market place. Now it was muted into cynicism: they had suffered too much in the meantime. Their hopes of a free and more just society were dashed. The dreams of idealism were being snuffed out.

John Roberts' reactions are not documented by his son Daniel, but we do know that locally, in Nailsworth, as elsewhere across the country, groups of people were forming to search for an alterna-tive society. Meeting together in one another's houses, largely unplanned and spontaneous, and only loosely coordinated, if at all, they all had a politico-religious basis, some going by particular names – True Levellers, Diggers, Grindletonians, Muggletonians, Fifth Monarchists – or others known just as Seekers. One such group of Seekers was associated with John's house in Siddington.

Writing in retrospect in 1694, William Penn describes these groups of Seekers:

> 'many left them [the Puritans], and all visible churches and societies, and wandered up and down, as sheep without a shep-herd, and as doves without mates, seeking their beloved, but could not find Him (as their souls desired to know Him), whom their souls loved above their chiefest joy. These people were

called Seekers by some, and the Family of Love by others, because, as they came to the knowledge of one another, they sometimes met together, not formally to pray or preach, at appointed times or places, in their own wills, as in times past they were accustomed to do, but waited together in silence, and as anything rose in any one of their minds, that they savoured of a Divine spring, so they sometimes spoke.[1]

In significant proportions within these groups were disenchanted idealists from the New Model Army. One such was Richard Smith who became prominent among the Seekers in Nailsworth.[2]

For many the time was so out of joint that the Day of Judgment could not be far off. Their reading of the prophecies of the Bible, particularly of the Book of Revelation, led some to predict with confidence the year 1656 as the End of the Age when King Jesus would come to claim His Throne.[3] Despairing of earthly political solutions, they waited patiently and looked for the New Jerusalem coming down from heaven. It was among such people and in such an atmosphere of excitement and expectancy that George Fox began to move in the north of England from 1649 onwards, and particularly among the Seekers of Westmorland in 1652.

Born in 1624, son of a Leicestershire weaver, and himself apprenticed to a shoemaker, Fox had left home and regular employment in his late teens in 1643. After some years in a spiritual wilderness, wandering, unable to settle, searching, agonizing, consulting priests, visiting religious groups, as far south as London, but mainly in the East Midlands, he began to reach a number of, for him, unexpected conclusions.

He recalls in 1646:

> As I was walking in a field on a First-day [Sunday] morning, the Lord opened unto me that being bred at Oxford or Cambridge was not enough to fit and qualify men to be ministers of Christ; and I stranged [was surprised] at it because it was a common belief of the people.[4]

He found himself moving away from an outward, formalized religion, which his own searching had shown him to be empty and unsatisfying, towards a process of looking inward:

> At another time it was opened in me that God, who made the world, did not dwell in temples made with hands. This at first

seemed a strange word because both priests and people used to call their temples or churches dreadful places, and holy ground, and the temples of God. But the Lord showed me, so that I did see clearly, that he did not dwell in these temples, which men had commanded and set up, but in people's hearts.[5]

Without any formal education, and like so many of his unlettered contemporaries, he began to explore the Bible for himself, derive insight and come to his own judgments:

And I had great openings concerning the things written in Revelations; and when I spoke of them, the priests and professors [religious people] would say that was a sealed book, and would have kept me out of it, but I told them Christ could open seals, and that they were the nearest things to us, for the Epistles were written to the saints who lived in former ages, but Revelations were written of things to come.[5]

Finally came the religious experience that was to answer all his questing:

And when all my hopes in them [the dissenting people] and in all men were gone, so that I had nothing outwardly to help me, nor could tell me what to do, then, Oh then, I heard a voice which said, 'There is one even Christ Jesus, that can speak to thy condition.' and when I heard it my heart did leap for joy ... And this I knew experimentally [from my own experience].[6]

This was for him a liberating experience, an inward discovery, a sense of being freed from all the endless wrangling over church doctrine, church furnishings, church ceremony and vestments, church organization. God is within; Christ is within; the Light of life is within.

Now the Lord God hath opened to me by his invisible power how that every man was enlightened by the divine light of Christ ... they that believed in it came out of condemnation and came to the light of life.[7]

In contrast to a post-war world of shattered lives and buildings, struggling agriculture, economic depression, with soldiery marching up and down the land, and no sign of a lasting peace, Fox describes the visionary experience that came to him in 1648:

> Now was I come in spirit through the flaming sword into the paradise of God. All things were new, and all creation gave another smell unto me than before, beyond what words can utter. I knew nothing but pureness, and innocency, and right-eousness, being renewed up into the image of God by Christ Jesus, so that I say I was come up to the state of Adam which he was in before he fell ... And the Lord showed me that such as were faithful to him in the power and light of Christ, should come up into that state in which Adam was before he fell.[8]

These sentiments led him into serious difficulties in Derby in 1650 where he was brought before the magistrates:

> They asked me whether I was sanctified.
> I said, 'Sanctified? yes' for I was in the Paradise of God.
> They said, had I no sin?
> 'Sin?' said I. 'Christ my Saviour hath taken away my sin and in him there is no sin.'[9]

He was sentenced to six months in the house of correction for blasphemy, but in 1651, on the outbreak of the Third Civil War, the prisoners were brought out to fight as soldiers in the parlia-mentary cause. Fox was offered a commission as their captain:

> They proffered that preferment because of my virtue [valour], as they said, with many other compliments, and asked me if I would not take up arms for the Commonwealth against the King. But I told them I lived in the virtue of that life and power that took away the occasion of all wars, and I knew from whence wars did arise, from the lust according to James' doctrine [James iv.1]. Still they courted me to accept their offer and thought that I did but compliment with them. But I told them I was come into the covenant of peace which was before wars and strifes were.[10]

His steadfast refusal to take up arms, then or shortly afterwards on the eve of the Battle of Worcester, resulted in his being thrown into the dungeon, 'a lousy stinking low place in the ground', for a further six months.

This time of imprisonment in Derby, however, proved to be a formative period, during which Fox gave shape to what was becoming a radical protest against the politico-religious settlement under the Commonwealth. Either verbally with a succession of 'professors' [professed church people] who came 'to dispute and discourse' or in writing in a series of letters addressed to the justices, the priests of Derby or for general circulation, he developed a critique which had as its centre the value of each individual and the possibility of their personal encounter with God, and a mission of proclaiming this 'inward' religion:

> Now the Lord showed to me, while I was in Derby prison, that I should speak in steeplehouses [churches] to gather people from thence; and a concern sometimes would come upon my mind about the pulpits that the priests lolled in. For the steeplehouses and pulpits were offensive to my mind, because both priests and people called them 'the house of God', and idolized them, reckoning that God dwelt there in an outward house. Whereas they should have looked for God and Christ to dwell in their hearts, and their bodies to be made the temple of God.[11]

Moving through the north-eastern midlands he attracted future leaders of the movement as his travelling companions, two of whom appear later in our story: William Dewsbury and Richard Farnsworth. The latter was with him in 1652 when he climbed Pendle Hill in Lancashire:

> when I came atop of it I saw the Lancashire sea; and there atop of the hill I was moved to sound the Day of the Lord; and the Lord let me see atop of the hill in what places he had a great people to be gathered.[12]

His vision of 'a people in white raiment' led him northwards into the dales of the West Pennines towards Sedbergh where, at the time of the Whitsun hiring fair, a thousand people gathered on Firbank Fell to hear him preach.

These were the Westmorland Seekers, Separatist groups who, though Puritan in outlook, could not find their spiritual home among the Presbyterians, Baptists or Independents, but met in small numbers for meditation and reading the Bible. They 'waited' in prayer and did not claim any infallible interpretation of Scripture for themselves. Drawing their inspiration from the Early Church of the Acts of the Apostles, where everything was under the guidance of the Holy Spirit, they 'waited' for power from on high and looked for an Apostle with a visible glory and power. He had now come, and the Quaker movement was born.

Fox stayed in the north over the next two years, either among such groups or in prison in Carlisle. Swarthmoor Hall near Ulverston, the home of Judge Fell, whose wife Margaret had become a 'convinced' Friend, developed as the nerve centre of the movement: a place of recuperation and consultation for the itinerant preachers, or an address to which they sent their reports and from which they received both moral and financial support.

In 1654 a period of expansion began:

> And so when the churches were settled in the north, the Lord raised up many and sent them forth into his vineyard to preach his everlasting Gospel, as Francis Howgill and Edward Burrough to London, John Camm and John Audland to Bristol through the countries, Richard Hubberthorne and George Whitehead towards Norwich, and Thomas Holme into Wales, a matter of seventy ministers did the Lord raise up and send abroad out of the north countries.[13]

Similarities with Christ's sending forth the Seventy[14] are unmistakable. They went in twos, and true to their message that 'there is that of God in everyone', not men only but several pairs of women went as missionaries. Two such Quaker women arrived in Cirencester in 1655.

For a number of years there had been a group of Seekers in Nailsworth, meeting in the house of William Beale. In 1655 they were visited by Humphrey Smith, once a priest in Stoke Bliss in Herefordshire, now turned Quaker:

> And in the same year came the said Humphrey Smith to Naylsworth, and had ameeting at one William Beales, where had been ameeting for some years of apeople called puritans or Independants, a seeking people to know the way of truth and most of those meeters came to here Humphrey Smith and were mightily affected with him, believing it was the way of truth; and many in and about Naylsworth were convinced by Humphrey.[15]

He also visited Painswick where 'some were convinced and were Redy and willing to Receive Friends into their houses ... and a fine people have Rison in that town, and truth is of agood esteem in that place'.[16] Moving on to Evesham, he was arrested with three Friends at the instigation of the local clergy and imprisoned for refusing to take the oath of allegiance. It was to visit him in prison that Margaret Newby and Elizabeth Cowart from Westmorland arrived in the town in mid-November.

Writing to Margaret Fell at Swarthmoor Hall on 25 November, Margaret described their experiences:

> A Friend did hold me in her arms, the power of the Lord was so strong in me, and I cleared my conscience, and I was moved to sing, and Friends was much broken and the heathen was much astonished. And one of them said that if we were let alone we would destroy the whole town. And the mayor came ... and took hold on me, and Friends did hold me and strove with him, and at length he tore me from them, and .... put me in the same stocks it being the fifth hour at night, and said we should sit there till the morrow, being the market day, and we should be whipped and sent with a pass [as vagrants] to our own country, and charged us we should not sing, and if we did, he would put both our hands in also. Nevertheless we did not forbear, being both moved eternally by the Lord to sing in the stocks, each of us both legs in, and so remained till the tenth hour the next day. And then the mayor ... sent his officers to fetch us out, the which officers said that these stocks were prepared for George Fox, against he came to the town, and then ... we were by the officers conveyed away on the backside of the town.[17]

She does not mention that these were special punishment stocks in the house of correction where a spell of three hours was considered as much as any prisoner could stand. Not allowed a seat, the two women were forced to lie on their backs on ground lower than the stocks. Margaret's health never recovered from the exposure for 17 hours through a freezing night and she died two years later. She writes her letter from Tewkesbury and ends with a request for more money to be forwarded as, undaunted, they move into Gloucestershire.

When Quaker missionaries were arrested, they were often found to be carrying papers containing an itinerary and people's names (which made them doubly suspicious to the authorities). It is almost certain that the brief for Margaret and Elizabeth was to 'go through the countries', visiting imprisoned Friends on their way. It would seem that after Evesham their route lay in a sweep through Gloucestershire, taking them through Cirencester, on their way to north Oxfordshire and Banbury. On reaching Cirencester, as Daniel records, they 'enquired if there were any people there abouts who were Seeking after the way of the Lord, and they were Directed to my father as the Likelyest person there abouts to give them Entertainment'.[18] This seems to have been a practice of the Quaker missionaries, as it was of George Fox himself, to ask after Seekers or any 'sober' ['serious-minded', perhaps 'Puritan'] people in the locality whenever they visited a town for the first time, and thus to make contact with like-minded or sympathetic groups. It is significant that when the two Northerners make their enquiries, John Roberts is sufficiently well-known as a Seeker in the town (of some 4,000 inhabitants) for them to be directed to his farm out at Siddington Peter.

John is now in his mid-thirties. His father has died some two years earlier, and John has taken over running the farm. He is married, with a growing young family: John aged eight, Lydia four, Thomas two and baby Nathaniel, a few months old; a fifth child, Joseph, died in infancy. Daniel has not yet been born.

In Siddington the Quaker women attempt no polemics; instead they request John to hold a meeting for worship in his house which they can attend. He readily complies and invites 'severall of his Acquaintance', probably other Seekers who frequent his house. They meet in silence, and after some time the visitors speak a few words. After this meeting for worship John attempts to engage them in discussion, but they have little to say and suggest that if he really wants to discuss more, he visit Richard Farnsworth who is in Banbury gaol. Daniel records that 'my father had the Curiosity to see him and talk with him.'[18]

The simplicity of the women's approach and their studied avoidance of debate stand in contrast with John's wish to talk more, an activity in which he and his acquaintances, presumably, frequently engaged in their search for 'Truth'. Religious controversy was the spirit of the age. Argument was entered into with vigour, although questioning or challenging the creed and practices of the established church courted the risk of having it dubbed as heresy, blasphemy or even sedition, and being punished accordingly. It was also often entered into with some viciousness. In a

sermon in January 1648 Alexander Gregory, the vicar of
Cirencester, had caused quite a stir among the Anabaptists and
Presbyterians, who then issued a pamphlet attacking him. This, in
turn, provoked Gregory's colleague in Kemble to respond with his
broadsheet *Gainsayer Convinced: An Answer to a certain scandalous
Paper subscribed and sent by certain seduced and seditious people to a
Minister.*[19] The main issues of contention were: the calling of the
ministry of the Church of England; the nature of the Visible
Church; the power of the magistrate under the Gospel; the right
of tithes.

The contemporary Isaac Pennington discerned in such controversies a progression reflecting as much an intellectual as a
spiritual search. He wrote that when there was a stirring against
Popery, Satan

> tempted them aside into Episcopacy; when that would hold
> no longer, then to Presbytery: when that will not serve, into
> Independency: when that will not keep quiet, but still there
> are searchings further, into Anabaptism: if that will not do,
> into a way of Seeking and Waiting: if this will not satisfy, they
> shall have high notions, yea, most pleasant notions concerning
> the Spirit, and concerning the life, if they will but be satisfied
> without the life.[20]

As will become clear, John Roberts was reaching this last stage
of cutting himself off from recognized church groups and of enter-
taining 'high notions'; of holding a set of free-thinking intellectual
tenets on religious matters, but without any corresponding depth
of spiritual experience. Curiosity, his intellectual search, was
leading him on.

At the gaol-house in Banbury John met up with Margaret
Newby and Elizabeth Cowart again, and after some difficulty with
the gaoler they gained admittance to Richard Farnsworth who was
being kept in the dungeon, a dark, cold, stinking place. Initially,
Richard had been arrested and imprisoned for failing to doff his
hat and offer the customary courtesies to the mayor and a justice
of the peace as they passed in the street. The situation, however,
had since deteriorated in that, when offered his release the next
day, Richard had insisted on knowing the charge against him and
why he had been imprisoned without trial. Instead of being given

an answer, he had been tendered the oath of abjuration, which he had refused to take. Now he was being confined indefinitely in the foulest part of the prison as a dangerous and seditious person.

As John and the two women Quakers are let into the dungeon the stench catches at their throats. They keep near the door, unwilling to venture further across a floor fouled with excreta and urine. Light comes into the gloom through a small grating set in the wall, to which a shadowy figure clings. He is preoccupied, calling through it to whoever is passing outside in the street. Not vituperation, but a sermon with urgency in its message. He becomes aware that there are people behind in the dungeon, turns to face his visitors and falls silent. Then, after a lengthy pause, he begins to speak again, quietly and firmly, and tells the story of Zacchaeus the tax-gather, a little man, who, because he wanted to see Jesus, ran ahead of the crowd and climbed a sycamore tree and waited for him to come that way. 'Our Saviour, knowing his good Desires, called to him, "Zacchaeus, come Down. This Day Salvation has come to thy House." – Richard Farnsworth then continued: 'Like Some in our Day who are Climbing up into the tree of Knowledge, thinking to find Christ there. But the Word now is, "Zacchaeus, come down! Come down!" for that which is to be known of God is manifest within.'[21]

That bizarre scene John Roberts never forgot; it marked a turning point in his life. Farnsworth's words rang in his ears – the words and the authority of the voice. Yes, he did want to see Jesus. Yes, he was only a little man, lost in the crowd; standing on tip-toe was not enough. In his desperation he had tried to run ahead of the crowd; he had been climbing higher and higher into the Tree of Knowledge. Now Jesus was calling to him by name: 'John, come down. Come down. What you are looking for is down here. You don't need more learning. Look within. It's in your own heart.' As John told his wife Lydia on reaching home, those words had 'spoken to his condition'. He felt that Farnsworth had known him from his youth – through all the years of searching.

That story was told over and over again – within the family circle in Siddington, and in the Quaker meeting that grew around him in the village and in Cirencester. Daniel knew it by heart.

Richard Farnsworth had pointed John Roberts to the Inner Light, 'the true light that enlightens every man'.[22] Here was the message of George Fox, that the God who had made the earth and sky did not dwell in temples made by human hands, but in the heart; that Christ, the Life, the Teacher, was the light of men. It was based on a growing understanding of Paul's phrase 'the glorious liberty of the sons of God', and particularly on the vision that Fox had shared with Farnsworth 'atop' of Pendle Hill.

John's experience was one of release. At a later stage, amidst the determined persecution of Quakers in 1671, John Roberts recalls in a letter to the rector of Siddington Mary:

> for I can truly say, in the fear of God, that I was long seeking the living among the dead, going from one form of religion to another, without ever finding a real peace or rest to my soul. But now, when I can say to His praise that I have found Him whom my soul loveth, I am made willing in odedience to Him to bear the reproaches of men, and to suffer joyfully the spoiling of my goods.[23]

At last he had found, in the most unlikely place, the freedom that he had fought and searched for; and with it the promise of a New Order, an emancipated society of fellow discoverers of the Truth. The Kingdom of God was not only within, but without [outside] as well. For him, the New Age, prophesied for 1656, had come.

NOTES

[1] Preface to *George Fox's Journal*, 1694 ed., p.xxv.
[2] 'And also there was one Richard Smith belonging to the county aforesaid [Gloucestershire], who had been a souldier for many years, but sone after friends came about, he was convinced, and Layd down his Arms, and came and Dwelt at Naylsworth, and continued there to his dying Day. And the said Robert Langley, ye younger, and Richard Smith, Married two sisters and thereby came to be Brother Laws. Pen would be to short here in this place to write the vallue of those two men and their wives. They were an upright hearted people and of a clean conversation, and freely given up to serve the Lord and his Blessed truth, and the Lord mightily Indued them with his wisdom above many.' (N. Penny: *First Publishers of Truth*, p.107).

[3] C. Hill: *The World Turned Upside Down*, p.91ff. George Fox, in prison in Launceston Castle from January to September 1656, writes: 'Now while I was in prison here the Baptists and Fifth Monarchy-Men prophesied that this year Christ would come and reign upon earth a thousand years. And they looked upon this reign to be outward, whenas he was come inwardly in the hearts of his people to reign and rule there, these professors would not receive him there. So they failed in their prophesy and expectation.' (*Journal*, p.261).

[4] G. Fox: *Journal of George Fox*, p.7.

[5] *Ibid*, p.8.

[6] *Ibid*, p.11.

[7] *Ibid*, p.33.

[8] *Ibid*, p.27.

[9] *Ibid*, p.51.

[10] *Ibid*, p.65.

[11] *Ibid*, p.85.

[12] *Ibid*, p. 104.

[13] *Ibid*, p.174.

[14] *Luke* 10, v.1 ff.

[15] N. Penny: *First Publishers of Truth*, p.106. At the Yearly Meeting of Quakers held in London on 18 May 1676 it was agreed and concluded 'that friends of the Monthly and Quarterly meetings of each County be reminded to keep an exact account among themselves of those that first brought the message of glad tydeings among them'.

[16] *Ibid*, p.105.

[17] *Swarthmoor Collection* 1.359, Friends House Library, London.

[18] *Memoir*, p.71 (*OR* p.4). The manuscript version reads: 'they were directed to my Father, he being a Seeking Man after the way of the Lord' (*MSS Memoir*, p.4).

[19] *Gainsayer Convinced* referred to in H.J. Wicks (1899): *Chronicles of the Baptist Church in Coxwell Street, Cirencester*, Harmer, Cirencester.

[20] Quoted in R.T. Vann: *The Social Development of Early Quakerism 1655-1755*, p.27.

[21] *Memoir*, p.72 (*OR* p.6).

[22] *John* 1, v.9.

[23] Given in E.T. Lawrence, *op.cit.*, p.325.

CHAPTER 6

The New Arrival

IN 1655, THE YEAR THAT marked for John Roberts the coming of the New Age, a young man of 21, less dramatically, but as excitedly, embarked on his professional career. His name was George Bull.

Born into a Somerset family of good estate, George was dedicated by his father to holy orders at baptism. He never knew his mother, who died in child-birth; and when George was four, his father also died. Brought up by guardians, he was left a small estate, sufficient to pay for a good education and, eventually, an extensive library. He attended Wells Grammar School, then Tiverton Free School, where he showed promise in classics. In July 1648 he was admitted to Exeter College, Oxford, as a commoner.

Six months later, after the execution of King Charles, students were required to take an oath that they would be 'true and faithful to the Commonwealth of England, as it is now established, without a King or House of Lords'. This George refused to do, and left Oxford with his tutor and other students to continue his studies in North Cadbury, Somerset; though not altogether seriously according to his biographer, Robert Nelson (1713): 'Thus transplanted from the strict discipline of a school to manly liberty he was overpowered by love of pleasure and diversions'.[1]

At the prompting of his guardians George put himself under the tutelage of an eminent Puritan divine, the Rev. William Thomas, rector of Ubley. He soon grew quite out of sympathy with the latter's austere Presbyterianism and eventually applied for holy orders to the one Anglican bishop still functioning, the ejected

Bishop of Oxford, and was ordained priest. In 1655, at the age of twenty-one, he took the first living available to him, St. George's, Easton-in-Gordano, Bristol, worth £30 per annum.

Nelson is of the opinion that the living was so small that no one paid much attention to George's Anglican opinions, nor took the trouble to dispossess him for using the then proscribed Book of Common Prayer at public worship.[2] The post was not without its challenges. George 'found the parish to abound with Quakers and other wild sectaries who held very extravagant opinions, which people there and in the adjacent parts were very ready to run into'.[3]

One story which Nelson heard him tell was of a Quaker who disrupted his sermon with the words 'George, come down; thou art a false prophet and hireling.' The unfortunate Quaker was immediately set upon by the congregation and had to be rescued by George, who then defeated him in argument. Again the Quaker was attacked by the congregation. Again George came to his rescue, bustled him out of the church, shut the door and returned to the pulpit to finish his sermon.[4] Nelson has other stories of George's work with recalcitrant parishioners, led astray by the sectaries.

It became George Bull's practice to make an extended visit to Oxford each year to use the libraries, and he found it convenient to break his journey in Cirencester to stay with Sir William Master.[5] Soon he was introduced to the vicar, Alexander Gregory,[6] and sometimes George preached for him because of his great age and infirmities.[7] He also became acquainted with the vicar's family, in particular, with his daughter Bridget. A friendship developed, and they eventually got engaged and were married by another William Master, vicar of the neighbouring village of Preston, on 20 May 1658, using the Anglican rite.

A month later, on 19 June 1658, George Spurrett, rector of Siddington Mary, died, and on 4 August 1658 the 24 year old George Bull was presented to the living by the patron and principal landowner, Dame Anne Poole of Oakley House, Cirencester, 'having a respect for Mr. Gregory'.[8]

There may also have been political motives for the appointment, for although the presentation document was issued by His Highness the Lord Protector [Oliver Cromwell] in all good faith as to one who would uphold the Commonwealth, known royalist sympathisers, Lady Poole and the Masters family, were behind the move and had assessed George's usefulness to them. Nelson explains:

> Several gentlemen in Mr. Bull's neighbourhood had frequent meetings to consult how they might contribute their share of advice and strength towards setting the nation upon a right foundation, by restoring the heir of the kingdom to the throne of his ancestors. And Mr. Bull was at that time [1659] so well esteemed for his loyalty and prudence that the gentlemen admitted him to their secret; and had confidence in his wise management, as well as his good dispositions to the Church of England and the royal family.[9]

Not only did George become deeply drawn into this intrigue, but it was also the decision of the local royalist gentry to make the rectory of Siddington Mary a regular place of their meetings.

The spirit of insurrection against the military regime of the later Commonwealth was in the air. In 1655 there had been rumours of 'some desperate design on foot' involving some 2,000-3,000 armed horse foregathering in neighbouring Wiltshire; ports had been watched, the guards on board men-of-war doubled, and horse-racing (as a cover for assembling horsemen) banned for six months.[10] This widespread plot for restoring the monarchy under Charles Stuart, in exile in the Netherlands, erupted in a royalist rising under Colonel Penruddock and was crushed in Salisbury that year.

The North Wiltshire social gossip, John Aubrey, relates the intrigues between his friend Tom Mariet and Major General Edward Massey, former parliamentary defender of Gloucester now turned royalist agent.[11] Correspondence between the king's secretary and such agents was couched in commercial language, sensitive information being written in cypher and individuals given pseudonyms. In the following example words in italics are in cypher decoded.

> 6 December 1655 *Dick Pile* to Sec. Nicholas. I am encouraged by *Halsey* ... to get commodities from France quickly, as it would be advantageous if, after the concluding of peace, I first had them to dispose of, so I have got 1,500 *foot* and 500 *horse*,

Dr. George Bull.

> but before I open shop you will be in *Gloucestershire*. I hear that
> the *King* is getting the like commodities. I want to know when
> he will come over, as I shall be 2 days before him. I want 2
> journeymen; I shall take *Massey* for one, and *Wilmot* for the
> other.[12]

This letter, from a collection of correspondence from T. Ross
to Secretary Nicholas, confirms the involvement of Massey and
focuses on Gloucestershire. Later that month Ross writes to
Secretary Nicholas to ensure that he has received the cypher: 'I
hope that you now have the character [cypher] from Mr. Lane, but
you will not find the word *Glasier* which I think is put for Massey.'[13]
This letter also refers to 'the token of taking him by the thumb', a
secret sign between royalist sympathisers, who refer to one another
as 'thumb-friends'.

Later, after Cromwell's death in 1658, Aubrey tells how Mariet
kept him informed each night of his 'tampering' with General
Monck, commander of the Commonwealth army in Scotland, to
see if he could be drawn into being 'instrumentall to bring in the
king'.[11] On 23 May 1659 the president of the Lord Protector's
Council instructed Captain Crofts of the militia troop in
Gloucestershire to investigate reports of a plot for an uprising:

> Council is informed of a very dangerous design against the
> public peace, by adherents of Charles Stuart and other ill-
> affected persons, and of meetings held and arms secretly sent
> down from London in trunks by carriers, to various parts of
> the kingdom. They therefore desire your utmost vigilance to
> prevent such meetings, and preserve the peace, and they
> empower you to search suspected houses for arms etc. and
> seize any you may find, and also any suspected persons whom
> you find consulting about taking up arms and disturbing the
> peace.[14]

In particular, Captain Crofts was to interrogate Mr. Overbury
over a trunk of arms sent down to his country seat at Bourton on
the Hill, Glos. Massey himself attempted an abortive rising in the
county in 1659, at the fringes of which would have stood the group
of plotters now centred on George Bull.

*   *   *

Despite these influential connections the young George Bull
was faced with the very practical question of how he was to maintain Bridget and himself in an appropriate style. They had moved
into the large rambling rectory, assessed at 7 hearths in the 1671/72
hearth tax returns[15] (John Roberts' substantial farmhouse was
assessed for 3 hearths), together with its garden, orchard and
stables; then there were 5 closes or enclosures of pasture, in all 17
acres, and another 8 acres of arable.[16] The rector also held 42 acres
in the common fields. While some of this ground might be rented
out, such an establishment needed considerable resources to be
staffed and maintained.

His predecessor, George Spurrett, appointed to the living in
1608, had grasped the opportunity presented in 1617/19 (as had
John Roberts *alias* Hayward the elder) of acquiring part of William
Welden's estate. He bought some 45 acres, the Old Parke, to the
north-west of the parish, which he farmed to supplement whatever
income he derived from the living. For the same purpose Edward
Allaway, George Bull's colleague in Siddington Peter, had taken
the lease of the water grist mill.[17] But George Bull lacked the financial resources to make such investments. At this date no regular
stipend to the incumbent was payable. He would have benefited
from the Easter offerings and the fees charged for conducting the
small number of marriages and funerals in his parish, but his principal source of income was from tithes.[18]

Tithe income consisted of two kinds: predial or great tithes,
and small tithes.[19] The predial or great tithes required the payment
to the incumbent of a tenth of the commodities which arose directly
from the land – corn, hay, wood, herbs, fruits, wine. Small tithes
were subdivided into mixed and personal tithes. Mixed tithes were
paid on animals receiving nourishment from the land (lambs,
calves, kids, etc.), on wool, milk, cheese and eggs, and on beans,
peas, hops, turnips. Personal tithes were paid on the industry of
man, mainly on mills and fish; profits from a trade, or as an
innkeeper or on money put out at interest were exempt.

From time to time surveys of the Gloucester diocese contain
assessments of the value of each incumbent's living. One such is
the Valor Ecclesiasticus Henricus VIII made in 1534/5, which
assesses the value of the rectory of Siddington Mary at £8, and that

of the vicarage of Siddington Peter at £5.[20] A breakdown of the the income and outgoings of the rector and vicar are given in Fig. 6.1. These figures are given again in the survey of 1603.[21] Towards the end of the seventeenth century the survey made by the Chancellor of the Diocese, Richard Parsons, and completed and published by Sir Robert Atkins, values the rectory at £80 and the vicarage at £25.[22]

These last figures reflect inflationary trends over 150 years, but allowance must also be made for a complication to the system of tithe collection, the practice of impropriation. In the case of the parish of Siddington Peter the full value of the tithe was £55; the Coxwell family took £30.

★   ★   ★

Before the monasteries were disolved in the reign of Henry VIII, the prior of the Hospital of the Knights of St. John of Jerusalem at Quennington was the appropriator [owner] of the tithes of Siddington Peter, choosing to receive a regular annual payment of 26s.8d. from his vicar there, rather than collect the tithes himself. The abbot of Cirencester Abbey and the prior of Monmouth had a financial interest in the tithes of Siddington Mary. At the dissolution of the religious houses these financial interests passed to the Crown, which retained them or sold them at will, in the same manner as it did the monastic buildings and estates. This lay ownership of a rectory or parsonage, comprising the parish church with the glebe, its right to tithes and other profits whatsoever, is known as impropriation;[23] and as with any other piece of property, an impropriate rectory could be bought, sold, inherited or willed away.

The 1603 survey[21] shows the rectory of Siddington Peter as impropriate to the king, worth £60, the annual value to the vicar being £5. Ownership appears to have passed to the Coxwell family soon afterwards, the right to tithes forming part of a marriage settlement in 1615.[24] Mrs Coxwell as the impropriatrix is presented at the consistory court in October 1677, 'the paveing and seats of the Chancell ... greatly out of repair'.[25] In September 1716 Sir Montague Nelthorpe acquires 'all and every the Lands Tenements and Meadows Pastures Feedings Tenths and Tythes of Corne

Graine and Hay Wooll Lamb And all and singular the Tythes as well as Great as Small Oblations Obventions Profitts Commodityes Emoluments and Advantages whatsoever to the Rectory [of Siddington Peter] belonging or in any wise appurteining'.[26]

Impropriators did not necessarily collect the annual tithes themselves but often leased their rights or used the services of tax farmers. The 1603 survey shows the rectory of Cirencester as impropriate to Mr. Butcher [Bourchier] of Barnsley. 'One of the Exchequer is farmer. The curate has no certain stipend but the courtesy of the inhabitants.'[27] The rectory of South Cerney was impropriate to the Bishop of Gloucester, worth £50; Thomas Cam was the tax farmer; the annual value to the vicar was £6.10s. The rectory of Coln Aldwyns was impropriate to the Dean and Chapter of Gloucester Cathedral; the Fettiplace family, whom we shall meet later, leased the right of tithes, paying an annual rent of £40 but the tithes being valued at £120. Percival and Sheils are able to demonstrate that over two fifths of the livings in the diocese of Gloucester in 1603 were impropriate. Thirty impropriations were held by the Crown, yielding £1,000 per annum, and 30 impropriations were held by senior clerics in the diocese.

Atkyns' survey of Gloucestershire, made towards the end of the century, also provides full details of the ownership and value of the right to tithes. The Cirencester tithing of Chesterton, adjacent to Siddington, was also impropriate to the Coxwells, worth £60. Another Cirencester tithing, Wigold, was impropriate to Mr. Georges, worth £20. The vicar of Cirencester benefited from the tithe of hay and all personal tithes from these tithings.[28]

*   *   *

Whereas Edward Allaway in Siddington Peter was dependent on the Coxwell family for whatever allowance they made him out of the tithe income, George Bull enjoyed independence and the potential of a considerably larger income. But he also carried the burden of collecting the tithes. This meant that he or his servant, because harvesting the various crops and commodities came at differing times of the year, would be moving among the farms and common fields almost constantly through the spring and summer seasons, collecting their dues: lambs in spring, wool in March, hay in May, peas and beans in June, etc. The size of his income depended on his diligence.

The 1534/5 valuation (Fig. 6.1) suggests that at least three individuals had reached an accommodation with the incumbents and were paying a modus, an annual cash payment, rather than paying in kind, but the glebe terriers of 1624 and 1677 make no reference to this practice being either continued or extended.[29]

Nor was George Bull entirely free of the Coxwells. Since the single village, with its one set of common fields, hay mows, pasture and water meadows, enclosures and waste, comprised two ecclesiastical parishes, there was always the need to clarify how the profits of the land were to be divided between the clergy. How the tithe for each field was to be allocated was stipulated in detail in the glebe terriers of 1677 and 1698. For example:

> Item the Twenty acres all to the Parson.
> Item the Gaston halfe to the Parson and halfe to the Vicar.
> Item the North hill parte to the Parson yet not neere the Third parte but the Vicar to have the most parte.

.That such divisions were a source of friction is indicated by several legal disputes in the village in the sixteenth century, before and after the dissolution of the monasteries. Even in the seventeenth century, where the principle of division was more defined, George Bull would have been caught up from time to time in dispute, suspicion and recrimination both with the husbandmen and yeomen of the village and the Coxwells.

Not all the land in the village was tithable, since it had become the practice, as enclosure of the waste progressed, to allocate the parson a tenth of such enclosures in lieu of tithes, thus steadily increasing the size of the glebe. This had happened in the case of Bidsmore and Black Pit in the sixteenth century, and the rector, George Spurrett, refers to the general consent of the parishioners given to further enclosures on this basis in 1623, which he confirms in the glebe terrier of a year later. Piecemeal enclosure thus followed until the Enclosure Act of 1778, when the incumbent, John Washbourne, was allocated 271 acres to compensate him for loss of tithes great and small.[30]

Figure 6.1: The annual value of the rectories of Siddington Mary and
Siddington Peter 1534/5
(after 'Valor Ecclesiasticus Henricus VIII')[20]

Income		Sid. Mary	Sid. Peter
Glebe:	arable	10s.	–
	meadow	9s.2d.	8s.4d.
	pasture	16s.	–
Tithes:	wheat	42s.	37s.5d.
	from W. Mann (wheat and hay)	53s.4d.	26s.8d.
	hay	5s.	26s.8d.
	wool	8s.	12s.
	pigs, sheep, hens, geese, cheese	7s.10d.	8s.2d.
	lambs	12s.	12s.
	personal	8s.6d.	12s.2d.
	John Skidmore	6s.8d.	–
	John Jeffreys	3s.4d.	–
	pension from abbot of Cirencester	8s.4d.	–
		£9.19s.2d.	£7. 8s.5d.
Outgoings		17s.8d.*	1.16s.2d.**
		£8.11s.8d.	£5.12s.2d.

* payments:	to Archdeaconry of Gloucester	6s. 8d.
	to Bishop of Worcester	2s.
	for Bishop's visitation	1s. 2d.
	to Prior of Monmouth	7s.10d.

** payments:	to Archdeaconry of Gloucester	6s. 8d.
	to Bishop of Worcester	2s.
	for Bishop's visitation	10d.
	to Knights of St. John	£1.6s. 8d.

But in 1658 George Bull was afforded no such relief from his unpopular task. A system of financial support for the church introduced under the Saxon kings, tithes had become a focus for resentment and resistance with country folk by the seventeenth century. John Roberts was only voicing common opinion when he said to Samuel Rich, minister of North Cerney: 'We Husbandmen ... Call them Caterpillars that live on the fruits of other men's fields and on the sweat of other men's Brows and, if thou dost so, Thou may'st be one of them.'[31] But such was the strength of vested financial interest for its retention that attempts at reform of the tithe system by both James I and Charles I had failed. The abolition of tithes had been a major aim of the Levellers, who were crushed, as we saw, in the early years of the Commonwealth. Four years later the Barebones Parliament was actually successful in rejecting, but only by a narrow margin, a committee's report to retain tithes: two days later, on 12 December 1653, the radical members of parliament were dispersed by soldiers.

John Roberts, though his farmhouse stood in the parish of Siddington Peter, held land in the Furzen Leaze and in the common fields, for which tithes were payable, half to the parson, George Bull, and half to the vicar, Edward Allaway. He refused to pay. We hear of no conflict between John and the ageing Edward Allaway or with the Coxwells as impropriators. Perhaps they chose to ignore the protest or, without further ado, sent in their man to collect the dues. But with the youthful, determined and possibly less pragmatic George Bull there came a head-on ideological collision. For John's refusal to pay his tithes was not out of dissatisfaction with the practice, or even a sectary's reluctance to finance his parish church. It arose from the Quaker testimony or witness against the very principle of tithes.

Writing in 1657, Anthony Pearson expresses the Quaker argument:

> The Basis of our Religion is the universal Manifestation and immediate Teaching of the holy Spirit; from which arises a Faith, that all acceptable Worship is performed in and under its Influence; that all Gospel Ministry flows from its Emanations; that this in Vessels prepared and sanctified by the Divine Hand, is the sole essential Qualification to that Work.

> That as the Gift is divine, the Service is free, and must be faith-
> fully discharg'd without any Object or Reward from Man. That
> Study, Learning or Art are no essential Parts of the Character
> of a Gospel Minister.[32]

The points of departure for this argument are the experience
of the Light within and the belief that this Seed of God lies in each
of us. Here we have mirrored Richard Farnsworth's appeal to John
Roberts in Banbury jail:

> Some, said he, in our Day ... are Climbing up into the tree of
> Knowledge thinking to find Christ there. But the Word now
> is 'Zacchaeus, come down! come down!' for that which is to
> be known of God is manifest within.[33]

The argument is anti-intellectual: illumination is not to be
achieved through learning and the possession of academic skills.
The argument is also anti-clerical and, thus, anti-establishment:
the word of God comes from the Inward Teacher. It became encapsulated in the Quaker slogans: 'Let Christ be your Teacher' or,
using Jesus Christ's injunction to his disciples: 'Freely have you
received; freely give'.[34] For the polemics which ensued the battle-
ground was the Bible, rather than the injustices and corruptions of
the tithe system.

Defenders of what was claimed to be the Divine Right of tithes
turned to the requirements under Mosaic law to pay a tenth to the
priests of Israel. Quakers argued largely from the *Letter to the
Hebrews* in the New Testament:

> The Lord did not command any People to pay Tithes but Israel
> ... Neither were they ever payable but by the Jews, after they
> came to the Land of Canaan, and to Levi's tribe only, to the
> Jewish Priests.[35]
>
> Now in the Fulness of Time, God raised up another Priest,
> Christ Jesus, who was not of the Tribe of Levi, neither made
> after any Carnal Commandment, *Heb.* 7.12-18, as the first
> Priesthood was; For he pertained to another Tribe, sprang out
> of Judah, of which no Man gave attendance at the altar, and
> therefore no Tithes were due to them for that Service.[36]
>
> [He] hath put an end to the first Priesthood, with its
> Shadow and carnal Ordinances; and changing the Priesthood,
> which had a Command to take Tithes of their Brethren (mark

that), not of those that did not own their Worship, there was a Necessity also of the Change of Law, and a Disannulling also of the Commandment going before.[37]

The Quaker argument concluded that to pay tithes would be tantamount to rejecting the high priestly function of Jesus Christ.

Writing in defence of tithes in 1700, Lesley observes:

'The Subject of Tythes is the Great DIANA of the Quakers. They have Bent their Whole Force against Tythes as the likeliest Means to overthrow the Church. And herein they have many Abettors. ...

But it is very observable, to what an Excess of Fury and Madness against all the Institutions of God that Spirit of Delusion which Possess'd the Quakers did Hurry them. Even to Account this part of the Worship of God, the Offering of His Tythe, to be a Renouncing of CHRIST, a Denial of his having come in the Flesh, and a Mark of Antichrist.'[38]

Undoubtedly Lesley was correct in his assessment that the Quaker refusal to pay tithes was more than a moral scruple, that it was also an attempt to break and dismantle the absolute power of the established church. As the Bishop of Gloucester accused John Roberts, 'I observe you, of all others [other sects], Strike at the very Root and basis of our Religion.'[39]

So the warfare of words continued from the presses over two centuries. But whatever might be pleaded in debate, payment of tithes in 1658 was a legal requirement by act of parliament, and the centre of most bitter contention was within the farming communities at the local level. It required considerable courage to face out the incumbent of the parish or the impropriator, and to take the consequences; it can be argued that only those who enjoyed some economic independence were in a position to do so. Similarly, those who held the right to tithes were presented with the quandary as to how to respond to such a challenge: whether to risk confrontation and resultant unpopularity, or to ignore the gauntlet. George Bull, out of principle or necessity, risked confrontation.

He had open to him several courses of action to obtain redress.[40] The first was to go himself, or send his man, to help himself: this was quite illegal, but effective, and was used by George on subsequent occasions.[41] A second avenue was to obtain an order for distraint from a justice of the peace: though practised, the legality of this was questionable. A third was the costly process of obtaining a judgment from the assize court for treble damages under a statute of Edward VI:[42] this appears to have been little used. The course he almost certainly did follow was to pursue his legal remedy in the ecclesiastical courts. The court could find in his favour and make an order for payment. If this produced no result, then he could apply to two justices to have the defaulter committed to prison until the debt was paid.

Following, then, the due process of law, George Bull had John Roberts imprisoned in Cirencester in 1658/9.[43] This was in the old Tudor workhouse, used also as a bridewell and debtor's prison, that stood in Dyer Street adjoining the *Bear Inn* on the east side.[44] The bridewell was in use during our period, regular quarterly payments of £3.15s.0d. being made to the master through the Quarter Sessions Order Book,[45] though by 1687 it seems to have been abandoned[44] and the building converted into a bakery.[46]

There John was joined by Elizabeth Hewlings of Harnhill, also from the Siddington Quaker meeting and also imprisoned as a debtor for non-payment of tithes. The Hewlings family were determined sectaries who provoked the ire of John Ham, the incumbent of the parish, and the men folk ran foul of the justices in Cirencester in the bursts of persecution over the next twenty-five years.[47]

Elizabeth Hewlings, a widow by this time, also acted as midwife in the Ampney villages to the south-east of Cirencester, and especially to the families of the well-to-do, where her services were particularly valued.[48] She may have helped at the birth of Edmund Dunch in 1657 at the manor in Down Ampney. Such was her skill and reputation that soon after John Roberts' imprisonment in the Cirencester bridewell Lady Dunch herself came in her coach to Dyer Street to have Mistress Hewlings released and restored to her duties.[49] Elizabeth's present unavailability had become a matter of some concern to the local gentry, and perhaps Lady Dunch's own daughter-in-law was pregnant again and nearing her time.

Her man, Alexander Cornwall, was sent into the bridewell to find Elizabeth and, in doing so, encountered John Roberts who

took him to her. They entered into some conversation as she got
ready to leave:

A.C.: What! Are you that John Hayward of Siddington who
keeps great conventicles at your house?

J.R.: The Church of Christ do often meet at my house – I
suppose I am the man thou meanest.

A.C.: I have often heard my lady speak of you, and I am sure
she would willingly be acquainted with you.[50]

The *Memoir* captures this dramatic turn in events as the narrative gives way to dialogue. Alexander Cornwall's keenness to get
John Roberts released, and both his and his lady's sympathy with
the Quaker cause are juxtaposed with John's concern to do nothing
underhand, and John's first preference to sit it out in the bridewell.

John is brought out into Dyer Street to stand at her Ladyship's
coach door. Lady Dunch puts 'on a majistick air' to see how the
Quaker would greet her. He goes up to her and says bluntly –
'Woman! wouldst thou speak with me?' There is banter and good
humour as a rapport between them develops, but her Ladyship
soon gets the measure of this stubborn Quaker, has her way, has
him released and tries to organize him into following her to Down
Ampney on horseback. But John still has his dignity.

J.R.: I don't know that thou art to have me, when thou hast
Bought and paid for me; for if I have my Liberty, I shall
think it my place to be at home with my wife and family.

L.D.: I have Some Skill in Physiognomy, and you don't look like
a man who can deny a Gentle-woman any Civil Request.

J.R.: If thou dost desire it, I intend to come and see thee at
Down Amny Some Other time.

L.D.: That will Suitt me much better than now ... But when will
you come? You must Sett your day, and I will lay a Side
all Business to have your Company.

J.R.: If it please God to Give me Life, Health and Liberty, I
intend to come on 7th day next – the day thou call'st
Saterday.

L.D.: Is that as far as you Used to promise?

J.R.: Yes.[51]

Dunch coat of arms.

His visit that Saturday was the first of several, and 'he found her very Inquisitive after the things of God'. Lady Dunch appears to have been something of a hypochondriac and enjoyed poor health, keeping to her room for much of the day. By 1658 John had already gained a local reputation for being a 'wise man' or healer.[52] He is, however, quite short with her over her maladies, in particular 'a fit of the Stone'. Quoting the instance of a man known to him who had suffered from gall stones while 'he Lived at Ease and faired Dilliciously as thou mayest do', he suggests to her a change to 'a more regular and temperate Life'. 'Aye', she replies, 'I know what you aim at. You want to have me a Quaker. And I confess, if I could be such a Quaker as you are, I'de be a Quaker tomorrow.'[53]

Later, she asks if she can attend one of the Quaker meetings for worship in Siddington, particularly if there is to be a visiting speaker. One seventh day in the winter two Friends from the north country arrive.[54] Ignoring the hard frost and snow, and with further disregard for her delicate health, John rides over to Down Ampney early on the Sunday morning to inform Lady Dunch, who is quite taken aback.

> 'How can you expect,' said she, 'that I should go out such weather as this? You know I Seldom go out of my Chamber – and to go so far Such Weather might Hazard my Health.' He reply'd, 'I would not have thee plead Excuses as some of old Did, and were not found worthy. Thou knowest time is none of ours, and we know not whither we may have the Like opportunity. As to the snow, it need not much incommode thee, for thou mayst soon be in thy Coach, and, pulling up the Glasses [window], be pretty warm. And when thou comest there, I know my wife will do her best for thee.'[55]

Her resistance crumbles, and she sends for Alexander Cornwall to have the coach got ready. 'For', said she, 'John is like Death – he will not be deneyed.'

She enjoyed this meeting and was noticeably attentive when the visiting Friends spoke, but restless during the periods of silent worship. Afterwards she stayed to a meal with the the Roberts family and their visitors in the farmhouse, sitting at the oak tableboard. Misunderstanding the silent Quaker grace before the meal, she whispered through it to Lydia Roberts until one of the visiting

Friends asked a blessing on the food. Afterwards she felt quite embarrassed and 'told my Mother that when she was at Court or Elsewhere among great persons she was accounted a wise woman; 'But', said She, 'Now I am among Quakers I am a very fooll.'[56]

Subsequently she came several times to meeting for worship in Siddington, and Friends were 'fully perswaded she was convinced of the Truth'. Soon afterwards, however, she moved up to London, where she was taken ill and died.

If John showed little sympathy for Lady Dunch's real or imaginary ailments, then she, in turn, was unsparing towards whatever sensitivities he may have entertained in the growing conflict with the local clergy. Though he may have shown a blunt and uncompromising exterior, with bluff good humour, it is quite clear from the *Memoir* that John Roberts suffered from times of self-doubt and considerable anxiety. The developing rift with George Bull in the small Siddington village community, with families and individuals taking sides, peddling tittle-tattle and back-biting, could have brought him little peace or pleasure; and the humiliation of being consigned to the debtors' prison would have taken some living down. Nevertheless, for the third of his invitations to Down Ampney manor Lady Dunch developed a scheme to create some entertainment for herself. Unbeknown to either of them, she invited the young vicar of Barnsley, Thomas Careles,[57] to the house at the same time as John.

The full surprise of her stratagem was diminished by the two men encountering one another on the way there and discovering that their appointments were for the same time. This, however, did not save them from having to engage in impromptu religious argument in front of her Ladyship. The debate centred on the 'Damnable Doctrine and Daingerous Tenett of perfection in this Life',[58] a matter which, as we have seen, had had George Fox thrown into Derby jail some eight years earlier. For holding to this teaching John was accused of being a papist, but he, according to Daniel, was able to get the better of Thomas by reductionist argument, much to her Ladyship's surprise.

★   ★   ★

Controversy over doctrine, which provided Lady Dunch with an amusing diversion, was a matter of serious concern to other women in the county. These were the 229 Quaker women from Gloucestershire who sent their names and petition to Parliament. Their petition joined the 7,000 names of Quaker women throughout the country who, on 20 July 1659, were protesting at the oppression of tithes, the sufferings of their families and the arrest of their menfolk.[59] One of the Gloucestershire signatories was John's wife, Lydia Roberts, and it could well be that this petition coincided with her husband's imprisonment in Cirencester.

The Gloucestershire petition challenges the unassailable position assumed by priests in doctrinal matters. The clergy 'will not suffer us to try [examine] their doctrine, but we must receive all whether bad or good; and if we do question it, six months in the house of correction, or five pounds fine .... it is an unrighteous thing that [people] should not have their liberty to question and try their doctrine without imprisonment'.[60]

Their other grievance centred on the clergy's right to tithes, and particularly on the excesses of some ministers in collecting them and the extreme harshness of some justices in upholding, to the women, an unjust law. 'It is an unrighteous thing to force people to maintain a Minister that they know in their consciences they are [he is] contrary to God ... And if the Priest come and pretend £15 Tythes they will take a hundred pounds; You grant them fifteen pound of us whom they do not work for, and they will take a hundred pounds and drive away our horses and oxen, and plough geer, and take ten times as much as the value, as they have done, which is upon record ... yet this unrighteous Ministry shall have their liberty, and be tolerated by the power of the Nation, to spoil [plunder] the goods, to summon to Courts, to prison, to death'.[60]

We have here not the polished arguments of the pamphleteer, but the heart-felt cry of women who have reached a point of desperation. Their generalisations can be challenged; their language is at times intemperate and ungrammatical; but the reader is left in no doubt as to the passion with which they demand justice and religious liberty. Their anger is vented against 'these Priests which are the bringers of the Nations into troubles, setting them one against the other ... whose throates are as open Sepulchres, who drinks up iniquity, and who swallowes down all.'[61]

John Roberts used equally vivid and intemperate language when trying to persuade Lady Dunch not settle with Mr. Brereton, George Bull's lawyer, but to leave him in prison and to spend her money on more deserving charitable causes than to pay off George Bull. 'To feed Such Devourers as these [the clergy] I do not account Charity, but rather like Pharaoh's lean kine they Eat up the fatt and the Goodly and look not a whitt the Better.'[62]

★   ★   ★

The arrival of George Bull at the rectory of Siddington Mary would have caused no small stir in the village. He made no secret of his high-church sympathies in the largely Presbyterian and Puritan neighbourhood, and it could only have been the death of Oliver Cromwell shortly afterwards that saved him from the attention of the Commonwealth authorities. In the following period of flux and uncertainty Bull was able to survive, uphold his principles and practices, and be drawn, unscathed, into the web of political intrigue which centred on his rectory.

The issue of tithes has high-lighted latent conflicts in this rural community. The financial interests of a monied *élite*, whether gentry or commercial entrepreneur, have been seen to lend support to a beleaguered clergy whose very livelihoods are threatened, as mounting criticism of an unpopular method of funding is translated into a refusal to pay up. Exploring this community further has revealed that the monied *élite* is populated with individuals who do not necessarily concur with the status quo and are prepared to circumvent punitive measures applied for its protection.

Contrasting images are presented of two young families. At one end of the village, up the long drive to the rambling rectory, upper class upholders of a vanished royalist establishment meet in secret with the young rector to plot for its return by force of arms. At the other end of the village, fronting the Ashton Keynes road, the coach of a high-born lady is publicly stationed in front of a farmhouse while, inside, her Ladyship and man-servant sit with a young yeoman, his family and egalitarian friends in silent worship of God, and later share their simple meal. They also are working for the return of a vanished order, 'the state [of perfection] when Adam was'. They have forsworn the use of force of arms, but their methods, already hinted at, still bring them into direct conflict with the authorities. Further examination of these methods becomes the focus of our next chapter.

*   *   *

On 9 August 1659, or thereabouts, John Roberts' only daughter Lydia died, aged eight. One can imagine the anguish within the family at the loss of the little girl: a favourite with her parents and granny; the one her older brother John had always protected; playmate of Thomas, aged seven; and nursemaid to Nathaniel aged two and Daniel aged one.

George Bull's stand over the non-payment of tithes and decision to have John Roberts put into the debtor's prison in Cirencester made it unthinkable to ask this 'hireling priest' to conduct the funeral in the village 'steeplehouse' across the field and to have her buried over there in the 'steeplehouse yard'. John and Lydia were aware that the issue of burials was a matter which other Friends' meetings were having to face, now that they had broken with the practices of the Established Church, and that plots of lands were being purchased or orchards used for the purpose.

Heartbroken at their loss, but resolved to face the likely condemnation from relations, John and Lydia decided that their orchard could become the burial ground for the Siddington Friends' meeting. Accordingly, Lydia was buried on 12 August with a simple service in the orchard at the end of their garden, not far from the little stream where she used to play. John's uncles and cousins, particularly the Solaces, were likely to be scandalized; the Solaces planned to have brass plates for themselves in the Lady Chapel in Cirencester parish church.

The following February there was another death within the meeting: Katherine, the wife of Roger Sparkes, died. On the blank page of the Second Book of Maccabees in the family bible, printed in 1551, where such records were kept, her husband wrote:

> Katharen wife of Roger Sparkes was taken out of the body the seaventeenth day of the twelfe mont called February in the yeare (1659) [1660] about the fourth houre in the affter none:

and buryed the eighteenth day of the same month; at Siddinton
in the County of Gloster in apercel of ground; of John Roberts
given by him for aburying place; for the people of the Lord to
be laid in; who are called in scorne by the world quackers.

He must have felt this loss keenly, for during the next few weeks
he endeavoured to regularize what for the moment was certainly a
generous act on John's part but still no more than a private arrangement with the present members of the Roberts *alias* Hayward
family. Discussions took place, and Roger appears as the prime-
mover in putting the matter on a legal footing. Consequently a
deed, dated 3 April 1660,[63] was drawn up conveying the burial
ground to Friends in consideration of £12 of good and lawful
money of England.

The first party to the conveyance comprise John Roberts
Hayward, yeoman of Siddington, and his mother, Mary, now a
widow, and for the other party are four Friends: Roger Sparkes,
Richard Townsend, Thomas Knight and Walter Hewlings (mis-
spelt as Hewlands). Later in the lengthy document these four are
referred to as Roger Sparkes etc., suggesting his prominence or
special interest. The conveyance was to last 1,000 years, with the
rent of one peppercorn payable, 'only if the same should be law-
fully demanded', on 20th March. The burial ground, no longer
open for burials, measures some 76 feet long and 40 feet wide (23m
x 12m), access to the ground being from the east across a brook
running north to south.

At the same time a narrow ledger, 150mm x 380 mm,[64] was
prepared and the first page entitled:

A Record of the Laying downe of the body of ffreinds and theyr
children and theyr burialls at Siddonton in a parcell of Ground
bought of John Roberts for that use and is neare adjoyning to
his house in the County of Glouc

The first two entries read:

Liddia the daughter of John Roberts was buried at Siddonton
the 12 day of the 6 month in the yeare 1659

Katheren the wife of Roger Sparkes of Cirencester layed downe
the body the 17 day 12 month & was buryed at Siddonton the
18 day of the same month in the yeare 1659 [1660]

Roger was buried at Siddington on 21 December 1665, and his son Jacob on 8 October 1666. The burials of John and Lydia Roberts *alias* Hayward, and their sons Thomas, John and Nathaniel are entered. The ledger record ends with Nathaniel's burial on 30 December 1707. Their youngest son, Daniel, was buried at Chesham, Bucks, in February 1726. However, John's mother Mary, although apparently in agreement with setting aside part of their orchard as a Friends' burial ground, was not buried there. Perhaps her relatives, the Solaces, prevailed.

When the meeting house in Thomas Street was built in 1673, the ground at the rear was also used as a burial ground. The first interment there was the burial of Thomas Barnfield on 27 September. Burials of Cirencester Friends then continued either at Thomas Street or at Siddington. The last burial at Siddington was in 1783.

NOTES

1. R. Nelson, *op. cit.* Nelson was one of George Bull's students in Siddington and is reliant on George's anecdotes for the account of his early life.

2. *Ibid*, pp.45 and 59. The Book of Common Prayer was rigidly disallowed under the Commonwealth. See Proceedings of Council, 21 December 1658, and the issue of letters to abolish Christmas and prevent the use of Common Prayer (*CSPD* 1658/9, p.225).

3. R. Nelson, *op. cit.*, p.45.

4. *Ibid*, p.48.

5. George Bull became acquainted with the Master family under unusual circumstances. His lodgings in the parish of St. George's were next to a gunpowder mill. This caused the parishioners some concern, and he was eventually persuaded to live with some local gentry, the Morgans. Mr. Morgan's wife was the daughter of Sir William Master of Cirencester. Later the powder mill exploded and George's earlier lodgings were demolished (Nelson, p.62). He may also have known William, George and John Master, who were his contemporaries at Oxford.

6 We encountered Alexander Gregory in Chapter 3 at the head of the column of Cirencester prisoners being marched off to Oxford in 1643; and again in Chapter 5 in dispute with local Anabaptists in 1648 over a number of matters, including the ministry of the Church of England, the calling of the ministry, and the right of tithes. As we shall see, these issues were still being lively contended ten years later.

7 R. Nelson, *op. cit.*, p.75.

8 *Ibid*, p.73.

9 *Ibid*, p.75.

10 *CSPD* 1655, p.vii.

11 A. Powell, *op. cit.*, p.92.

12 *CSPD* 1655, p.49, 6 December 1655.

13 *Ibid*, p.69, 26 December 1655.

14 *CSPD* 1658/9, p.353.

15 GRO D383.

16 GRO GDR V5 270T.

17 GRO wills Allaway 1662/24.

18 The Cirencester Parish Book (GRO P86 IN 6/3), a document confidential to the incumbent, provides details of the customary dues of the minister in 1706: 'for mortuaries the minister has twelve pence for Reading the Service at the Grave when the Corpse is buried with tolling of the Great Bell, and two shillings and sixpence for Reading the full Evening Service in the Church at whatever Funeral it is desired. For breaking the ground in the chancel ten shillings. For every woman that is churched fourpence; for everyone in the Parish above 16 years of age twopence at Easter, except hired servants, whether men or women, and their Easter due is sixpence a piece.' The customary due for a woman getting married, whether in the parish or not, was five shillings. Reading the banns for a man cost him two shillings.

19 G. Brocklehurst, *op. cit.*, p.5ff.

20 *Valor Ecclesiasticus Henricus VIII*, Vol.2, p.245.

21 A.C. Percival and W.J. Sheils: 'A Survey of the Diocese of Gloucester 1603' in *Ecclesiastical Miscellany*, Bristol and Gloucestershire Archaeological Society, pp.96/7.

22 Sir Richard Atkyns, *op. cit.*, pp.651/2.

23 G. Brocklehurst, *op. cit.*, p.16.

24 GRO D269 B/T1.

25 GRO GDR 231. It was the responsibility of the owner of the rectory, rector or impropriator, to keep the chancel in good repair. The nave was the responsibility of the parish through the churchwardens.

26 GRO D2525 Box 17.

27 Further, the vicar of Cirencester had to find his own accommodation until 1695, when at last a vicarage was purchased; up till then an allowance of £4 per annum had been made to him for rent (Cirencester Parish Book, *op.cit.*). An augmentation of £30 was made to the vicar's income by the Trustees for the Maintenance of Ministers, a government body, during the Commonwealth period, in December 1655, with a further increase in March 1659. (*CSPD* 1655, p.71; 1658/9 p.295). In January 1699 the sum of £616 was raised by public subscription to buy the vicar an annuity of £30. (Cirencester Parish Book, *op. cit.*).

28 Sir Richard Atkyns, *op. cit.*, p.344.

29 Glebe terriers 1624 (GRO GDR V5 270T) and 1677 (GRO P293 IN 3/2). The glebe terrier of 1698 (GRO P293 IN 3/3), however, makes reference to a 'composition' or modus agreed between the incumbent and the lord of the manor for the latter to pay £38 each 1st August in lieu of hay and privy [personal] tithes on specified meadow, pasture ground and arable. It would seem that George Bull's successor, Joseph Stephens, had come to this arrangement with the Bathurst family, the new lords of the manor.

30 GRO Q/R1 127 Siddington.

31 *Memoir*, p.146 (omitted in *OR*).

32 A. Pearson, *op. cit.*, p.vii.

33 *Memoir*, p.72 (*OR* p.6).

34 *Matthew* 10.8.

35 J. Gratton, *op. cit.*, p.300.

36 *Ibid*, p.303.

37 *Ibid*, p.304.

38 C. Lesley, *op.cit.*, p.i.

39 *Memoir*, p.129 (*OR* p.43). Ten Quakers gave as the reason for their imprisonment in Gloucester Castle in September 1658: 'for that they cannot pay tythes unto A man they know is not of gods sending, noe minister of Christs, that teacheth for filthy Lucur and miends Earthly things, such mind not the Lord Jesus but theire owne bodyes.' *CSPD* 1658/9, p.149.

40 A.C. Braithwaite: 'Early Tithe Persecutions – Friends as Outlaws'. *Journal of the Friends Historical Society*, Vol. 49, No. 3, p.149.

41 *Memoir*, p.126 (*OR* p.41).

42 2 & 3 Ed.VI c.13 Sect. 1.

43 The account of this imprisonment and the events that followed appear early on in the *Memoir* (pp 84-102; *OR* pp.14-19) and are placed before John Roberts' debates with Bishop William Nicholson, who was appointed to the see of Gloucester in 1660/1. In the Great Book

of Sufferings, however, the story appears, undated, on the page for 1681; this date is used by Besse. I follow Lawrence in seeing this imprisonment as occurring before the Restoration. I base this on biographical data of characters who are about to be introduced in the story. Alexander Cornwall, who *subsequently* became a Quaker, was arrested with other Friends in Cirencester on 13 January 1661.

Elizabeth Hewlings was buried in the Friends' burial ground at Siddington on 7 August 1670. Thomas Car(e)les(s) was not yet vicar of Cirencester in 1658/9, but still the up-and-coming young vicar of nearby Barnsley; however, he died in 1675, making 1681 an impossible date.

44 GRO P86/CH 12/2.

45 GRO Q/SO1.

46 GRO D182 III 79.

47 The Quarter Sessions Indictment Book (GRO Q/SIb1) opens with Elizabeth senior, Elizabeth junior, Mary and Jacob and three other Quakers from Harnhill presented for not having attended national worship for three months since September 1660. Jacob Hewlings was a particular focus for attack in the 1680s and was regularly pursued through the consistory court for his church rate of 3s.4d. in the 1690s, when such prosecutions had died down elsewhere in the deanery or diocese. They were a prosperous and influential family who would not be subdued; the hearth tax returns for 1671[15] show Jacob occupying a considerable establishment assessed at 8 hearths in Harnhill.

48 *A Short Relation of some part of the Sad Sufferings and Cruel Havock and Spoil Inflicted on the Persons and Estates of the People of God, in scorn called Quakers, for meeting together to Worship God in Spirit and Truth Since the late Act against Conventicles*, London 1670.

49 According to Lawrence (E.T. Lawrence, *op.cit.*, p.329), Lady Dunch was the daughter and sole heiress of Sir Anthony Hungerford, who was buried on 18 October 1653. She married Edmund Dunch of Little Wittenham, Bucks., in 1645 (?), bringing with her a fortune of £60,000; this included the manor of Down Ampney. Her mother, Lady Jane, who died 29 January 1652, is described in the Down Ampney parish register as 'a very religious woman, full of good works'. The Hungerford manor house, where these events take place, had been built during the reign of Henry VIII. Her husband had been created Baron Burnell of East Wittenham in 1658. Lawrence is less precise on their dates: Edmund Dunch 'did not long survive his elevation' and the death of his lady 'occurred not long after'.

50 Adapted from *Memoir*, p.87 (*OR* p.16).

51 *Memoir*, p.91 (*OR* p.18).

52 This is to be explored more fully in Chapter 9.
53 *Memoir*, pp.93-94 (*OR* p.19-24).
54 *MS Memoir*, p.14.
55 *Memoir*, p.101 (*OR* p.25).
56 *Ibid*, p.102 (*OR* p.25).
57 Thomas' surname is variously spelt: Carles, Careles and Careless. The latter spelling is used consistently in the *Memoir*, reflecting local pronunciation or even local humour. Son of Philip Careles of Lothbury, London, he matriculated at Balliol College, Oxford in 1641 at the age of 15. He gained his B.A. in February 1644/5, and his M.A. in December 1649. In 1652 he became a fellow of his college and was appointed preacher in St. Aldates church, Oxford. In 1654 he was appointed to the rectory of Barnsley, which he held until his death in 1675. In March 1663 he assumed the additional responsibility of vicar of Cirencester. He died on 7 October 1675, aged 50, and was buried in Cirencester. There was formerly a monument to him in Cirencester parish church (S. Rudder).
58 *Memoir*, pp.95-99 (*OR* pp.21-24).
59 *These several Papers was sent to the Parliament the twentieth day of the fifth Month 1659. Being above seven thousand of the Names of the Handmaids and Daughters of the Lord and such as feels the oppression of Tithes*, London 1659.
60 *Ibid*, pp.51-52. At Lady Dunch's instigation John Roberts had been drawn into debate with Thomas Careles, defending what had been termed a 'Damnable Doctrine and Daingerous Tenett', and courting these risks.
61 *Ibid*, p.51.
62 *Memoir*, p.90 (*OR* p.18).
63 GRO R96/1432 6401.
64 GRO R96/1432 6401.

CHAPTER 7

Threshing the Mountain

Behold, I will make you a threshing sledge, new sharp and having teeth; you shall thresh the mountains and crush them, and you shall make the hills like chaff;

You shall winnow them and the wind shall carry them away, and the tempest shall scatter them. And you shall rejoice in the LORD; in the Holy One of Israel you shall glory.

Isaiah 41, vv 15-16

OUR LAST CHAPTER, SET principally in the village of Siddington, saw two of its inhabitants locked in an ideological struggle. The arrival of the well-connected young rector, of a strong Anglican persuasion, with his new bride to occupy the rectory of Siddington Mary, not fifteen minutes walk away from the Roberts' home, overturned whatever understandings and accommodations the villagers had reached with his predecessor. He laid claim to his divine right to tithes. Come the corn harvest of 1658, George Bull faced up to the established and respected Roberts family, demanded his dues and, meeting resistance, sought satisfaction through the ecclesiastical courts. We glimpsed a little of this young man's background and education, identified his leanings in church and national politics, and followed his first steps in a promising career. There was a logic to his actions in Siddington: they appear predictable, consistent and justified. Whatever personal qualms he may have felt, he was assured of the legal, moral and political support not only of the established church, but of an influential section of the local gentry as well.

111

The case with John Roberts is rather different. He has abandoned all previous caution, regardless of the inevitable outcome, and has refused to pay the rector's due. His stand on the issue of tithes, though perhaps secretly admired by a proportion of the farming community, would have been regarded as little more than foolhardy. It could only court the wrath of the social establishment and would mean financial ruin for himself and family. John appears fired with emotion, speaks with a strong inner conviction and will not be deterred. The incident occurs less than three years after the visit of the north country Quaker women to his farmhouse in Siddington Peter. What has taken place in the intervening period to explain his behaviour?

At the end of 1655 we left him, a thirty-four year old yeoman, at his meeting with Richard Farnsworth in Banbury gaol. It had been a time of revelation and discovery as John had been pointed to look to the 'light within'. But the implications which the spiritual experience carried with it could only have become clear to him as the days and months passed. Being a Quaker was not something one could or did keep secret. It implied a change in life style and led to a stand that would provoke conflict. Daniel Roberts describes it as: 'after that time he patiently bore the Cross'[1] and suggests that it was some time later before 'it had pleased God to Communicate to him the Knowledge of his blessed Truth'.[2]

But John Roberts would have had few role models on which to base a new life style, and only his local friends to turn to for support. It would be a mistake to see the Quakerism of this period as much more than a wave building on the ground-swell of radical Puritan opinion. A rudimentary network of missionary preachers based on Swarthmoor Hall in north Lancashire had emerged, and these were moving south, contacting pockets of radicalism and gaining adherents. To understand this incipient movement as a religious sect in any modern sense would be quite anachronistic.[3] It had as yet no defined structure, no buildings, no tests for membership and little literature. Rather, it was composed of clusters of amorphous local groups, visited from time to time by charismatic preachers. Its centre was the silent meeting for worship and waiting on God, its handbook the Bible, but not in any literal sense for it looked to the Spirit that gave forth the scriptures to reveal God's truth. This, in turn, invited an individual quest.

On his return to Siddington John Roberts shared his experience at Banbury with his wife Lydia and, without doubt, with the group of Seekers who met in his house. He would also have begun to make contact with other Quaker groups that were springing up in the vicinity. In Nailsworth there had also been a group of Seekers: these had turned Quaker following a visit from the itinerant Herefordshire preacher, Humphrey Smith, in 1655. In the same year Humphrey Smith had visited Thomas Loveday and his wife and John Mason and his wife in Painswick, who had then begun to hold meetings for worship in their homes.[4] It is likely that some sort of loose association developed between these groups, and that joint meetings began to be held at perhaps monthly intervals.

A significant event for all these emerging Quaker groups would have been the visit of George Fox to Tetbury on 5 October 1656. Freed from six month's incarceration in the foul dungeon of Doomsdale in Launceston Castle on 9 September, Fox was visiting Quaker groups along his route from the west country up to London. He records his recollection of the open-air meeting held on the estate of Justice Nathaniel Cripps at Upton, near Tetbury:

> And from thence we passed the next First-day [Sunday] to Justice Nathaniel Cripps's in Wiltshire where there were about two or three thousand people, and all was quiet. And the mighty power of God was manifested and people were turned to the grace and Truth that came by Jesus in their hearts, which would teach them to deny all manner of ungodliness and worldly lust and would teach them to live soberly and godly in the present world .... So here was their teacher, the grace of God, that would teach them how to live and what to deny .... and this was a free teacher to every one of them, and they might come to be heirs of this grace and of Christ from whence it came; who ended the prophets and the priests that took tithes, and the temple. And as for the hireling priests that took tithes, and their temples (which priests were made at schools and colleges and not by Christ), with all their inventions they were to be denied.[5]

He spoke to the crowd for several hours 'and the people turned to the spirit of God in their hearts, that by it they might be led into all Truth ... And all people generally went away satisfied and admired [amazed] and were glad they were turned to Christ Jesus their teacher and saviour'.[6]

Was this point at which it pleased God to communicate to John Roberts the knowledge of his Truth? Fox had given the same Quaker message as Richard Farnsworth: that the grace of God in their hearts – or the light within – or Christ – would be their teacher; it was available to every one of them, not just to God's elect as taught by Calvinists; this inward teacher would show them how to live and what to deny. The corollary was that they had now no need of human teachers, particularly the paid clergy who did not follow Christ's injunction: 'Freely have you received; freely give'.[7] These should be denied.

It was to counter such teaching that in February 1655 a Commonwealth proclamation, specifically mentioning Quakers and Ranters, had warned against disrupting church services. Further, General Desborow, the military commander for the south-west (for the country was under military rule), had re-iterated the point in detailed instructions to his lieutenants in Gloucestershire in January 1656.[8]

Fox's appeal led to attempts by a number of Quakers in Gloucestershire to confront the clergy publicly. In May 1657 Samuel Clift, a clothier from Avening, the adjoining village to Upton, 'was moved to goe to the steeplehouse [church] upon the first day of the week [Sunday] and there stood patiently among the people for the space of an houre or thereabouts while [the priest] was preaching and praying'. Imprisoned in Gloucester Castle on a charge that he 'volluntarily and maliciously did by word and deed and overture molest and interrupt Samuel Hierne Clerk', Samuel Clift was acquitted at the quarter sessions.[9] In Dursley, again a few miles from Upton, in 1658, Deborah Harding waited for the minister to finish his sermon before standing up to give a Christian exhortation to the congregation, as was her right under the Commonwealth Directory, but 'they fell into an Uproar, some crying 'Kill her', and others 'Strike her down', others 'Tear her in pieces'. The Magistrates, to secure her from the Rabble, sent her to Prison'.[10]

In contrast to a later stage, when persecution against Quakers became intense and it was their practice to keep careful records of incidents, there was little systematic record-keeping among Quakers during the final years of the Commonwealth,[11] and any records that have survived from this period must be treated as minimal accounts. There would have been a number of similar incidents in Gloucestershire in this period for which we have no official record. The national picture that George Fox gained from his travels in 1656 was that there were seldom less than a thousand Quakers in prison.[12]

One incident for which we have no official record is Daniel Roberts' account of how his father felt the necessity 'Laid upon him to go on a first-day, in the Morning, to the public Worship-house in Cirencester, in the time of Worship, not knowing what might be required of him when he came there'.[13] The parish church has the proportions of a small cathedral, and in those days had two galleries on the north side of the nave, one for Lady Poole and her family, and the other for the Hungerfords. It would have been well filled, each family of the middle and better sort in its assigned pew, in social ranking, with the Master family sitting at the front of the central aisle in the nave, and the Georges prominently in the first pew in the chancel. The common sort were consigned to benches at the rear where unruly elements and restless children would have been kept in check by the patrolling of the specially appointed Church Walker.[14]

While the rest of the congregation were thus seated in enforced decorum, John Roberts stood up with his hat on, a sign of protest in the manner of Samuel Clift of Avening. The minister, Alexander Gregory, refused to continue with the service, and John was escorted to the door by the churchwardens who stood there to ensure that he did not return. Daniel says that his father stood outside, waiting a little time in stillness, then made off across the market place to go home. There is the suggestion of self-restraint on the part of the minister and the churchwardens, possibly in deference to John's social standing; from their point of view, a regrettable incident which was passed off with dignity.

But the story does not end there. Crossing the market place, John stopped to tie his shoe-lace when 'there came a man behind him with a Stone in his hand and Strook [struck] him a hard blow on the Back – saying 'There! take that for Jesus Christ sake!' He [John] Reply'd, 'So I do,' not Looking back to See who it was, but went his way.' Some days later the man called on John to ask his pardon because he could find no peace until he had. It was the man's visit, rather than his own protest in Cirencester parish church, that held the greater significance for John. Initially very unsure of himself and the rightness of his action afterwards, John found in the man's contrition 'great Confirmation that he was in the Right way'.[15]

★   ★   ★

John Roberts' example was soon followed by others. In the summer of 1657 Robert Sylvester, a leading Quaker from Nailsworth, and Philip Gray, a glover, and Thomas Onion, both from Cirencester, made a similar protest in Cirencester parish church, standing silently with their hats on during the Sunday service.[15] On this occasion Alexander Gregory was much less patient. He stopped the service, saying that 'he could not go forward while those Dumb Dogs Stood there'. Members of the congregation seized the Quakers and dragged them out of the church. At the first opportunity the minister made a complaint to the justices that his service had been disrupted, and the three Quakers were bound over to appear at the Quarter Sessions at Gloucester at the beginning of September.

The county Quarter Sessions Indictment and Order books for the Commonwealth period have not survived, so that an official version of the proceedings against the Quakers is not available to us. We do not know, for example, the composition of the bench on this occasion but we can anticipate, judging from county records four years later in the early Restoration period,[16] that some dozen justices of the peace would have been present, and a similar number of respected citizens forming the Magna Inquisitio (grand jury). The Quarter Sessions became, therefore, something of a social occasion (but not quite to the same extent as the twice-yearly assizes) when prominent landed gentry, the legal fraternity, the litigants, the witnesses and the defendants would make their way to the county town and fill its inns, as Ceilia Fiennes found to her annoyance thirty years later.[17] Justices, who had dealt with particular cases at the local petty sessions and referred them higher, would make it their business to be present and sit with their colleagues on the bench.

In contrast to our present-day ideal of formality and impartiality in court, we must imagine a more individual, personal and on occasion convivial character to the proceedings that, from time to time, could get out of hand. At the Trinity [June] Sessions of 1674 orders were made, reminding the Gloucestershire justices that only one piece of business might be dealt with at one time, that they were not to speak publicly to other men in court during the 'agitation' of any business, that others disturbing the court would be reproved by the chairman of the bench and removed.[18] At the Epiphany [January] Sessions of 1676 the lawyers present were reminded that attorneys could practise only as seconds, except in the default of counsel, that the court would hear no case unless counsel be retained, and that counsel were to attend in their bar gowns.[19]

That the three men engaged counsel is unlikely: for the next twenty-five years Quakers attempted to conduct their own defence. But they did ask John Roberts to accompany them into court – because of his courage and outspokenness, or his education and experience, or perhaps his social standing. When their case came up they would have attempted to appear before the justices wearing their hats, which would have caused great offence. Alexander Gregory's evidence, that they had disturbed divine service, certainly would have enraged the justices still further. Without calling for the defence, the justices found them guilty and ordered the mittimus[20] to be made, consigning them to the county gaol.

With 'the Zeal of the Lord kindled in him', John Roberts stepped forward and in open court challenged the chairman of the bench, John Stephens.[21]

J.R.: Are not those who Sit on the Bench Sworn to do Justice? Is there not a man amonge you will do the thing that is Just and Right?

J.S.: Who are you, Sarrah? What is your name?

J.R.: John Roberts.

J.S.:   I am glad I have you here, I have heard of you. You deserve a Stone-Dublett (meaning a Jayl). There is many an honester man than you hang'd.

J.R.:   It may be so. But what dost thou think becoms of those who Hang Honest Men?

J.S.:   I will send you to prison; and if any Insurrection or tumult be in the Land, I will come and cutt your throat, first, with my own Sword; for I fear to Sleep in my bed at night Lest Such phanaticks as you Should come and cut my throat.

And in the heat of passion 'he took up a ball of Wax, which Lay near him, and violently threw it at my Father; but he, haveing timely warning, avoided the blow by Steping aside'.[22]

The justice was furious. And the Quakers had deliberately provoked him, as they had Alexander Gregory. It is difficult for us, at this distance removed in time, to comprehend the sense of outrage felt by these twin pillars of the politico-ecclesiastical establishment, justice of the peace and minister of the church, as their authority was flaunted. To us there is a quaintness to the conflict over hat honour and plain speech: to them, however, it was an open challenge to their status and power.

Hierarchical society of the seventeenth century had evolved its elaborated codes of deference – both within the family itself and in the gradations of society. Hats, universally worn, were doffed by men to a recognised social superior, who was greeted with a *congée*, that is bowing with the knee slightly bent and the other foot drawn back along the ground, and offering an appropriate salutation, such as 'Your humble servant, sir'.[23] There were gradations of salutation, many of which persist to this day: your grace, your honour, my lord, master or plain Tom.

The 'thou' form of the verb, used consistently by John Roberts to Justice Stephens, was the appropriate mode of address to children, pets, very close friends, a servant; more widely used among the common sort, it was excluded from the mannered society of the gentry and above. Used inappropriately, 'thou' became a term of over-familiarity, condescension, contempt or even abuse. However, believing that all were equal in the sight of God, Quakers were not willing to follow these codes of behaviour: 'thou' was the second person of the verb singular, and 'you' the plural.[24]

Why did these Quakers want to cause offence? Abrupt reactions of outrage are symptomatic of those whose values, frequently unrecognised and subconsciously held, are being challenged. Acceptance of a stratified patriarchical society, ordained by God, and preserved in turn by king, bishop, justice, priest, down to the venerable head of each family, was here being confronted by an egalitarian ideal, also believed to be ordained by God, whereby all are His children, recipients of His free grace, endowed with the gifts of His free Spirit, and called to His service as they are led. That all should be equal in the sight of God and man, greeted as equals and addressed as equals, could only be seen by the squirearchy as a dangerous 'levelling' principle, harking back to the preposterous claims of the mutinous troops finally cornered at Burford: reform of parliament, almost universal male suffrage, reform of the legal system, abolition of tithes, religious toleration.[25] In brief, this meant their ordered (and privileged) world turned upside down. It was sedition, and those that wanted it so were lumped together as that 'levelling crew' or 'phanaticks'. The finer distinctions that we, with detachment and hindsight, can make between Levellers, True Levellers or Diggers, Muggletonians, Fifth Monarchists, or Quakers, were then less easily visible. Such people were to be recognised by their uncouth manners and obstinacy.

Justice Stephens' outburst in court serves as a barometer for the political climate of 1657. To us it may seem extreme, even unbalanced, but such was the neurosis prevalent in the administration. Our introduction to George Bull in the last chapter revealed the existence of a pro-royalist faction active in Gloucestershire, with royalist agents preparing for an uprising.[26] To these worries should be added the authorities' concern for the personal safety of Oliver Cromwell. A government report of 15 January 1657 reads:

> Last week a plot was discovered: in the chapel of Whitehall were trains of [gun]powder and other combustibles to fire it, and meantime some desperadoes were to assassinate the Protector.[27]

This abortive coup was the work of disaffected officers of the New Model Army and Fifth Monarchy men: nine of Cromwell's own bodyguard were arrested on suspicion of being implicated. The issue was the belief that Cromwell would accept the Crown which was being offered him: the Fifth Monarchy men would have no other king but King Jesus.

On 9 April 1657, writing to Ambassador Lockhardt in Paris, Secretary Thurloe reports another attempted uprising:

> The fifth monarchy men designed an insurrection and were so ready that they had appointed their rendezvous this night at Mile End Green, but we had notice of it and seized some 20 of their ringleaders, as they were ready to take horse, took many arms and ammunition ... There was a declaration which set forth a new government.[28]

But before the end of the month popular belief would have it otherwise:

> On the discovery of the late plot against his Highness Major General Harrison, Captain Lawson and Colonel Danvers have been secured in custody by the sergeant-at-arms attending Council ... It is said that Anabaptists and Quakers were chiefly active in the conspiracy.[29]

It is against this background that Justice Stephens wants to have John Roberts and his fellow Quakers secure inside Gloucester Castle, where, should there be a local uprising, he will personally slit their throats.

Little wonder, then, that the court dispenses with the defendants' defence. The issue before the justices is no longer the vicar's exasperation with troublesome dissenters: it is replaced by their primary concern for keeping the peace and the safety of the state.

John Roberts, Robert Sylvester, Philip Gray and Thomas Onion were conveyed on 7 September 1657 to the gaoler of Gloucester Castle, the county gaol, situated on the site of the present-day H.M. prison near the water front, then busy with shipping. That afternoon John composed an affectionate letter to Lydia, his wife, offering her reassurance and consolation:

> Dear Heart, be not discouraged but wait on him [God] in the Light of himself, who is able to supply all thy wants: & be a Husband to thee, & a Father to thy Children, & a present help in trouble. Dear Friend, I have found the fathers Love much to me, who hath counted me worthy to suffer for his truths sake...[30]

He asks her to visit him as soon as possible, and to bring his eldest son John so that he can learn the way. In seventeenth century gaols prisoners were expected to provide their own necessities, and his son would have to make the 40 mile round trip quite frequently.

But the letter was never delivered. Its despatch was overtaken by a visit that evening from John's uncle, Justice Andrew Solace, who had secured John's release, offering to stand security for him until the next Quarter Sessions, when the gaoler would present the calendar of the prisoners and his case would be reviewed.

It was a frosty encounter between uncle and nephew, the justice embarrassed by his nephew's behaviour in court, and the Quaker still smarting from what he saw as a gross miscarriage of justice:

A.S.:   Coussin, are you willing to Except your Liberty to go home to your wife and famiely?

J.R.:   On what terms, Uncle?

A.S.:   On Such Terms that the Jayler open the Door and let you out.

J.R.:   What! without entering into any Recognizances?

A.S.:   Yes.

J.R.:   Then I except of my Liberty. But I admire [am astonished], Uncle, how thou, and Severall others of you who Satt on the Bench, could Sitt as with your thumbs in your Mouths when you Should Speak a word in behalf of the Innocent.

A.S.:   You must Learn to Live under a Law, Cousin, and if you accept of your Liberty till Sessions you may have it. If not, Stay where you are.[31]

The next day, with the gaoler's permission, John Roberts returned home. And the letter? – Lydia kept it, her three sons in turn kept it, her granddaughter Elizabeth transcribed it, and it was preserved among the treasured possessions of the family.

★   ★   ★

That night John simply could not sleep. Lydia watched him tossing and turning in bed as she got up to breast-feed Nathaniel. John became convinced that God was calling him to confront Justice John Stephens but he could not bear the thought. In the early hours

husband and wife talked it through, and in the end Lydia provided
the moral support he needed:

> If thou are fully perswaded that the Lord requires it of thee, I
> would not have thee Disobey him, for he will require nothing
> of us but what he will enable us to go through; therefore we
> have good cause to trust in him.[32]

John could not face any breakfast and in the first light saddled
his horse. Mounted and ready to set off down the Cirencester road,
he felt that the command of the Lord was: 'Remember Lot's wife:
do not look back'. Passing through the deserted streets and market
place of the town, he took the Bisley road, out up Cecily Hill, past
Oakley Wood, across the steep valley of the Frome and then right
to Lypiatt. The fresh morning air was a tonic; in fact, he began to
enjoy the nine-mile ride. But once in sight of Justice Stephens'
mansion[20] the earlier panic feelings returned. He argued to himself:
he was sure to be arrested again; Uncle Andrew would not rescue
him another time; he was abandoning his wife and family – and
what would his neighbours say?

In the end he reined in his horse, dismounted and sat down by
the track. He laid his fears before God:

> after some time of waiting in Silence, the Lord appeared again,
> and the Cloud was soon gone, and the word of the Lord was
> to him, 'Go, and I will go with thee, and will give thee a new
> Sharp Threshing Instrument, and thou shalt Thresh the
> Mountain'.[33]

He was filled with a sense of the love and goodness of God, and
said quietly: 'Thy presence is enough'.

To the modern reader it is bewildering that John Roberts should
associate the violent imagery of a mighty threshing sledge, crushing
mountains as chaff, with the love and goodness of God. Further
examination of the biblical text, *Isaiah* Chapter 41, may provide an
explanation. The quotation itself is taken from verse 15, but it is
earlier verses in the chapter that could well have provided the reassurance and strength that John was looking for. 'I have called you
my servant, have chosen you and not cast you off' (v.9); 'be not
afraid, for I am your God (v.10); 'all who set themselves against
you shall be as nothing' (v.11); 'I say to you, Do not fear; it is I who
help you' (v.13). Perhaps the narrative has become elided, and

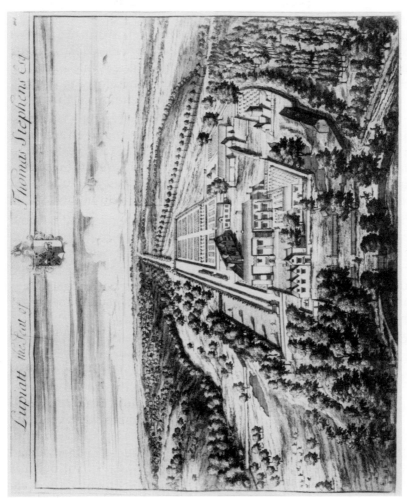

Lipiatt Manor, seat of Justice Stephens.

reference to these verses lost in the telling. What has remained, since it held particular significance for John and Daniel Roberts and their audience of early Quakers, is the image of the powerful threshing sledge, taken from the prophet's vision of the end of time, and speaking of God's judgment and sovereign power. It was their belief that they were called by God to be his servants in the last throes of a cosmic struggle between good and evil; that the Antichrist was about to be overthrown and a new rule of justice and righteousness ushered in; that there was, therefore, an urgency to warn their contemporaries against the impending cataclysm.[34]

From the narrative it is clear that these were John Roberts' sentiments when he rode into Justice Stephens' stable yard, left his horse with the groom, encountered the clerk to the Quarter Sessions (surprised and irritated to see John out of prison), waited in the large hall of the manor house, and eventually was shown into the justice's presence. He felt he had a message to deliver.

A tense and gauche John Roberts, who had paced the hall and prepared his speech, was quite disarmed by the manner of John Stephens. His 'greatest enemy', who had 'before behaved himself very feirce, like a Lyon', came forward to greet him, shook his hand and, with a smile, asked, 'Friend Hayward, how do you do?' Nonplussed, John replied, 'Pretty well' – and, then, remembering the purpose of his visit, launched on his declaration.

J.R.: I am come in the fear and Dread of the God of Heaven to warn thee to repent of thy wickedness with Speed, Least he cutt the thread of thy Life and Send thee to the pitt that is bottomless. I am come to warn thee in Great Love, whether thou wilt hear or for bare, that I may be clear of thy Blood in the day of account, and preach the Everlasting Gospell to thee.

J.S.: You are a Welcome Messenger to me. – That is what I have Long desired to hear.

J.R.: The Everlasting Gospell is the same God Sent his Servant John to declare, when he saw an Angell fly through the midst of Heaven, Saying with a Loud Voyce, 'Fear God and give Glory to him; for the hour of his Judgment is come: and worship him who made heaven and Earth, the Sea, and fountains of Water'.

The justice took the Quaker by the arm, and they sat down side by side on the couch. He said quietly, 'I believe your Mission is of God, and I Receive it as Such. I am Sorrey I have done you wrong, but I will never wrong you more. I would pray you to forgive me, and to pray God to forgive me.' They talked for a long time. The justice asked, 'Would you like to eat and drink, for the best in my house is at your disposal?', but the Quaker declined and eventually took his leave. 'So they parted in much Love.'[35]

The four Quakers appeared again before the justices of the peace at the Epiphany Quarter Sessions 1658 in Gloucester. Before their case came up, Justice Stephens had caught sight of them and called across the court, 'John, I accept of your appearance and Discharge you, and the Court discharges you, So you may go about your business'.

The clerk of the court was less generous and demanded his fees, which the Quakers refused to pay, believing themselves to be innocent of any crime. John Roberts stoutly maintained, 'I don't know that I owe any man here anything but Love, and must I now purchase my Liberty with my money?' Another area of conflict had thus arisen, which Justice Stephens then attempted to circumvent. After considerable pestering by the clerk, he announced, 'John, you are discharged paying the fees of the Court'. But the Quakers were not prepared to accept their liberty on such terms; they wanted to be found 'not guilty'. So they were taken off again to Gloucester Castle by the gaoler . That night, however, Justice Stephens came to the prison in person and had them released.[36]

★   ★   ★

There is one more side to this story – that of Lydia Roberts. On the day of her husband's visit to Lypiatt manor she and their eldest son John had ridden across to a Quaker gathering at Justice Nathaniel Cripps' house at Upton, near Tetbury. A prominent Quaker, William Dewsbury, was to speak. She kept her worries to herself and gained little from the meeting. When it was over, William Dewsbury began to pace up and down, in a very agitated manner, along the corridor where people had collected. Eventually he came across to Lydia, took her by the hand and said, 'Woman, thy Sorrow is Great, I Sorrow with thee'.

He resumed his pacing. Then, after some time, he came back to her, 'Now the time has come that those who marry must be as though they married not – those that have Husbands as though they had none, for the Lord now calls for all to be offer'd up'. Lydia and the preacher had never met before. The conviction that God had given this stranger a sense of her burden produced in her a feeling of release and she 'went home rejoicing in the Lord'.

John had got back to Siddington before her. When they shared their experiences with one another the emotion was too great. They simply burst into tears 'in a Sence of the Lord's so Eminently making way for and helping them that day'.[37]

★   ★   ★

This chapter has focused on the turn of events in Cirencester in the latter half of 1657 when four Quakers decided to take their protest against tithes and 'hireling priests' into the public arena. It became rapidly apparent that the authorities would not permit their action to remain an unwelcome extension of the religious debate, but would summarily treat it as a threat to public order and possible sedition. Social processes at work in the mid-seventeenth century legal system have been brought into view, and we have been introduced to the system's main pillar of support, the justice of the peace.

The story, on this occasion, has a happy ending, with almost all the parties reaching an understanding and achieving greater mutual respect. Long imprisonment has been avoided, and we do not read of the four affronting the vicar in his church again. To this extent, a tenuous, localized instance of toleration, if not tolerance, can be recognized. But this was not universally the case. The events here described occurred against a background of scattered pockets of persecution – in Evesham and Banbury, as we have already seen, or, as the State Papers reveal, in Colchester, Dorset and Exeter.[38] If four Quakers were released from Gloucester Castle in 1658, ten more were detained.[39]

This led, as we saw in the last chapter, to a mass petition of 7,000 Quaker women and sympathizers in 1659. It was preceded, in September 1658, by Quaker lobbying of the Protector and his Council:

> Many of these prisoners have been in 2 years; some for bidding
> the priest repent and the people fear God; some for not
> swearing [taking an oath]; others for not doffing their hats to
> a proud man; all for conscience' sake and not for evil doing.
> Some are hauled out of their meetings and whipped; some are
> almost killed going to meetings.[40]

The term 'prisoners for conscience sake' and the tactics of
silent, non-violent public protest in churches, or of lobbying the
civil authorities by letter and petition have a ring of modernity about
them. The arena of confrontation was being shifted from the rule
of might to the power of moral argument.

In the same month John Fielder and 19 Quakers pushed this
argument still further: if Quakers were being persecuted and
unjustly imprisoned for conscience sake, then did this not call into
question the very *raison d'être* of the Commonwealth, brought in
to safeguard individual liberty?

> It may seem strange to you that so many friends [Quakers]
> should be cast into prison that there is hardly a gaol where
> there are not some. It is no less strange to us that such suffer-
> ings should come for conscience' sake, when most of us have
> been instruments with you in casting off the burden of oppres-
> sion, and when you have pretended [promised] so much liberty
> of conscience and have practised the same things for which we
> suffer.
>
> What have we done? What laws have we broken? What
> plots are we engaged in? ... We have been persecuted, beaten,
> stoned, stocked, hauled out of our synagogues, cast into
> dungeons and noisome [stinking] vaults, denied food for days
> together, not allowed pen, ink and paper, and a legal trial
> refused or postponed for months, during which some have died
> ... Was not freedom of conscience the great cause in the late
> wars?[41]

But granting liberty of conscience on the Quakers' terms was
not an option for the Protector's Council. It suspected that the
Quaker demands contained a dangerous and seditious levelling
principle which would dismantle the structure of seventeenth
century hierarchical society. Quaker irreverence in refusing to doff
the hat or bow and scrape did more than transgress the social codes
of deference: it also carried messages of radicalism, subversion and

a collapse of authority. It was met not only by indignation, but also by fear. This was particularly felt in the army and navy where converts to Quaker principles among the officers and other ranks were seen as a corrupting influence and prejudicial to sound military discipline.[42]

This chapter has demonstrated how the neurosis which gripped civil government in the final years of the Commonwealth generated a siege mentality. Fears of plots from within and without led to reactions of panic and scapegoating which find their parallel in our own century in the McCarthyist communist witch-hunts. At the national level a Committee of Safety was formed to purge the judiciary and army of unreliable elements. With puzzling mental dexterity it was able to lump together Quakers and Anabaptists with Catholics as the 'reds' of the time.[43]

There is here a double irony: firstly, that while John Roberts and his Quaker friends were being abused and punished as the perpetrators of insurrections, the actual subversives, the more socially respectable group of plotters centred on the Siddington Mary rectory, went unnoticed and unscathed; and secondly, that for the Royalists, too, the Quakers were the 'baddies'. After the fall of Richard Cromwell it was the Quakers, Brownists and Anabaptists who, the Royalists maintained, were in the ascendant with Sir Henry Vane, who were strongest in Parliament, who composed the new regiments of foot being raised under a famous Quaker from New England.[44] While this scaremongering was rife among the Royalists, more quietly and realistically, the Commonwealth Committee of Safety steadily continued its work of purging the army of any Quaker officers.[45]

Daniel Roberts' narrative, however, takes us away from the rhetoric of central government and the exiled faction, and makes available to us the authentic voices of local people. Again he skilfully contrasts the registers of language – of polite society, of anger, scorn, consolation and what may be termed 'Quaker-speak'. The latter may be postulated to have developed among the Puritan sects and the soldiers of the New Model Army, revealing the strong influence of the King James version of the Bible both in its cadences and imagery. Daniel shows that 'Quaker-speak' was by no means restricted to religious gatherings, but was employed in public places, its distinctiveness marking off its users as Quakers as easily as bluntness of manner or simplicity of dress.[46] Its declamatory style lent to such pronouncements the quality of prophetic utterance.

But then the Quakers were engaged in what George Fox termed the 'Lamb's War', a spiritual warfare, in which the forces of darkness would be finally defeated. The horrors of the Thirty Years War on the Continent and the Civil War in England had convinced them that the end of time was at hand. John Roberts proclaims the angel of the Apocalypse flying across heaven and warning mankind, and it is with the eschatological imagery of the prophet that he hears God speaking to him: the Lord is now sending his servants to thresh the mountains, symbols of idolatrous worship.[47] Quakers, too, were caught up in the tensions of the age and there is a tautness and urgency in their speech.

However, the significance of this story for the Roberts family and for early Quakers does not lie in the exhilaration of public protest in church or of court room scene or the Quaker rallies of Fox and Dewsbury. It centres around the issue of certainty. Despite an outer appearance of unshakable confidence and unswerving commitment to Quaker testimonies, we glimpse here a very human, private world of dilemma and unsureness. We see, particularly, a man and his wife discovering together the loneliness of their religious stand, and beginning to comprehend the power of their adversaries. This brings to them the heights and depths of emotion, of hope and despair, as the commands of the voice of God are pitted against the hosts of their enemies. But inner certainty and final confirmation are not to be found in this conflict: they come in that quiet place where spirit speaks to spirit, as the enraged church-goer makes his peace with John Roberts, and as the country gentleman justice of the peace and the yeoman Quaker sit side by side on a couch and experience the moment of reconciliation. The core of the Quaker message, that there is that of God in everyone, had received its confirmation.

NOTES

1 *Memoir*, p.72 (OR p.6).
2 *Ibid*, p.73 (omitted in *OR*).
3 C. Hill: *A Nation of Change and Novelty*, p.154.
4 N. Penny: *First Publishers of Truth*, pp.105/6.
5 G. Fox: *Journal*, pp.272/3.
6 *Ibid*, p.273.
7 *Matthew* 10, v.8.
8 *CSPD* 1655/6, p.103.
9 *GBS* Vol.1, p.421.
10 J. Besse, *op.cit.*, Vol.1, p.209.
11 See W.C. Braithwaite: *The Beginnings of Quakerism*, p.316. As early as 1657 George Fox was urging Quakers to keep a record of all their sufferings, so that they could be compiled and laid before the judges on circuit and Oliver Cromwell himself, in an attempt to achieve some redress.
12 G. Fox: *Journal*, p.280.
13 *Memoir*, p.73 (*OR* p.6).
14 Cirencester Parish Book (GRO P86 IN 6/3). The more modest gallery of Lady Poole and her son-in-law and daughter, Lord and Lady Newburgh, was replaced by 'a large handsome gallery' in 1711 when Allen Bathurst was created Lord Bathurst. The Hungerford gallery was emblazoned with their coat of arms. Would Sir Edmund and Lady Dunch have been seated in it when John Roberts made his public protest?
15 *Memoir*, p.74 (*OR* p.7).
16 The first extant quarter sessions indictment book (GRO Q/SIb1) runs from 1660 to 1668/9. Two volumes of the quarter sessions order books are relevant to our period: the first (GRO Q/SO1) from Easter 1672 to Michaelmas 1681, and the second (GRO Q/SO2) from Epiphany 1681 to Trinity 1692.
17 C. Fiennes: *Through England on a Side Saddle in the Time of William and Mary*, p.197.
18 GRO Q/SO1 f. 74a.
19 GRO Q/SO1 f. 128.
20 A mittimus is a precept in writing, under the hand and seal of a justice of the peace, directed to the gaoler, for the receiving and safe keeping of an offender until he is delivered by law (*Jacob's Dictionary*). An example for Gloucestershire is given in J. Besse, *op.cit.*, Vol.1, p.224.

21 Justice John Stephens was the second son of Thomas Stephens and lord of the manor of Lypiatt. His father, who purchased the manor in the reign of James I from the Throckmorton family, had been Attorney General to Prince Henry and Prince Charles, the future Charles I. Atkyns (*op. cit.*, p.701) describes the manor as having 'a large and ancient Seat and a great Estate in this and other places'. John Stephens continued on the commission of the peace after the Restoration and attended the quarter sessions until 1666 (GRO Q/SIb).

22 Based on the *Memoir*, pp.75/6 (*OR* p.7/8).

23 See Ellwood, T.: *The History of the Life of Thomas Ellwood*, p.33. Ellwood's autobiography is illuminating as to the very real social predicament faced by this son of a country justice of the peace when turning Quaker in 1659 (p.30ff). His testimony over hat honour caused him extreme problems at home, where refusing to show deference to his father by removing his hat brought him, in turn, a physical attack with both fists, imprisonment at home and a bizarre chase across the fields (p.46ff).

24 See Ellwood, T., *op. cit.*, p.31, where the use of the 'you' form for polite speech in the singular is described as 'corrupt language'. Quakers 'must keep to the plain and true language of 'thou' and 'thee''.

25 Gerard Winstanly and a number of his followers became Quakers after the suppression of the Leveller movement. Leveller concerns for reforming the legal system and abolishing tithes were certainly shared by Quakers, but there is little evidence that they were in sympathy with the Diggers' pretensions to communism.

26 A royalist invasion was confidently expected to occur in the spring of 1658. Ambassador Lockhardt reported to Secretary Thurloe that the king planned to land his army in Plymouth and hoped to be favoured with insurrections in Bristol and Gloucester. *CSPD* 1657/8, p.352.

27 *CSPD* 1656/7, p.243.

28 *Ibid*, 1656/7, p.335.

29 *Ibid*, 1656/7, p.351.

30 A facsimile of a manuscript copy of the letter is given in E.T. Lawrence, *op. cit.*, p.300.

31 Adapted from the *Memoir*, pp.76/7 (*OR* p.10).

32 *Memoir*, pp.77/78 (*OR* p.11).

33 *Ibid*, p.78 (*OR* p.11).

34 To this extent early Quakers shared the beliefs, if not the methods, of the Fifth Monarchists.

35 *Memoir*, pp.79-82 (*OR* p.12-13).

36 *Ibid*, pp.83/84 (*OR* p.14).

37 *Ibid*, pp.82/3 (*OR* p.13).

38 *CSPD* 1656/57, pp.122/3, 2 October 1656.

39 *Ibid*, 1658/59, pp.148/9, September 1658.

40 *Ibid*, 1658/59, pp.147, 30 September 1658.

41 *Ibid*, 1658/59, p.138, 30 September 1658.

42 Henry Cromwell felt that Quaker principles were incompatible with civil government or with discipline in the army. 'Our most considerable enemy now is the Quakers.' See C. Hill: *A Nation of Change and Novelty*, p.246. Compare also the difficulties experienced by the navy when gunners turned Quaker: the master of gunner of the 'Limehouse' 'said that no power on earth will compel him to fire a gun, lest blood should be spilt', *CSPD* 1656/57, p.548, 22 April 1657. See also *ibid*, p.326, 4 April 1657.

43 O'Malley identifies a smear campaign against Quakers in the newsbooks of the later Commonwealth period. 'A typical example of this reporting, the type that sees their [Quaker] actions as a social and religious threat, is to be found in 1655 in a report from Gloucestershire which manages to combine suspicion of their motives, criticism of their methods of gaining converts, with the suggestion that they are associated with the 'malignants' or cavaliers'. (T.P. O'Malley: 'The Press and Quakerism 1653-1659', *Journal of the Friends Historical Society*, Vol.54, 1979, p.181).

44 *CSPD* 1659/60, p.5, 2 July 1659; p.156, 27 August 1659; p.171, 3 September 1659.

45 *Ibid*, 1659/60, p.240, 4 October 1659.

46 Commenting on one of the villagers who joined the Quakers for dishonest motives, Gough makes reference to their distinctive style of speaking: 'Hee came home the next day a perfect Quaker in appearance, and had gott theire canting way of discourse as readly as if hee had beene seven years apprentice' (R. Gough, *op.cit.*, p.172). See R. Baumann: *Let Your Words be Few*.

47 His youngest son was born later that year and, after the manner of the Old Testament prophets, was given a symbolic name – Daniel, champion of God against the idolatrous worship of rulers. The *Book of Daniel*, of course, forms part of the Old Testament apocalyptic writings.

CHAPTER 8

Restoration of the Kingdom

For what is a King, and what is Parliament, what is a Protector and what is a Council, while the presence of the Lord is not with them? And we are not for names, nor men, nor titles of Government.

Edward Burrough

THE PERIOD OF INCREASING political uncertainty ushered in by the death of the Lord Protector, Oliver Cromwell, in September 1658 came to an end some eighteen months later. Charles Stuart, exiled in the Low Countries, was invited by the English Parliament to ascend the throne. The plotters of Siddington rectory and the failed rising of Major-General Edward Massey were overtaken by events, and England's hereditary monarchy was restored without further bloodshed. An account of how this political *volte-face* was achieved does not fall within the ambit of this study. Suffice it to say that General Monck, commander of the Commonwealth army in Scotland, was a key player, marching south and taking control of London. There he restored to the Rump those members of the Long Parliament who had been excluded for their moderate opinions or royalist sympathies by Pride's Purge in 1648. The North Wiltshire gossip, John Aubrey, suggests that expediency, rather than principle, may have been uppermost in these developments, acidly observing that the royalist agents 'tampering' with Monck 'were satisfied he had no more intended or designed the king's restauration when he [Monck] came into England or first came to London, then his horse did'.[1]

Of some significance for our story, however, is the Declaration of Breda, made by the future Charles II on 4 April 1660 as a basis for a *rapprochement* with the English Parliament. A general pardon was extended to all the king's subjects, except to the 50 or so directly involved in the trial and execution of his father; the army was to be paid, and the soldiers accepted into the king's service on the same terms as before; Parliament itself was to settle all matters relating to grants and forced sales of land; and there was the offer of some form of religious toleration:

> because the passion and uncharitableness of the times have produced several opinions in religion, by which men are engaged in parties and animosities against each other ... we do declare a liberty to tender consciences, and that no man shall be disquieted or called in question for differences of opinion in the matter of religion which do not disturb the peace of the kingdom.[2]

Charles Stuart landed at Dover on 25 May 1660 and proceeded by degrees to London, where he was greeted with great acclamation on 29 May. Addresses of laudation and congratulation were made by the gentry of Gloucestershire, numerously signed, and by the officers of the county militia.[3] The euphoria of the London crowds was echoed in celebrations up and down the land, and there would have been much drinking of toasts of loyalty. At the end of June the mayor and corporation of Gloucester sent a transparently disingenuous address to the king to 'congratulate his safe arrival, the blessed return of many prayers of pious hearts in his behalf; [to] detest and abhor the execrable murder of his late father and laud his singular patience in his long and disconsolate exilement'. They went on to 'implore pardon and confirmation of privileges to themselves, and cheerfully yield the fee-farm rents due to the Crown, which they were forced to purchase by the threatening violence of the times'.[4] But the king, not convinced of their professed loyalty, instructed Lord Herbert to slight the city's defences at an estimated cost of £1,200 two years later.[5]

The State Papers for the early months of the Restoration are quite exceptional in that they are packed with petitions to the new monarch from a multitude of individuals, suggesting a vast throng of claimants and opportunists jostling one another for the benefactions and restitutions he might bestow. His supporters, whose property had been destroyed or sequestered, demanded it to be restored, while its new occupiers defended their right to retain it. Ejected clergy or those formerly with plural livings pleaded the return of their parishes. Pensions for loyal service and grants to relieve hardship were all sought.

Major-General Edward Massey, now Sir Edward, had become a significant figure nationally, and a number of petitions were made on the strength of services rendered to him. Retrospectively, these petitions provide insight into his activities in the last years of the Commonwealth. Sir Fulk Greville petitioned for a place as Gentleman Usher or Cupbearer since 'he and his sons risked life and estate with Major-General Massey for the recovery of his Majesty's title'.[6] Sam Farley of Bristol was seeking a surveyorship of the Land Waiters as 'he was useful to Sir Edward Massey and others of the adjoining counties in conveying letters and intelligence'; Massey certifies that this was in connection with his designs on Bristol and Gloucester.[7] Thomas Fry wanted to be appointed a Messenger of the Council Chamber 'in reward for good service ... in privately conveying to London [*inter al.*] Sir Edward Massey, and in shipping persons of quality beyond seas'.[8] The mayor and deputy lieutenants of Bristol petitioned 'for leave to retain in their city armoury 315 muskets, 216 pikes, 245 pairs of bandoliers belonging to five companies of Sir Edward Massey's regiment, disbanded: their arms were taken away from them during the troubles'.[9] Massey himself petitioned for the return of his ironworks 'yet standing in the Forest of Dean, with iron of all sorts, cut wood, coal etc. for making it (confiscated by the Rump Parliament)',[10] and was voted £3,000 by Parliament in recognition of his services to the royalist cause.[11] His action in successfully defending Gloucester against the former king, critical to the fortunes of the then parliament, had been forgiven and forgotten.

★   ★   ★

By early August 1660 the monarchy seemed firmly established, and Secretary Nicholas was able to write confidently to Sir Henry Bennet: 'Notwithstanding the dying struggles of fanatics and sectaries, things go on daily to fix a happy settlement'.[12] Whatever his majesty may have intended at Breda towards the tender consciences of non-conformity, his officers still considered Anabaptists and Quakers, the fanatics and sectaries, as a threat to the new regime, though now diminishing, and made it their duty actively to suppress them.

The behaviour of some of the restored royalists in Gloucestershire scandalized the god-fearing Puritans:

> The most eminent Cavaliers, imbittered persecutors in the County, ride about with sword and Pistols, pretending to bee a Troop. The last week they rid madly about to disarm the Fanaticks, and all the pastors of the Congregational Churches, and officers that had formerly served Parliament ... together with all Church members, whether Souldiers or not, they ransacked for Arms ... They drink the King's health stoutly and rage against any who have the face of Godliness. And not only souldiers, but the people who had long obscured their malice to the people of God, are now confident and act barbarously.[13]

As early as 8 May the mayor of Gloucester had sent a constable with a drawn sword to break up a Quaker meeting at Maisemore.

> Friends [Quakers] being peaceably met together to wait upon the Lord, there came one John Coney of that place, with a sword in his hand and struck Nicholas Wasfield several blows.[14]

In Nailsworth on 16 May

> There came a wicked man (that is a great professor [religious person], with others with him, with their swords drawn and their pistols cocked, and lighted matches [tapers] in their hands) into the meeting, and laid hands on one Friend and had him before the Mayor of Gloucester.[14]

Later the same month a Quaker meeting at Shortwood was broken up by armed soldiers and three of the Friends were imprisoned by the governor of Gloucester. At the beginning of June a Quaker meeting in Gloucester was broken up and three Friends sent to prison.[15]

It was at this time that we have the first record of a Quaker meeting being broken up in Cirencester, when Philip Gray and John Roberts were arrested again, together with John Ovenell, who worked for John Roberts, Thomas Barnfield, Henry Stacy and blind

William Bowly, all of Cirencester, Jacob Hewlings and William Hinton from Harnhill, and Thomas Eldridge from Driffield.[15] Imprisonment of the nine Cirencester Friends probably lasted 14 weeks, with their being released at the Michaelmas Sessions in September 1660, though they are not entered in the Quarter Sessions Indictment Book.

We have suggested that from the first days of the movement Quakers made it their practice to keep records of injustice and persecution, but that these, on the whole, were spasmodically kept. Hitherto, imprisonments or instances of violence, particularly at the hands of the clergy, were usually recorded, but reports of losses of goods incurred for tithes, for example, or for church dues had become commonplace and tended to be neglected in the record. There needed to be a sense of outrage to trigger an entry being made.

But in the summer of 1660 one senses a change. Whereas before persecution had been of an individual, provoked by a public protest or by flouting the codes of deference, now persecution is of the group, and for no other reason than that the group comes together to worship. The local Quaker meeting, by its existence, is being brought into confrontation with authority. Greater diligence in maintaining documentation has now become urgent if redress is ever to be achieved.

★ ★ ★

It is in the autumn of 1660 that we observe the first signs of unease on the part of the government as to whether the former promoters of republicanism were prepared to accept the return to monarchy. Success was measured by the numbers willing to swear the new oath of allegiance to the king, but reports were coming in that Anabaptists and Quakers were attempting to obstruct the king's officers. They could not be ignored since loyal people would complain 'if these [the sectaries] are excused from the oath, being of dangerous principles and ready to spurn Government'.[16] In November the mayor of Bristol requested 'instructions whether they are to be imprisoned or bound to answer their contempt at the sessions. These monsters are more numerous here than in all the West of England, and have meetings of 1,000 or 1,200 to the great alarm of the city'.[17]

The concern of the mayor of Bristol is mirrored in Cirencester where the justices decided to act again, sending the constables to break up the Sunday meeting for worship:

> On 18 9mo 1660 [18 November 1660] Friends being mett peaceably together in the feare of the Lord there came amongst them two Constables and other officers who charged Friends in the Kings name to goe along with them but Friends could not break up at their time wherefore they halled [hauled], pulled and pusht them forth and had them to prison and thrust them in and gave the Goaler orders to keep them there till the Commissioners [justices] came to Towne.[18]

This time the local Quakers were kept in Cirencester and taken to the bridewell in Dyer Street. The names of the earlier nine Friends recur, with the addition of those of John Cripps, Roger Sparkes and Richard Townsend, all of Cirencester. It is to be assumed that, after their short spell of imprisonment and having been reprimanded by the justices, the twelve were then released.

We know that almost all the men arrested were married, with growing families, suggesting a gathering of 30-40 people. It is unclear where this Quaker meeting had been held. Ten years later Cirencester Friends were meeting in an upstairs room of a private house in the town, rather than at John Roberts' house in Siddington.[19]

These attempts by the authorities to suppress the supposedly disaffected proved ineffective, and only served to heighten tensions. In turn, this confirmed the hard-line policy. There were rumours of an uprising, and later that year Parliament formally rejected the promises of the Breda Declaration to those with tender consciences. 'The bill on the king's declaration about religion was cast out by 20 voices. ... There is a great stir about the plot, and many are troubled about it, though there are doubts whether there was one', wrote a London correspondent.[20] A more careful watch was mounted on Anabaptists and Quakers.[21] Secretary Nicholas now was writing to Sir Henry Bennet: 'More and more is daily discovered of the restless malice of the plotting traitors, who design to embroil the kingdom in new troubles'.[22] There were even rumours implicating General Monck, now the Duke of Albemarle, who, to his great annoyance, was falsely accused of storing gunpowder.

The revelations of Shadrach Moring, a worsted comber, to the authorities in the October had been that the planned rising in London was deferred, that the king was to be seized on his way to Portsmouth, that Ludlow was in Gloucester, and that if Shadrach's wife were to hear a soft knocking at the door, it was the signal of the rising and she was to wake him.[23] After the sighting in Gloucester, Ludlow was feared to be in Wiltshire in December 1660. The deputy lieutenants of the county were away in London, with Richard Davy left in charge. The latter wrote urgently for an order to search for arms, ammunition and trumpets since he had intercepted a barrel of gunpowder being delivered to a commonwealth man in Salisbury: 'these people have plots in hand, talk high and hope to have a turn [revolution] and see the Cavaliers beg their bread before Christmas'.[24]

It is against this background of growing panic that the justices in Cirencester again act. This time it is not the constables but the military that are sent to deal with the local Quakers. In addition to their regular and known meetings for worship each Sunday, Cirencester Friends were also meeting regularly for worship on a Thursday, an important meeting that all were expected to attend.[25] It is to this, probably evening, meeting that the deputy lieutenant, John Howe, brought a platoon of soldiers, armed with swords and pistols.

> The 20th of the 10mo 1660 [20 December 1660] Friends being mett together at Cirencester there came apartye of souldiers, horse and foot, Commanded by John Howe, Deputy Lieutenant of the County, who sent fower souldiers to the meeting who went in with their swords and pistolls and commanded five persons to goe along with them before John Howe, John George and John Fettiplace, Commissioners [justices], who had nothing to lay to their charge but confessed they did believe they were honest men. Notwithstanding, they tendered unto them the oath of Allegiance and because for Conscience sake they could not sweare they were committed to prison 14 weeks. R. Townsend, Roger Sparks, J. Roberts.[26]

Unable to accept double standards of speaking the truth, and
as a protest against blatant perjury in the courts and an open practice of lying, cheating and dishonesty in trade, Friends, from the
earliest days, had refused to take oaths. They followed Jesus Christ's
injunction, letting their yea be yea, and their nay nay.[27] Their stand
was now used against them. Their refusal to take the oath of
allegiance could be taken as an admission of treasonable intentions,
required no trial and meant immediate imprisonment. As a swift
and effective ploy for dealing with these troublesome people, the
justices came to use it more and more.

Less certain and more cautious, Marmeduke Lord Langdale
was writing to Secretary Nicholas from Holme in January 1661 for
instructions:

> There is a sect of persons, called Quakers, who hold meetings
> in several parts, and lead most exemplary lives, accounting
> persecution an honour. Asks how the King wishes them to be
> dealt with, and whether they fall within the last concessions.
> Some wish him to interrupt their meetings and imprison them,
> and offer to raise volunteer troops of horse.[28]

In this latter, more belligerent group must have fallen Sir Henry
Bennet, who wrote to Secretary Nicholas from Wiltshire:
'Anabaptists and Quakers swarm in every corner of the county'.[29]
Writing to Secretary Nicholas from Wakefield, William Lowther
was finding that the discontented had grown more bold and were
abusing their liberty; he had heard tales that 'in all the great towns
Quakers go naked on market days through the town, crying, 'Woe
to Yorkshire' and declare strange doctrine against the Government,
some officers being amongst them'.[30]

★   ★   ★

But what of the Fifth Monarchy men? We have already considered their implacable refusal to have any king except King Jesus
and their attempted risings in 1657 when it was proposed to crown
Oliver Cromwell. How had they reacted to the restoration of
Charles Stuart? Quite distraught, they looked for the hand of God
to smite the 'house of Belial'. But to their gratification Prince Henry
died in the autumn of 1660, and in the December the Princess of
Orange fell ill and died of measles. This was taken by them to be

a clear sign from God that the time had now come to restore the kingdom of Jesus.

Under their leader, Thomas Venner, a cooper, they staged a revolt in London on the Lord's day, 6 January 1661. Sir John Finch, writing to Lord Conway, describes events:

> On Sunday 50 Fifth-Monarchy men went to Mr. Johnson, a bookseller near St. Paul's, and demanded the church keys; being refused, they broke open the door, and setting sentries, demanded of passengers [passers-by] whom they were for: one answered for King Charles, on which they replied they were for King Jesus, and shot him through the heart; they put to flight some musketeers sent to reduce them, and the Lord Mayor came in person, whereupon they retreated to Highgate; on Wednesday morning they returned to the city with mad courage, fell on the guard, and beat the Life Guard and a whole regiment in half-an-hour, refusing all quarter. Venner, their captain, was taken, with 9 more, and 20 slain. The Dukes of York and Albemarle marched with 700 horse into the city, but all was over ... No man is now allowed to have arms unless registered; nor to live in the city without taking the Oath of Allegiance; nor to exercise religious duties out of his house; nor to admit others into it under penalty of a riot. This troubles Anabaptists and Quakers who had nothing to do with this business.[31]

Finch's view as to the non-involvement of Anabaptists and Quakers was not shared by the authorities.[32] A royal proclamation was made, clearly implicating them, and across England there was a round-up of 'fanatics and sectaries'. On 21 January George Fox and 11 other Friends made 'a Declaration from the harmlesse and innocent people of God, called Quakers, against all plotters and fighters in the world, for removing the ground of suspition from both magistrates and people in the kingdom, concerning wars and fightings',[33] but they were too late to prevent the imprisonment of more than 4,000 Quakers.

★ ★ ★

In Cirencester 18 Friends sign an account of their arrest, the new names of Nathaniel Cripps, Richard Arnell, Walter Hewlings, Thomas Knight, Thomas Onion, John Clark, Richard Crowther and Lady Dunch's servant, Alexander Cornwall, appearing.

> Upon the 13th day of the 11mo 1660 [13 January 1661] being
> the first day of the week one Robert Morse, an Attorney, being
> a Lieutenant to John Howe, came to the place of Meeting at
> Cirencester and brought one of the Constables along with him
> and the said Morse violently pulled them out of the Meeting,
> strikeing and beating of them, and hayling [hauling] them by
> the haire of the head. Then the said Constable went before
> and Morse followed behind friends, pulling a staffe from a
> blind man [William Bowly] and beat the blind Man with his
> own stafe, and strikeing and driveing friends forceably to the
> prison where they putt them, and wished the Goaler to bind
> them neck and heels together, and next day they were brought
> before John Howe who had nothing to accuse them of, but
> tendered the oath of allegiance, and because they could not
> sweare he committed them to prison.[34]

Binding a prisoner neck and heels together was the practice of
roping or chaining the neck and the heels, and then drawing them
either forwards or backwards tightly together.[35] These eighteen
men must have been left to lie in this contorted position for more
than twenty hours in the bridewell in Dyer Street before their brief
appearance before Justice Howe. Afterwards they were probably
kept on in the Cirencester bridewell, the other jails – and particularly Gloucester Castle – being so full of sectaries under arrest. And
there they stayed until released following the royal proclamation of
11 May 1661.[36]

On 15 January 1661, two days after the arrests in Cirencester,
a party of soldiers was despatched to the country seat of Nathaniel
Cripps, the former justice, at Upton, near Tetbury, scene of George
Fox's large gathering in 1656 and William Dewsbury's meeting in
1657. Their instructions were to search for arms. The house was
searched from top to bottom, but all they could find to take away
was a fowling piece. Nathaniel was arrested as he was returning
home across the fields, brought to Cirencester, tendered the oath
of allegiance and, on his refusal to take it, imprisoned.[37]

On 16 January, following up a lead from two informers, the
under-sheriff of the county and his bailiffs made three night arrests:
a cooper and a woolcomber, who opened the door to their knocking,
and a second woolcomber, whose door they broke down and who
was then pulled out of bed. Held at an inn over night, the three

were forced to watch while the bailiffs and informers passed the night in 'drinking Healths, playing at Cards, quarrelling and belching out Oaths and Curses, to the Dishonour of God, and Grief of the Prisoners'. The next morning they were taken before the justices, tendered the oath of allegiance and, refusing it, also imprisoned.[37]

★   ★   ★

For the Epiphany Quarter Sessions, held that month, Jacob Hewlings of Harnhill was taken to Gloucester from the Cirencester bridewell, after his arrest on the 13th, to appear with six other Quakers from the village: his relations Elizabeth Hewlings senior (released from the bridewell just over twelve months earlier by Lady Dunch), Elizabeth Hewlings junior and Mary Hewlings; and Richard Craddock, Charles Kilmaster and Elinor Harding. They were charged by the tithing man with not having attended their parish church for the last three months.[38] There is no record of how they were sentenced. It would be surprising if they, too, were not tendered the oath of allegiance and then imprisoned.

This case would have been registered with the clerk of the Sessions before the rising of the Fifth Monarchy men and is unusual. Non-attendance at the parish church had formerly been the proper concern of the consistory court of the bishop, until bishops and the church courts were dispensed with under the Commonwealth and a measure of religious toleration permitted. It became again the regular concern of the re-established consistory courts, as we shall see, under the Restoration.

For the tithing man, a civil appointee, to bring the action before the justices, rather than the churchwardens to make a presentment before the bishop, may well indicate the beginnings of a policy on the part of the civil authorities to coerce the sectaries back into conformity; a policy which was then overtaken by the swift measures needed to handle the January insurrection.

★   ★   ★

Nationally, there followed a period of vigorous investigation of suspected persons, providing the new royalist commanders with an opportunity to show their mettle; and, undoubtedly, old scores were settled, as in the case of Nathaniel Cripps at Upton. Letters were being regularly intercepted[39] and were found to contain suspicious expressions.[40] To the consternation of the authorities, their searches revealed a developing organization and communication network among the Quakers. Meetings of representatives of local meetings for an area were coming together each month, funds were being raised,[41] publications were being printed and disseminated,[42] and information was swiftly circulated. 'Quakers get hold of any thing [news] and send it abroad, the nation over, in a week', complained John Dickson to the Duke of Buckingham.[43]

Tensions and a pervading sense of insecurity in the face of plots, real and imaginary, were to characterize the remainder of the Restoration period. The initial euphoria was gone; unresolved social, political and religious conflicts remained. In June 1661 Secretary Nicholas believed that he had unearthed a rising of the Anabaptists and the Fifth Monarchy men.[44] In Essex he found dangerous meetings of both Quakers and Fifth Monarchy men.[45] In February 1662 a Quaker's letter intercepted at Cockermouth gave rise to fears that 'their meetings contrary to proclamation, their collection etc. may give opportunities to effect dangerous designs'.[46]

To deal more firmly with such threats, legislation had been prepared during the latter half of 1661; and prominent Quakers had appeared at the bar of the House of Commons to speak against it. However, the bill, known to history as the Quaker Act,[47] passed through both Houses and had returned to the Commons by February 1662, though it did not gain the royal assent until May 1662. There were doubts as to its likely effectiveness, Secretary Nicholas receiving the report in April 1662: 'There is general discontent for want of bread: if the Act of Conformity comes forth, they will not submit to it. There are agents among them ... The Quakers are buying up the best horses in the country' – a sure sign that there was to be a rising.[48]

The Act provided for the punishment of any person who maintained that the taking of an oath in any case whatsoever is altogether unlawful and contrary to the word of God and who wilfully refused an oath when tendered. Further, it was made an offence for Quakers to leave their habitations and assemble, five or more, under pretence of worship not authorized by law. A first and a second offence would incur fines, but for a third the punishment was transportation.

★   ★   ★

It is at this period, between Easter and Trinity [April and June 1662], that Cirencester Friends were brought before the Quarter Sessions in Gloucester. The indictment book[49] retains most of its names index, from which can be found page references to given individuals. However, when one tries to refer to the indictments of known Quakers (for example, John Roberts, listed as Hayward, or Philip Gray), a difficulty is encountered: pages 54 and 67 have been neatly excised from the record. If one uses the name of Richard Townsend as a guide, then one finds that page 109, on which his third indictment was recorded, has also been excised; this page falls in the period Michaelmas 1663-Epiphany 1664 [September 1663-January 1664].

Fig. 8.1 contains the names of individuals, derived from the extant pages of the names index, who have indictments on one or more of these three missing pages, 54, 67 and 109. An asterisk marks the names of those whose Quaker affiliation can be established from Quaker records.

What of the unmarked names? Does this mean that William Gwilliam, for example, was also a Quaker in Cirencester? Were the Baptists William Chance and Robert Wilkins associating with the Friends Meeting? The presence of names of women in our list is also of interest since in all our quoted accounts of arrests of Cirencester Quakers to date only the men were taken. Alice Clutterbuck is of particular interest as she is the married sister of John Roberts,[50] and this is the first indication we have that she was linked with Cirencester Friends.

According to the names index, John Roberts (as Hayward) is indicted also on the missing page 66, together with Thomas Hayward. Could this also be Thomas Roberts *alias* Hayward? The latter was a prominent citizen of Cirencester, in the legal profession, occupying a house with three hearths next door to Mr. Morse,[51] the attorney who broke up the Quaker meeting in January 1661. Thomas Roberts was, in fact, prosecuting at the Easter Quarter Sessions in 1662 in two cases from Welford.[52] At the

Figure 8.1: The Gloucester Quarter Sessions Indictment Book 1660/1669.

Indictments traced to pages excised from the record

Defendant	page 54	page 67	page 109
*Thomas Barnfield	x		x
*Elinor Blagge	x	x	
John Bowly			x
*Richard Bowly		x	
*Thomas Bowly			x
†William Chance	x	x	x
Alice Clutterbuck	x		
*William Constable			x
*Philip Gray	x	x	
William Gwilliam		x	
*Elizabeth Harding	x	x	
*John Hayward	x	x	
*Ely Hewlings			x
*Walter Hewlings	x	x	x
Elizabeth Iles		x	
*Thomas Knight		x	
Anna Kent	x		
Mary Mann	x		
*John Timbrell			x
*Richard Townsend	x	x	x
†Robert Wilkins	x	x	

*names to be found in Quaker records.

†known Baptists.

Pages 54 and 67 fall in the period, Easter-Trinity Sessions 1662.

Page 109 falls in the period, Michaelmas Sessions 1663-Epiphany Sessions 1664.

episcopal visitation of June 1665 Thomas Roberts *alias* Hayward is presented as a churchwarden in Cirencester, then against his name is entered 'exco[mmunicatus] Roberts'.[53] Also intriguing are the names of Thomas and William Kite who are also indicted on page 66. Were they related to Elizabeth Kite who was buried in the Quaker burial ground in Cirencester in 1699, and were they also Quakers?

The missing pages, then, raise many lines of speculation. Particularly puzzling are the names which appear both on page 54 and 67. What were the two sets of indictments, and why should they appear so closely together? Does page 54 fall at the end of the Easter Sessions, when some or all of the defendants were consigned to Gloucester Castle? Their names would then appear again on the gaol delivery on page 67, given at the Trinity Sessions. But, finally, there remains the other unanswered puzzle: who suppressed these records, and for what purpose?

★   ★   ★

As some had predicted, the new legislation did little to deter Quakers from holding their meetings for worship. In June 1662 Secretary Nicholas was requiring the justices in Southwark to take orders to suppress the frequent unlawful meetings of Quakers and Fifth Monarchy men.[54] From Kent, that month, came reports of dangerous and ill-affected persons holding unlawful meetings at night.[55] Near Cranbrooke Quakers and Anabaptists had long been holding meetings, and lately strangers had been amongst them: 'At one meeting 150 Quakers stood silent, quaking and trembling two hours, till two letters were delivered to John Bennet, the master of the house, said to be from beyond the sea, while he and others read them privately'.[56] In July Lord Fauconberg warned Secretary Nicholas that he heard much of meetings and night ridings of disaffected persons, and was informed, by an Anabaptist near Beverley, of an intended general rising of Presbyterians, Quakers and Scots in the north.[57] Quakers were suspected and Quakers were feared.

In contrast to this scare-mongering, William Williamson reported to Secretary Nicholas also in July: 'The Commonwealth men still resolve to wait till the Presbyterians take the lead. They keep quiet themselves, and laugh to see the Quakers and others drawn to prison, while they blow the fire by seditious pamphlets'.[58]

By the autumn of 1662 the strain was beginning to tell on some of the king's officers. From Wrexham came the report in September that, undeterred by the new Act, a fanatic had walked naked through the fair with a pan of coals on his head, crying fire and brimstone on all who would not repent.[59] In October Thomas Leigh confided to a relative: 'Base lies are spread of the King and Government, just as of the late King. There is much running up and down, buying of horses, and night riding. The Quakers meet more boldly than ever. Since lenity nor the civil power can restrain them, they must be governed by the sword'. He went on to say that he would rather suffer a fine than be continued as sheriff another year as it had almost broken him.[60] An informant among the prisoners of Ivelchester [Ilchester] jail reported a plot intended for 5 November and 'that Anabaptists, Quakers and Presbyterians have articles agreed on and sealed between them, to fight against the King and his government'.[61]

★   ★   ★

Cirencester Friends seem to have missed the storm of persecution which descended on Quakers in London during the summer months of 1662,[62] the King using the arrival of the Queen in Westminster as an occasion to intervene and have them released in August.[63] But in October there was rumour of a Quaker and Anabaptist plot, either the one reported from Ivelchester jail or another, and on 26 October some hundreds in London were imprisoned, with yet further arrests made in November.[64] This time the wave of persecution reached Cirencester.

It came on the day of the Monday corn and cattle market, when country folk came into town to buy and sell. The attorney had gathered a troop of mounted soldiers and rode into the busy market scene at the top of Dyer Street:

> The 3rd day of the 9th mo 1662 [3 November 1662] Robert Morse aforesaid with severall other Troopers ridd about the Market in Cirencester and seized on severall friends [Quakers] and some they took out of their houses and one friend [Quaker] he struck such a blow over the head that he was almost aston-

ished [stunned], he had them to an Inn, and after a time took their words to appeare the next day, which they did but none came against them. but the next day he sent for them and they went, so he caused them before Fettiplace and Powell called Justices and Deputy Lieutenants. Comeing before them their hatts were taken away, but command was that they should be given them againe, that they might put them on soe them called Justices might know them from the rest of the prisoners, for there was some Baptists in the Roome taken up after the same manner, but Robert Morse pulled them off and beat one friend [Quaker] before the Commissioners faces alsoe Philip Breache called an Ensigne pluckt off some of their hatts and stampt on them and beat one face and head, soe they [the justices] asked them if they would give bond for their peaceable liveing and for refusing they were committed to prison and the said Philip Breache smote George Robinson (in another place afterwards) severall blows on the head, and haveing beat him downe stamped on his head and had his rapier drawn and severall times rann it neare to him and then made astopp swearing that he would run him through and struck him on the head with it, and all this for no other cause than keeping on his hat.[65]

This was a round-up of known Baptists and Quakers. George Robinson was a visiting Friend, staying over the weekend with a Cirencester family, and may have spoken at the Quaker meeting the previous day. He had been arrested at the point of a cocked pistol for speaking at a Quaker meeting at Shortwood in May 1660.[66] The inn in question, where they appeared before the justices on the Wednesday, was almost certainly the Ram Inn at the top of the market place, used by the justices for conducting their business.[67] After the hearing the group of Baptists and Quakers would have been marched, publicly, ignominiously and subjected to brutality, the length of the market place down to the bridewell in Dyer Street.

Three days later, the young ensign, Philip Breach, brought a platoon of soldiers, armed with muskets, to make further arrests at the Friends' Thursday evening meeting:

On the 6 day of the same month [6 November 1662] friends being peaceably mett together at Cirencester the said Philip Breache and other souldiers went to the Meeting place and he commanded the souldiers to charge their musketts and prime their panns, and soe they thrust out all the men being but 12 and then he smote two of them, and sweare he could find it in his heart to run one throw [through] and soe drove them up to the Inn where the Deputy Lieutenants were, where the souldiers testified that it was a Mute Meeting soe they took their Names and committed them to a Roome and a guard of souldiers were sett over them and gave Command to them that none should come at them and in a little time the Marshall came and took their names and the names of the rest that were taken before and had them all to prison.[65]

The 'meeting place' would have been the house of a Cirencester Quaker, which seems to have been not be far from the market place and the Ram Inn, possibly at the other end of Dyer Street. The soldiers' testimony that it had been a 'mute meeting' would have caused the authorities some difficulty, because if no one had spoken, how could the prisoners be accused of plotting and sedition? Nevertheless, the policy of arresting all the males among the Quakers proceeded.

The third eye-witness account is of events at the meeting for worship, in the same house, on the following Sunday:

On the 9th day of the same month [9 November 1662] the Constables and other officers and souldiers went into the same house where Friends were mett together and pulled out 7 which were all the men friends that were in the Meeting and had them to the Main guard and there kept them about an hour and then the Marshall had them to prison and on the 15th of the same month they were sent before the Commissioners [justices] who tendered them the oath of Allegiance, and soe friends refusing to sweare were sent back to prison againe.[65]

Thus, in three military operations, nearly all the male Quakers in Cirencester had been arrested within a week and had been quite summarily imprisoned in the local bridewell.

There are 28 signatures to the veracity of the these accounts, presumably from the individuals who were imprisoned. The names of the important visitor, George Robinson, and of John Roberts (given as Hayward) head the list. For ease of identification, they are given below in alphabetical order.

William Hogarth: Ram Inn, Cirencester.

Thomas Barnfield	Philip Gray	John Ovenell
Richard Bowly	John Hayward	Robert Penson
William Bowly	Ely Hewlings	George Robinson
John Clark	Jacob Hewlings	Roger Sparks
Thomas Cowly	Walter Hewlings	Henry Stacy
Samuel Clift	William Hinton	Robert Sylvester
John Cripps	Thomas Knight	Henry Symonds
Nathaniel Cripps	Robert Newcomb	John Timbrell
Thomas Eldridge	Thomas Onion	Richard Townsend
William England		

We have already met the clothier Samuel Clift from Avening and Robert Sylvester from Nailsworth in connection with public protests in churches in 1656/7; they may have travelled over to Cirencester on the Sunday to give support to the meeting. The rest provide us with a list of Quaker menfolk in 1662, suggesting at least 50 adults belonging to the movement, then seven years old in the district. These 28 Quakers, together with the men from the Baptist meeting arrested at the same time, would have remained in the Cirencester bridewell until after Charles II's first Declaration of Indulgence, made on 26 December 1662. The King followed this initiative by addressing Parliament in favour of indulgence in February 1663, but his Bill, introduced into the House of Lords, was defeated in the Commons.

*   *   *

Our consideration of the first eighteen months of the restored monarchy in England has been based, as far as has been possible, on contemporary accounts. Our focus has been the emergence of a radical social group in Cirencester and the conflict this engendered with the authorities. We have had available to us eye-witness accounts of incidents and encounters, made from the standpoint of the radicals, and the sketchiest of information from the official record. These accounts have proved invaluable, firstly in illustrating the limited viewpoint and paucity of detail, had we been dependent on official sources alone, and, secondly, in revealing the process of social interaction which otherwise would have lain hidden behind 'historical facts'. Graphically, we have been able to relive the dreaded tramp of soldiers boots, the hammering on the door and the threat of steel and bullets, as homes were broken into and ransacked, their occupiers abused and ill-treated, religious meetings rudely broken up, and men-folk frequently borne away to the local bridewell or even to endure the loathsome conditions of the county gaol.

Although such accounts are charged with a sense of outrage at injustice and brutality, they are relatively restrained and confine themselves to a narration of events. They need, of course, to be complemented by what might have been contained in the reports of the justices to their superiors, or of the attorney and ensign to the justices. Such accounts are no longer available to us, but to guide the imagination use has been of reports of officialdom attempting to deal with the radicals elsewhere. These exchanges between the centre and the periphery convey not only a changing climate of opinion and a hardening of attitudes, but also the role of personality and the strong opinions of individuals in the social process.

We are introduced, by turn, to the new civil authorities in Cirencester, drawn from the gentry of the neighbourhood: Justices Howe, Fettiplace and Powell, who were also deputy lieutenants of the county, and their subordinates, Mr. Robert Morse the attorney and Mr. Philip Breach the ensign. We also observe a main guard in the town and the existence of a garrison of soldiers, mounted and on foot, to support the civil powers. Their purposes may have been to preserve the peace and see the monarchy established, but the intemperate behaviour and vindictiveness of the subordinates and the arbitrary use of power by their superiors betray both an underlying insecurity and sore memories of the past. Prejudice, rumour, deliberate misinformation and scare-mongering all contribute to a climate of fear until these civil powers can see the work of seditious fanatics at every turn. The gentry's neurotic hatred for the sectaries, noted during the last years of the Commonwealth, is replicated under the Restoration.

In this sense there is a continuity of official policy, from the Commonwealth into the Restoration, towards an ongoing social conflict. Throughout this chapter the expressions 'Anabaptist' and 'Quaker', both terms of abuse, have been retained when reporting in order to recapture this anger. They are blanket terms, employed pejoratively for any active in their disaffection towards the new political establishment, and may, or may not, reflect the religious affiliation of individuals. To the extent that Baptists and Friends were developing an organisational structure, with movement of their leaders among groups, and containing networks of communication and the facility to print and distribute literature, the fears of the authorities were justified. In the case of Friends in Cirencester, or nationally, they had no justification in the frequent and wholesale arrests for fear of armed rebellion.

The strength of the growing Quaker movement has also been revealed. Not all the occupations of the 30 or so males can be established, but sufficient is known to suggest a robust group, mainly in their twenties and thirties, from the middling sort. Richard Bowly and Roger Sparks were cordwainers [shoemakers], John Timbrell a mercer, Philip Gray a glover, Richard Townsend a bodice-maker, John Cripps a woolcomber and Thomas Knight a card-maker (for wool carding). Thomas Eldridge and William Hinton came from the village of Driffield and were probably husbandmen, while John Ovenell worked as a farm labourer for the yeoman John Roberts in Siddington. Samuel Clift was a prosperous clothier, and Jacob Hewlings occupied a mansion with eight hearths in Harnhill. William England lived more modestly in a house with two hearths in the less salubrious Instrop ward.

Thus, by and large, the Quaker group was composed of individuals who, as trades people, craftsmen or farmers, were their own masters, enjoying a measure of economic independence. They had the opportunity and means to claim liberty to worship, denied to those ultimately financially dependent on the squirearchy or unsympathetic employers. Further, they were linked by trade or through the Quaker movement with similarly placed individuals across the nation and in the capital, from whom they received both moral and practical support. It is because of this broader dimension, beyond the parochialism of Cirencester, that much use has been made of contemporary material preserved in the State Papers.

The *Memoir* contains no reference to this period, concerned as it is with moments of religious experience rather than a history of John Roberts' life. This was a dark period for Friends, when concerted attempts were being mounted by the authorities to eradicate the movement. Believing that they were reviving a primitive form of Christianity, Friends gained consolation from the *New Testament* and the sufferings of the Early Church, finding that they were experiencing a re-run of injustice, persecution and harsh imprisonment. When we return to the *Memoir*, we shall observe high morale among Friends under such circumstances and a readiness to see the funny side of daunting situations. Two ironies which they must have later enjoyed were, firstly, that Giles, the son of Justice Fettiplace, became an ardent Friend, to the great annoyance of the local gentry; and, secondly, that Mary Rutter, the married sister of the ensign Philip Breach, sold to Friends the lease of the messuage, on which they built their meeting house.

But religious matters of doctrine and practice have become subordinated to the political conflict between the establishment and radicalism, and have been absorbed into it. The context has been the restoration of kingship to England, and differing concepts of such a kingdom have emerged. To the supporters of Charles II it was a reversion to legitimate government, albeit now circumscribed by an active and determined parliament. It implied a return to a hierarchy of power and privilege, bolstered by a universal state church, and commanding grateful obedience and loyalty from the restored king's subjects. Its maintenance and protection justified arbitrary and extreme measures against would-be opponents.

To the Fifth Monarchy men this kingdom represented a betrayal. But it was also confirmation that they were living in the last days, for Antichrist now ruled the land. The Lord was calling on his chosen to establish the true kingship of Jesus – by force of arms – to bring in that promised time when the saints would rule.

There is a third conception. As Friends revised their early millenarian expectations, they came to see that the Christ had already come and his kingdom of glory and power was indeed established in their hearts. This kingship was not dependent on force of arms; neither was it expressed in might and wealth. Its rule was contained in the moral imperatives of loving God and loving one's neighbour as oneself. Addressing the Commonwealth Committee of Safety two years earlier, when the restoration of the king and the allegiances of Quakers were in question, Edward Burrough expressed the Friends' position:

For what is a King, and what is Parliament, what is a Protector and what is a Council, while the presence of the Lord is not with them? And we are not for names, nor men, nor titles of Government but we are for justice and mercy and truth and peace and true freedom, that these may be exalted in our nation, and that goodness, righteousness, meekness, temperance, peace and unity with God and with one another, that these things may abound.[68]

NOTES

1 A. Powell, *op.cit.*, p.92.
2 Quoted in W.C. Braithwaite: *The Second Period of Quakerism*, p.6.
3 *CSPD* 1660/1, p.4, May 1660.
4 *Ibid*, 1660/1, p.66, 25 June 1660.
5 *Ibid*, 1661/2, p.424, 30 June 1662, and p.447, 26 July 1662.
6 *Ibid*, 1660/1, p.18, May 1660.
7 *Ibid*, 1660/1, p.153, July 1660.
8 *Ibid*, 1660/1, p.12, May 1660.
9 *Ibid*, 1660/1, p.393, November 1660.
10 *Ibid*, 1660/1, p.171, July 1660.
11 *Ibid*, 1660/1, p.423, December 1660.
12 *Ibid*, 1660/1, p.184, 9 August 1660.
13 H. Jessey: *The Lord's loud call to England, being a true relation of some Late, Various and Wonderful Judgments or Handyworks of God by Earthquake, Lightening, Whirlewind, great Multitudes of Toads and Flyes; and also the striking with Sudden Deaths of divers persons in several places*, published by H.J. a Servant of JESUS the Christ, and Lover of Peace and Holiness, London 1660.
14 *A Declaration of some of the Sufferings of the People of God called Quakers 1660*, p.7, quoted in Gloucestershire Notes and Queries Vol.2, p.37.
15 J. Besse, *op.cit.*, Vol.1, p.210.
16 *CSPD* 1660/61, p.359, 21 November 1660.
17 *Ibid*, 1660/1, p.363, 24 November 1660.
18 *GBS* Vol.1, p.424.
19 J. Besse, *op.cit.*, Vol.1, p.216.
20 *CSPD* 1660/1, pp.423/4.

21 *Ibid*, 1660/1, p.422, December 1660: Geo. Williamson to Jos. Williamson: Will look after the Quakers and Anabaptists against whom there has been more guard than formerly.

22 *Ibid*, 1660/1, p.425, 27 December 1660.

23 *Ibid*, 1660/1, p.310, 11 October 1660. Ludlow, Colonel Edmund Ludlow, arrested as one of the regicides, but now escaped, was a shadowy figure, moving among disaffected groups and hunted desperately by the authorities. Later he was reported as being in the Low Countries with John Desbrough, planning an insurrection; and he was certainly regarded by the inmates of Ivelchester [Ilchester] jail as their coming saviour. (*CSPD* 1660/1, p.550, 29 March 1661; 1661/2, p.596, 18 December 1662).

24 *Ibid*, 1660/1, p.412, 13 December 1660.

25 GRO D1340 A1/M1, 27 November 1693.

26 *GBS* Vol.1, p.424.

27 *Matthew* Chapter 5, verses 33-37: ... Do not swear at all ... Let what you say be simply 'Yes' or 'No'.
In an attempt to reassure the authorities and to avoid imprisonment for refusing to take the oath, Quakers in the North of England, meeting in Skipton on 23 November 1660, declared, 'because their conscience does not allow them to swear, and therefore, they may be liable to be misunderstood and persecuted, that they acknowledge Charles II as rightful supreme magistrate and will yield him due obedience in the Lord, will not conspire against him or the peace of the Kingdom; but if anything be required of them contrary to their conscience, will rather suffer than sin by resistance'.(*CSPD* 1660/1, p.361).

28 *CSPD* 1660/1, p.466, 3 January 1661.

29 *Ibid*, 1660/1, p.319, 22 October 1660.

30 *Ibid*, 1660/1, p.472, 12 January 1661.

31 *Ibid*, 1660/1, p.470, 11 January 1661.

32 Colonel Thomas Culpepper, writing to Secretary Bennet on 26 December 1662, refers back to 'the time of the Quaker rebellion'. (*CSPD* 1661/2, p.602).

33 *Ibid*, 1660/1, p.481, 21 January 1661.

34 *GBS* Vol.1, p.424.

35 See E.T. Lawrence, *op.cit.*, pp.338/9.

36 *CSPD* 1660/1, p.587. The proclamation commanded the liberation of all Quakers who were in prison on scruples of conscience only, for not taking oaths, etc., without their being at the trouble and charge of suing out particular pardons.

37 J. Besse, *op.cit.*, Vol.1, p.211.

38 GRO Q/SIb 1 Epiphany 1660/1.

39 T. Ellwood, *op.cit.*, p.77.
40 *CSPD* 1661/2, p.263, February 1662. Some of these intercepted letters find their way into the State Papers (*Ibid*, 1661/2, p.569, 25 November 1662).
41 *Ibid*, 1661/2, p.264, 3 February 1662.
42 *Ibid*, 1661/2, p.569, 25 November 1662.
43 *Ibid*, 1663/4, p.507, 7 March 1664.
44 *Ibid*, 1660/1, p.471, 12 June 1661.
45 *Ibid*, 1661/2, p.205, 1661?
46 *Ibid*, 1661/2, p.263, 3 February 1662.
47 St. 13 & 14 Car.II cap.1.
48 *CSPD* 1661/2, p.356, April 1662.
49 GRO Q/SIb 1.
50 The will of John Roberts *alias* Hayward the elder (PRO PROB11/234).
51 GRO D383.
52 GRO Q/SIb 1 folio 139v.
53 GRO GDR 213.
54 *CSPD* 1661/2, p.400, 6 June 1662.
55 *Ibid*, 1661/2, p.405, 12 June 1662.
56 *Ibid*, 1661/2, p.412, 19 June 1662.
57 *Ibid*, 1661/2, p.441, 16 July 1662.
58 *Ibid*, 1661/2, p.428, 3 July 1662.
59 *Ibid*, 1661/2, p.481, 2 September 1662.
60 *Ibid*, 1661/2, p.527, 25 October 1662.
61 *Ibid*, 1661/2, p.596, 18 December 1662.
62 See W.C. Braithwaite: *The Second Period of Quakerism*, pp.23/4.
63 *CSPD* 1661/2, p.466, 22 August 1662. 'The King to the Lord Mayor and Sheriffs. ... lays hold of this occasion of public joy, on the first coming of the Queen to the royal palace of Westminster, to order the release of Quakers and others, in gaol in London and Middlesex'.
64 See W.C. Braithwaite: *The Second Period of Quakerism*, p.25; T. Ellwood, *op.cit.*, p.126.
65 *GBS* Vol.1, p.426.
66 *Ibid*, Vol.1, p.423.
67 See *Memoir*, p.178 (*OR* p.78).
68 December 1659. Quoted in E.B. Emmott, *op.cit.*, p.215.

CHAPTER 9

Conventicles and Covens

The Mayor requiring Sureties for their good Behaviour, which
they knew, in his Sense, implied a Restraint from their religious Meetings, they refused, frankly telling the Magistrates,
that they might as well think to hinder the Sun from shining
or the Tide from flowing as to think to hinder the Lord's people
from meeting to wait upon him whilst but two of them were
left together.

Quakers in Bristol, January 1661 (J. Besse I, 42)

THE WINTER OF EARLY 1663 was exceptionally hard. In the
capital the Thames froze over and enterprising trades folk set
up a winter fair on the ice, with stalls, entertainments and even
bonfires. In the country any merry-making was short-lived and soon
was replaced with shortages and the grim struggle to survive as the
severe weather continued. Spring was late. From the west of
Gloucestershire came the report in April: 'By reason of the hard-
ness of the winter and the backwardness of the spring there has
scarce been fodder enough to keep the cattle alive'.[1]

There was excitement later in that year when news came that
the king and his new queen intended to take the waters at Bath,
visit Bristol, and return to London via Cirencester and Oxford.
William Godolphin, secretary to Sir Henry Bennet and accompanying the royal progress, had been deputed to keep Under-
Secretary Joseph Williamson in London posted with court news:

2 September: The King has reduced his diet. His Majesty and
the Queen have now only 12 dishes per meal, and Prince
Rupert 6.[2]

12 September: The King and Queen visited Longleat ... a stately and large house, where they were nobly treated. ... His Majesty goes to Cirencester on 22nd and the next day to Oxford, dining at Cornbury. The business of the court is follies, not worth writing about.[3]

18 September: The King dined at Badminton, Lord Raglan's house, and was handsomely entertained.[4]

28 September: The King and Queen left Bath on 27th instant and at their entrance into Gloucestershire were met by the high sheriff and a little after by the Lord Herbert of Raglan, Lord Lieutenant of that County, with a brave appearance of the Gentry of that County who all conducted their Majesties to Lord Herbert's house at Badminton, where their Majesties were nobly entertained at times, and at supper by the Lord Newburgh at Cirencester, where they lodged that night.[5]

James Livingston, Viscount Newburgh, host to their majesties, had married as his second wife Anne, the daughter of Sir Henry Poole of Sapperton, and was therefore the son-in-law of Dame Anne Poole, who had had George Bull installed as rector of Siddington Mary. He now held, in addition to his Scottish interests, Oakley House as his English seat, and sat as one of the two members of parliament for the town from 1661 until his death on 26 December 1671. Described as one of the finest gentlemen of the age, he had been appointed a Gentleman of the Bedchamber to Charles II and Captain of the King's Body Guard.[6]

The townsfolk would have caught a good view of the royal party approaching Cirencester down the Tetbury road that afternoon, and leaving through the town and along Akeman Street towards Oxford the following morning. Undoubtedly, it was all a grand affair, with an opportunity for the local gentry and notables of the town to be presented to their majesties.

The royal visit, especially a glimpse of Prince Rupert, would have evoked mixed feelings for a number of the older generation, with their memories of the sack of the town by the cavaliers some twenty years before and the march of the prisoners barefoot through the snow to Oxford. In particular, Alexander Gregory, the then vicar who had been driven along with the men, would not have been standing at the church porch among the crowd in the market place. His place would have been taken by Thomas Careles.[7] The previous August, at the age of 68, Alexander Gregory had been ejected from his living.

Edward Calamy describes Gregory as:

> a very humble, serious and affectionate Preacher and exceeding desirous to promote the Good of Souls. He was much belov'd and his Labours had great Success and he was therein unwearied. He kept up a Weekly Lecture every Tuesday, and on Thursdays in the afternoon he catechiz'd in his own House, taking great Care not to discourage such as were bashful or had bad Memories for whom he was solicitously concerned. ... He was always tender of giving Offence.[8]

When eventually released from Oxford in the mid 1640s, Gregory had not returned to royalist occupied Cirencester but had found himself a living in Camberwell, London. In 1648 Thomas Osborne, Thomas Shepherd and Caleb Selfe had been deputed by the town to attempt to persuade him to return, the parish book recording on 2 March payment to them for two journeys to Camberwell. At that date they had not been successful: 'And if they can make it appear that they want a third Journey for the good of the Towne they are to be payd for.'[9] Perhaps the third journey was necessary, for Calamy records: 'When the War was at an End, he settled at another Place at some considerable Distance where also he was well belov'd: But on earnest Solicitation of his old Friends at Cirencester he returned to them again though his Benefice there was of considerably less Value than the other.'[8]

But the Act of Uniformity of 1662 had required his unfeigned consent and assent to the Book of Common Prayer, an oath of non-resistance and a declaration that the Solemn League and Covenant of the Presbyterians was invalid, all to be made before his congregation assembled for religious worship. It meant a return to the Laudian practices of wearing a surplice, making the sign of the cross at baptisms, the parishioners' kneeling at communion before a re-positioned communion table, and, most especially, accepting the authority of bishops and the jurisdiction of the re-established consistory courts. This he had found himself unable to undertake, and on 24 August 1662, Black Bartholomew's Day, Alexander Gregory, with nearly 2,000 other clergy, was ejected from his living.

He took with him a number of his congregation, who established two Presbyterian meetings in the town. Three years later he was driven out of the town itself by the requirements of the Five Mile Act of 1665 and went to live in Minchinhampton, where he died the same year.

How many townsfolk, then, were lining the streets in September 1663 to watch the royal cavalcade, and did they all cheer? The euphoria of three years earlier had gone:

> When the King came in, all called Hosanna, but it is not so now ... the Presbyterians are disappointed because their ministers are turned out; the Independents because they have not their liberty, and some have lost their fortunes; the government is also a burden to Fifth Monarchy men and Quakers. They hope an alteration at the next Parliament.[10]

Earlier in the year an unsigned letter, intercepted by the authorities, to a correspondent in Boston, New England, reported:

> None of the ejected ministers durst act since August 24, there have been such watchings against private meetings. The gaols are so filled that many are stifled through thronging together. The Anabaptists hold out long and the Quakers to the last. Most of the Presbyterians have conformed to the present worship.[11]

Whatever hostility there was remained muted, for people had learned to keep their feelings to themselves, but coolness and disapproval were present. In November 1663 Colonel Slingsby complained to Secretary Bennet from the Isle of Wight that a paper had been slipped under his door condemning the Conformity Acts of Parliament as 'arrogant impositions of the sons of pride' and reflecting 'the imperious sect of the Church of England'.[12]

★   ★   ★

The newly introduced hearth tax was certainly unpopular,[13] but more so were the tales circulating of the loose morals prevalent at court.[14] At the time of the king's visit to Bath and Bristol, Charles Bailey, a prisoner in Newgate jail, Bristol, took the opportunity of writing to him, threatening him with a share of the whirlwind of the Lord that was coming over the nation, having seen in a vision those allied to the king feeding as for the slaughter. He had promised his majesty, when they had last spoken together, to reveal anything that would do him hurt: therefore he now advised him to 'avoid rioting and excess, chambering and wantonness, oppression for which the land mourns, and injuries to the Lord's people'.[15]

It was, however, the politico-religious issue, focused in the determination of parliament to bring dissenters to heel, that gave officials most concern. Another well-wisher, concerned at the coolness of the people's affections and the despondency of his majesty's former good subjects, pointed out to the king that 'in the church ceremonies are more thought of than learning and piety, so that thousands wish its utter overthrow, who, if more liberty had been given, would have supported it. Church offices are sold to persons who allow offenders to be bought off for money.'[16]

The Fifth Monarchy men were still giving the authorities concern. The day that the king and his party arrived in Cirencester, Peter Crabb was reporting to Secretary Bennet on the funeral of a leading Fifth Monarchist:

> 'Four or five thousand people attended Henry Jesse to the grave, and there would have been as many more, but it was not thought convenient. His dying words were that the Lord would destroy the powers in being, and he encouraged the people to help the great work.'[17]

His followers were to meet that week 'to conclude the time when to finish the Lord's work, as they call it'.

That autumn, then, was once more a time of growing nervousness and insecurity, which, in the October, erupted into panic over the Northern Plot. Whether there actually was a plot is questionable, as Sir Thomas Gower observed from Yorkshire: 'all the late rumours come from one man, whilst three others ... say the design is laid aside at present'.[18] But as a precautionary measure he confirmed that 'all the heads [leaders] of the fanatics are privately seized'. In Gloucestershire Lord Herbert sent orders to double the guard at Gloucester, drew together a troop of horse and ordered the volunteers to be as ready at a call as in so large a county.[19]

Almost certainly the one man referred to by Sir Thomas Gower was Thomas Denham, an *agent provocateur*, who had infiltrated radical groups and was trying to encourage them to mount an uprising.[20] Denham may well have been one of the two 'Quakers' who crossed into the north of Lancashire, bringing word that thousands of people from London, Durham and Yorkshire would join them in an uprising.[21] In an unaddressed letter, which may have been unearthed in one of the house searches that followed, the unsigned correspondent bewails the fact that the government was acting with such rigour toward men, some of whom were deluded and betrayed by informers.[22]

Rumours of a Northern Plot confirmed the fears of justices in Lancashire and Westmorland and provided them with an occasion to conduct house searches, and to arrest, imprison and interrogate at will. In the reports of Daniel Fleming and Sir Philip Musgrave to Secretary Williamson there seems to be almost a determination to implicate Quakers, Fleming advising in January 1664 that they had proceeded smartly at the Lancaster assizes against Quakers, committing George Fox and half a score more to close jail for refusing the Oath of Allegiance, and fining 60 on the new Act [Quaker Act].[23]

This is the very period of the appearance of the nine Cirencester Quakers at the Quarter Sessions, entered on the missing page 109 of the Indictment Book (Fig. 8.1). Were these there to answer charges of meeting for worship in contravention of the Quaker Act, or had they been held in jail since October on suspicion of plotting an insurrection? The absence of the names of John Roberts and Philip Gray from the list suggests the first possibility, with the likelihood that these two, now well known to the justices, were being held over for the assizes on more serious charges. This could even have been the time when the jailer at Gloucester Castle deliberately left the names of John Roberts and other Friends off the calendar of prisoners to appear at the assizes and sessions and ill-treated them; it was only a letter to the judge, written by John and smuggled out of the prison, that secured a court hearing and their release.[24]

That their policy of intimidation and repression was not succeeding with the Quakers, was becoming clear to the authorities. Cirencester Friends, as Friends elsewhere, continued to meet for worship twice a week, despite the legal penalties or the brutality used by officials when breaking up meetings.[25] Investigations continued into the so-called Northern Plot during the spring of 1664, with more attempts to implicate Quakers, and in the July further punitive legislation was enacted. The First Conventicle Act, as it became known, extended the provisions of the Quaker Act to all dissenting groups, with the added penalty that Quakers who refused to take any judicial oath should incur the judgment and punishment of transportation.

It was to quite severe measures that the authorities were looking, in order to deal with what they termed the insolence or impudence of the Quakers. Banishment seemed to be the answer. 'The Quakers multiply, though some are under the lash, yet for want of the executive part, transportation, little good is done', wrote Sir John Lowther from Whitehaven.[26] In October 1664, at a meeting for worship in London, 'George Whitehead and 50 more were taken. The sessions have been held. Twenty-eight are to be transported; 8 women are committed to Bridewell for 11 and 12 months'.[27] The same month, on the Isle of Wight, Quaker travelling preachers were arrested and pressed for the plantation in Guinea and sea service.[28] In December 1664 Sir John Lowther reported that he had proceeded against 20 or 30 on the Conventicle Act and, if encouraged, would sentence them to banishment; he asked to which plantation they should go.[29]

But their own harshness rebounded on the authorities. Eight Quakers, sentenced at the Hertford assizes, were put on board the *Ann* of London, four to be shipped to Barbadoes, four to Jamaica. But when, due to contrary winds, the ship had only reached Deal after two months at sea, the master put them ashore, 'certifying that from the disasters which befell him, he thought it unlawful to transport them against their consent'.[30] In Bristol 8 of the crew of the *Mary Fortune* refused to carry three Quakers to the Barbadoes since 'they durst not carry away innocent persons who walk in the fear of the Lord'.[31] In March 1665 Secretary Bennet was having to urge the Lord Chief Justice: 'There being now several ships in the Thames bound for the plantations, the King, wishing to repress the more than ordinary insolence of Quakers and other sectaries, orders that those condemned to transportation be sent off in these ships'.[32] Braithwaite estimates that about 243 Friends were sentenced to banishment, of whom less than a score were actually transported, the rest being held in prison until 1672.[33]

There were difficulties, too, with grand juries in the courts, and even with some of the judges. In Norwich the grand jury was fined £10 for every Quaker they acquitted,[34] and in London the grand jury brought in a verdict of not guilty for 16 Quakers: 'Lord Chief Hyde and Judge Kelynge, who were on the bench, were angry and disputed severally with the jurymen, with threats, and thus drew six of the twelve to their side. The judges would not take it for a verdict, but being Saturday night, dismissed them, binding the six [jurymen] who said 'not guilty' in £100 each, to answer for it on Monday at the King's Bench before the Lord Chief Justice'.[34] Anthony Cooley complained from Canterbury: 'Nothing was done at the sessions against the Quakers and that diabolical rabble, because most of the grand jury being fanatics, the bills of indictment were not found'.[35] From Westmorland Daniel Fleming reported that 'several justices are cool to commit Quakers because the judges have either set them at liberty or given them very small fines'; it was only by waiting on Judge Twysden, with other justices, that he had managed to persuade him to proceed against George Fox and Margaret Fell.[36] In Exeter Judge Hale had dismissed cases against Quakers, ruling that the Conventicle Act was not against religious meetings but against seditious conventicles.[38]

The steadfastness and resilience of Friends under persecution perplexed the authorities. By February 1665 the clerk of assize in York was writing in desperation for permission to release nine Quakers, already held in prison for two and a half years under sentence of *praemunire*.[39] He complained that although the Quakers had lost their estates, 'they are so infinitely impudent and provoking that all are tired out with them': they were released a week later.[40] By May 1665 Abraham Nelson was instructing Lord Arlington: 'No penalty should be inflicted on the Quakers in the meanwhile, but officers should be on the watch against insurrections'.[41] Even George Fox was released in September 1666, to the despair of Daniel Fleming who complained to Secretary Williamson: 'I perceive by several Quakers' letters (which I this day opened) that they are very glad that George Fox is set at liberty, and hope great things from him at his arrival at London'.[42]

*   *   *

Three events of national significance taking place in London during this period gain no mention in the *Memoir*, nor in the extant Cirencester records. The first of these was the outbreak of plague in the summer months of 1665, when between 70,000 and 100,000 persons, or up to a fifth of the inhabitants of the capital, died. The second was the Great Fire which swept through the city in September 1666, fanned by an 'east wind [which] blew as if it had a commission from heaven to execute on the city'.[43] Though largely passed over in the local records, these calamities befalling the capital were widely regarded as God's judgment on the city.[44]

This judgment had been foretold. In prison in Lancaster Castle in 1665, George Fox had had a vision of what was to come:

> As I was walking in my chamber, with my eye to the Lord, I saw the angel of the Lord drawn southward, as though the Court had been all of a fire; and not long after, the wars with Holland and the sickness [plague] began.[45]

Ellis Hookes recounts the warnings given to the king by a young Quaker from Huntingdonshire two days before the outbreak of the Great Fire,[46] while George Fox, released from Scarborough Castle on the day of the outbreak, observes:

> The first day I came out of that prison the fire broke out in London, that consumed most part of that city in three days time. And then I saw the Lord God was true and just in his word that he showed me before in Lancaster Gaol. The people in London were forewarned of this fire; yet few people laid it to heart but grew rather more wicked and higher in pride.[47]

Shortly afterwards Adam Barfoote, a Quaker from Staffordshire, met the king in his coach going hunting. 'And he stepped to the coachside, and laid his hand upon it and said 'King Charles, my message's this day unto thee, in behalfe of God's poor, afflicted, suffering people' ... And he told him that the Lord had pleaded with this City with plagues, sword, and with fire, and so left him.'[46]

Such warnings were not to be lightly dismissed. Still preserved among the State Papers is the report from John Allen to Secretary Williamson of an intercepted letter:

> J.C. a Quaker writes that being in Windsor, considering the
> sad state of London, and praying for those that were left, a
> bright cloud came about him, and a shrill child's voice said,
> 'They have had the pestilence and fire, and other calamities,
> and not yet amended, but a worse plague has yet to come on
> them and the nation'.[48]

This third calamity was a series of disasters in the war against
the Dutch, culminating in the daring foray of Dutch warships up
the Thames in June 1667. Shock waves were sent through the
capital. Not only was there widespread destruction of English shipping in the Medway, but, ignominiously, the flagship of the Duke
of York, Admiral of the Fleet, was captured. At the national level
this led to the fall of the king's chief minister, the Earl of Clarendon,
reputed architect of the punitive measures against the non-conformists. At the local level in Cirencester there would have been a
general easing of persecution by the justices and military against
Baptists, Presbyterians and Quakers.

★   ★   ★

There developed, then, an anomalous situation, whereby
severe penal laws against non-conformist conventicles continued
unrepealed, yet were no longer enforced. Quakers had never made
any secret of their meetings, but now Baptists and Presbyterians
were emboldened to assemble openly. Even during times of more
rigorous persecution it had been a Quaker practice to take a house
with indulgent neighbours and, from an upstairs room, for one of
their speakers to address the crowd assembled in the back garden.[49]
Now, to the horror of Thomas Holden in Falmouth in 1667, 'The
Quakers in these parts grow so impudent that they are building a
house purposely to meet in'.[50] A year later Francis Bellott complained to Secretary Williamson, 'The insolence of the [fanatics]
has grown so high that they build houses for their meetings, as well
nonconformist Presbyterians as Quakers'.[51] But it was still a few
years away before Cirencester Presbyterians or Quakers would be
so 'impudent' or 'insolent' as to acquire their own buildings.

The use of the words 'impudence' and 'insolence' betrays the
sense of outrage and frustration felt by Anglicans at the *de facto*
toleration of the nonconformists by the civil powers. But all was
not lost. If the justices were less enthusiastic to act, then recourse

could be made to the bishop's consistory court to curb the activities of the 'fanatics'. A census of its adherents was taken by the Church of England in 1665, and another in 1669. Bishops were required also to report on conventicles being held in the parishes of their diocese, the numbers and quality of those involved, with details of the abettors and teachers. Details of the returns for the Gloucester diocese are no longer available to us, but what we do have are the number of 'causes' laid before its consistory court in the months that followed.[52]

The consistory court was held in a railed off space, 22 feet by 17 feet (6.5m x 5.5m), in the south-west corner of the nave of Gloucester cathedral.[53] The judge, i.e. the bishop (but more usually the chancellor of the diocese), presided from a dais under the window of the south wall. The registrar sat at his desk in an enclosed well, which also contained a table with a seat round it. There was a narrow space between this well and a balustrade, which marked off the consistorial place from the rest of the nave. Parties in the suits and any spectators would *per force* have stood in the south aisle or nave. Proctors conducted the business of litigants, and apparitors would call the parties cited.

Proceedings were held in Latin. As a result 'many and great Mischiefs do frequently happen to the Subjects of this Kingdom from the Proceedings of the Courts of Justice being in an unknown language, those who are summoned or impleaded having no Knowledge or Understanding of what is alleged against them in the Pleadings of their Lawyers and Attornies, who use a Character not legible but to Persons practising the Law'.[54]

Ostensibly, the court concerned itself with the health of the soul and the correction and reformation of manners. Thirty years earlier there had been an annual hearing for each deanery. In Cirencester Charles Bragge, alehouse keeper, had been presented 'for incroaching upon the churchyard. The judge did enioyne him to remove his Brewhouse, his pigges stye before our lady day next'; Henry Topp had been presented for teaching without a licence, Richard Trinder 'for powling [pulling] down crabbes [apples] upon the sabbath day in tyme of divine service', John Freame, shoemaker, 'for working upon All Hallow Day in prayer tyme', William Horsell 'for a common swearer and filthy drunkard and railer against his neighbours'.[55] But in 1666 the preoccupation of the court was with church attendance.

In 1662 and 1663, in the Cirencester deanery, there had been occasional presentments for not attending church, usually one or two individuals from Harnhill, or the neighbouring parishes of the Ampneys or South Cerney.[56] On 10 January 1666, however, 21 persons from Cirencester were presented for not coming to church, 12 from Coln Aldwyns for not receiving the sacrament, the individuals again from the cluster of parishes around the Ampneys for not coming to the Communion at Easter or to church, and in the near-by parish of Meysey Hampton 14 for not paying the church rate. Two weeks later a further court hearing was held. Now 24 persons from Cirencester were presented, with 8 of them sentenced to excommunication; another 8 were excommunicated from Meysey Hampton; the individuals from Coln Aldwyns and the parishes around the Ampneys were again presented. A further two weeks later there was another court hearing for the deanery, with those refusing to conform being presented yet again: another 6 excommunications for Cirencester and 3 for Coln Aldwyns. A month later, on 8 March 1666, there was a fourth court hearing, leading to a further 18 excommunications.[57]

Who were these persons arraigned before the consistory court, and what was the significance of the sentence of excommunication?

A number of the names can be identified from Quaker records as Friends.[58] An asterisk denotes that they were excommunicated.

Cirencester

*Richard Bowly senior
 wife of Richard Bowly [Mary]
 William Bowly
 Richard Burdge
*William Constable
*Samuel Cripps
*Hanna England
*Ely Hewlings

Walter Hewlings
Catherine Iles
*Martha Lewis
 Thomas Onion
*William Petty
*Richard Townsend
*wife of Richard Townsend
 [Theophila]
*Roger Sparkes

Coln Aldwyns
Giles Fettiplace, Mary Fettiplace

Driffield
*Thomas Eldridge and *his wife [Amy], *William Hinton and *his wife [Sarah]

Harnhill
Thomas Hinton, Thomas Iles

Giles Fettiplace, son of the commander of parliamentary garrison in Cirencester in 1642/3, was lord of the manor of Coln Aldwyns. Two of the 13 in the parish who followed his example of not taking the sacrament were Roman Catholics. The others may have attended a Friends Meeting or have belonged to other dissenting groups.

The leaders of the Baptists in Cirencester, John Oates and Giles Watkins, and Joan Pelteare, in whose house the Baptists met, together with William Chance and Robert Wilkins were called four times before the consistory court and eventually excommunicated. The religious affiliation of the other names who resolutely defied the church authorities cannot, as yet, be established with certainty.

Excommunication could be of two types: lesser and greater. The lesser prohibited entry into a church or receiving the sacrament; it also barred the individual from acting as a witness or executor of a will, or from receiving Christian burial. The greater form of excommunication separated the individual from the mystical body of the church and from the society of the faithful in secular as well as spiritual matters; the individual was also denounced during divine service at the end of the Nicene Creed. More seriously, if excommunicated persons failed to submit themselves to the judge for forty days after denunciation, then a *significavit* or writ *de excommunicato capiendo* could be issued by the judge and directed to the justices of the peace: the persons 'signified' were apprehended and held in prison until they made their submission to the ecclesiastical judge.[59]

Since there is no record of the court pursuing these individuals to the length of indefinite imprisonment, it is to be assumed that the sentences of excommunication were of the lesser type and were intended to serve as a sharp reminder to the recalcitrant of the full scope of the bishop's powers.

*   *   *

But why was no example made of John and Lydia Roberts *alias* Hayward from Siddington Peter, or of John Ovenell, who worked on the farm for them? Although there were no presentments recorded from the parish, later that year or possibly early in 1667 John Roberts and John Ovenell were presented at the consistory court, the *Memoir* providing a lively and humorous account of how the hearing went.[60]

On this occasion John Roberts was in a truculent mood, playing to the gallery and challenging the bishop,[61] and winning from him, surprisingly, a sympathetic response. The bishop's treatment of this Quaker is contrasted in the narrative with that meted out to the luckless Baptist preacher who was heard next.

The bishop began the hearing by attempting to draw John on the Quaker position over baptism:

Bishop: But how many Children have you?

J.R.: It hath pleased God to give me six Children; three of which he was pleased to take from me, and the other three are living.

Bishop: And how many of them Have been Bishop'd [baptised]?

J.R.: None that I know of.

Bishop: What Reason can you give for that?

J.R.: I think a very good one.

Bishop: What is it?

J.R.: Most of my Children were born in Oliver's [Cromwell] days, when Bishops were out of fashion.

Then the Court fell a laughing'.[62]

The hearing then moves to the substance of the indictment: John Roberts and John Ovenell (who, John Roberts says, is too old and too busy about the farm to come) have been presented by the minister (George Bull) and churchwardens of Siddington Peter for not coming to church. This John Roberts stoutly denies:

Bishop: Do you deny matter of Fact?

J.R.: Yes, I do; for it is my Principle, and also my Practice, to go to Church.

Bishop: And do you go to Church?

J.R.: Yes. And sometimes the Church comes to me.

Bishop: The Church comes to you! I don't understand you,
            Friend. ...

Then the apparitor said, 'My Lord, he keeps meetings in his house,
and calls that a Church.'

J.R.:   No. I do no more believe my house to be a Church, than
           I believe what you call so to be one. But I call the People
           of God the Church of God, Wheresoever they are Mett
           to worship him, in spirit and Truth.[63]

We do not learn how John is eventually sentenced. From the
Memoir it would seem that the bishop was too busy or exhausted
to argue further. But this would have scarcely satisfied the minister
and churchwardens of Siddington Peter.

Some time later John was again summoned to appear. This
time the summons was delivered by the bishop's bailiffs who arrived
when John was away from home, travelling with George Fox.

Fox had been released from Scarborough Castle and was using
the temporary respite provided by the more relaxed attitude of the
civil authorities to begin the mammoth task of visiting all the Quaker
meetings in England and Wales. His purpose was to persuade them
to form themselves into small clusters, which would come together
monthly (monthly meetings), and to develop larger regional group-
ings which would meet quarterly (quarterly meetings). Fox came
to Gloucestershire in March 1668 and held a General Men's
Meeting at Nathaniel Cripps' house at Upton, outside Tetbury,[64]
when Nailsworth Monthly Meeting was agreed upon, comprising
the meetings at Nailsworth, Cirencester, Painswick, Tetbury and
Stinchcombe. John Roberts attended this meeting, and then
accompanied George Fox to Bristol.

On his way back from Bristol John learnt from Friends in
Tetbury that the bailiffs had been to his house. Hoping to evade
them, he chose to delay the rest of his journey until after dark.

> The Moon was shining bright as he rode through his own field
> about a Mile from his house. He thought he saw the shadow
> of a Man; upon which he ask'd, 'Who's there?'[65]

From the shadows stepped Sam Stubbs, a bailiff, waiting to
warn him that the bishop's bailiffs, the notorious Paytons, were out

searching for him. At first John thought that the bailiffs had, in fact, now caught up with him.

'Hast thou anything against me?'

'No, Master', replied Sam. 'I might, but I would not. I have wronged you enough already, God forgive me. But those who now lay await for you are the Paytons, my Lord Bishop's bailiffs; and I would not have you come into their hands, for they are merciless rogues. I would have you, Master, to take my counsel, and ever, while you live, please a knave, for an honest man will never wrong you.'[66]

The interest of this episode in the *Memoir* for Daniel and the Roberts family may well have centred on his mother's quiet handling of the Paytons, who wanted a bribe of 20 shillings to go away. Early Friends, too, would have been gripped by his father's vision that night (antedating Bunyan) of a fierce animal, barring the way he had to pass; resolutely John continues his way and the animal turns out to be chained up and harmless. Daniel also provides a lengthy treatment of the debate at the bishop's palace at Bishop's Cleeve, when John forcefully claims that the Common Prayer Book is no more than a human construct, a graven image, blindly worshipped; that God is beyond our human understanding and cannot be constrained in the doctrine of the trinity; that the established church has a preoccupation with sin; and that our civil laws need reforming, in particular the death penalty for stealing cattle. (Should readers wish to pursue John's critique of the assumptions and injustices of his contemporaries, they are directed to the *Memoir*.)

Perhaps of more significance for our study of social attitudes and social relationships is the preparedness of Sam Stubbs to wait patiently along Bear Gate, the country lane leading from the Fosse Way past the Furzen Leaze to Siddington, on a clear and cold March night to warn John Roberts against the bishop's bailiffs. What could have been the motive?

To this incident may be added the warning given by the appar- itor when he served the summons for John's earlier appearance at the consistory court: 'I cannot encourage you to come, for, 'tis likely, they may ensnare you and send you to prison'.[67] Then there are George Bull's servants [employees] who, as John informs the bishop at his palace, 'have come to me and confes't before my Family, that I might have their Ears [cut off for perjury]; for their master made them Drunk, and told them, they were set down in the List, as Witnesses against me, and they must swear to it; and so they did, and Brought Treble Damage, for a field of Corn – And the Servant owned, he had took the tythe from my Tennant, and Thrash'd it out and sold it for his master'.[68]

Why should these lay employees of the bishop and rector gratuitously volunteer warnings and confessions which could have cost them dearly? Their actions speak for the secret regard which the 'common sort' entertained for John Roberts, or Quakers in general; or, conversely, for the contempt in which they held the policies of their ecclesiastical masters. We shall come across other examples before our story is done.

★   ★   ★

Undoubtedly, the mood of 1667 and 1668 had much to do with it, emboldening fainter spirits to assert themselves a little. Not only were the Great Plague and the Great Fire seen as acts of God's judgment on king, state and church, but also, and directly connected with this, 1668 was another time when the second coming of Christ and the end of time were confidently expected to occur.[69] The itinerant Quaker preacher, John Banks, travelling from Warwickshire, through Gloucestershire to Bristol, wrote to his wife on 28 June 1668:

> The Truth of our God prospers and increaseth and gaineth a good report in these parts, and many other places where we have travelled; and many, yea very many, are coming in to partake thereof: for people in many places are weary of the hireling priests and dead worship in the world, and their assemblies grows thin. The Lord, by the all-sufficiency of his power, hath made our service effectual unto many, both Friends and other people, and very full and peaceable meetings we have had in several counties and shires.[70]

Earlier in 1668, when the King had addressed Parliament in February, requesting it to 'think of some course to settle the minds of his Protestant subjects in matters of religion, and induce them to support the Government',[71] there had even been hopes of a toleration act being passed. But this was not yet to be. In its place there came a backlash,[72] for the reaction of Parliament that April was to draft and pass a yet more stringent Bill for suppressing conventicles. This went to the House of Lords, but did not become law until May 1670.

★   ★   ★

And so May 1670 came. Andrew Marvell described this piece of legislation, the Second Conventicle Act, as 'the quintessence of arbitrary malice'.[73] Now juries were dispensed with; a single justice could convict in his own right, and this on the evidence of a paid informer. Penalties of imprisonment or transportation were dropped, the purpose of the new legislation being to ruin the offender financially. For those found at a conventicle of more than five persons there was a fine of 5s. for a first offence, and of 10s. for subsequent offences. For those found preaching at conventicles the fine was £20 for a first offence, and £40 for subsequent offences. There were also fines of £20 and £40 for those found harbouring a conventicle. Justices were empowered to break into houses to search out conventicles, and they could look to the militia for support. For officers neglecting to enforce this legislation there was a fine of £5, and for justices a fine of £100. Money raised by fines was to be divided into three parts: equal thirds to the king, to the poor and to the informer.

George Fox wrote a paper to the magistrates in protest at the injustice of the legislation, observing:

> Would not this Act have taken hold of the twelve apostles and seventy disciples, for they met often together? And if there had been any Act or a law made then, that not above five should have met with Christ, would not that have been a hindering of him from meeting with his disciples?[74]

The State Papers for May, June and July contain a spate of reports from Secretary Williamson's correspondents around the country, alarmed at the flagrant disregard of the new Act. Sir Thomas Gower complained that Whitby and the country adjacent were too much implanted with all sorts of dissenters and Quakers who herd together, and that most of the neighbouring justices were winking at it, if not favouring the proceedings.[75] From London James Hickes reported:

> A Quaker preaching near Devonshire House was seized and carried by the guard at the Change; thousands stopped to hear another at Bishopsgate Street, where the trained bands drew up as close as the multitude would admit, and an officer got in and pulled him down, but his crowd was so great that they carried him away; this caused a shout or two, but no harm was done.[76]

Lord Arlington was informed that from accounts of the prosecution of the Act in Somerset, Bristol and Wiltshire a great deal of moderation had been used, as upon the first Sunday when all the constables in Bristol absented themselves.[77] In Westmorland the Quakers had met numerously every Sunday since the Act had been in force, and at Looe in Cornwall the Quakers remained obstinate and were meeting on the sands.[78] In Chester all the goods of the Quakers had been distrained, who, undeterred, were still meeting twice every Sunday.[79]

A further development in London was to secure all the meeting houses by the military, and for the Bishop of London to install clergy in them to read divine service with an armed guard. George Alsop, rector of Chipping Ongar, complained that when he had attempted this at the Quaker meeting house in Gracechurch Street, he had been hindered from doing so by a great company of Quakers who got between him and the guard of soldiers.[80]

The Archbishop of Canterbury took the opportunity to write an *Epistola Archiepiscopica* to all the Anglican bishops, urging them to greater endeavours. The Bishop of Gloucester's copy was entered into the diocesan records:

> if wee doe our partes now at first seriously by Gods helpe and the Assistance of the Civill power considering the abundant care and provisions This Act containes for our Advantage wee shall within a few months see a great Alteration in the distractions [perplexities] of these times.[81]

The bishop was to require the clergy to perform their duties 'by an exemplary conformity in their own persons and practice', and to admonish and recommend to them 'strictness and sobriety of life and conversation'. The ecclesiastical judges, officers and clergy of the diocese were counselled 'that in their severall places they doe their best to persuade and wynne Nonconformists and Dissenters to obedience to his Majesties Lawes and Unity with the Church, And such as shall be refractory to endeavour to reduce by the Censures of the Church or such other good meanes and wayes as shall be most conducing thereunto.'

For the early summer of 1670 we have eye-witness accounts of two sets of incidents involving Cirencester residents, illustrating how the Bishop of Gloucester attempted to persuade and win Nonconformists to obedience, and how the refractory were 'reduced'.

★   ★   ★

The first, observed by the twelve year old Daniel Roberts,[82] is of the arrival of an imposing cavalcade in Siddington Peter: Bishop Nicholson in his coach, the Chancellor of the Diocese in a second coach, and Thomas Master, Esq.,[83] of Cirencester Abbey, in a third, accompanied by a retinue of 20 clergy on horseback. The bishop was on his way from Cirencester to perform his visitation at Tetbury and had decided to take a detour to call on John Roberts. One can imagine a warm afternoon in early summer with John Roberts busy about the farm, unaware of the arrival of these unexpected visitors.

The bishop remained in his coach at the gates and sent his secretary, George Evans, one of the horsemen, to ride down the short drive to announce him. Before reaching the house he encountered Lydia Roberts in the yard, who had heard the noise of the horses and was just coming round the house from the garden.

'Is your husband at home?'

'Who would speak with him?' She did not recognize this mounted, official-looking stranger and, seeing the coaches and the crowd of horse-riders, feared it was the sheriff come to arrest John.

'Here is my lord Bishop, and several Gentlemen, come to see him.'

Lydia fetched her husband. It was with some trepidation that John approached the bishop's coach, but the bishop reassuringly offered him his hand, which John took.

'I could not well go out of the country [district] without calling to see you, John', the bishop said disarmingly.

'That is very kind. Wilt thou please to alight and come in and those that are with you?'

'I thank you, John, but we are going to Tetbury, and time will not admit of it now. But I will drink with you, if you please.'

John asked Lydia to bring some beer and waited at the side of the bishop's coach. He was not convinced and was wary of trouble. The men, in high spirits after dining with Thomas Master at the Abbey, began to tease him. George Evans asked, half jokingly, half trying to lay a trap:

'John, is your house free to entertain such men as we?'

'Yes, George. I many times entertain honest men; and sometimes others', he drily replied. He remembered George Evans from of old.[84]

'My Lord, John's friends are the honest men, and we are the others.'

'That is not fair, George. For thee to put thy own constructions on my words. Thou shouldst leave me to do that.'

The beer had still not arrived. The Chancellor and Squire Master got out of their coaches and joined the little group at the bishop's coach door. Chancellor Parsons then took up the teasing, suggesting to John that the bishop had come to inspect the Quaker burial ground.

'My Lord and these Gentlemen have been to see your church yard, or burying ground, which you call it – where you inter your dead, and I think that you keep it very decent.'

'Yes, although we are not for pride, yet, to be decent we think is commendable.'

'But there is one thing which I did not expect to see among you', observed the Chancellor, 'and I think it looks a little superstitious, and that is those grave stones, at the heads and feet of your graves.'

'That', admitted John, 'is what I cannot plead much for; but it was permitted to be done, to gratify some who have had their relatives there interred; but we propose, ere long, to have them taken up, and converted to some better use. But, I desire thee to take notice, we had it from among you. And I have observed that in many things, wherein we have taken you for our pattern, you have led us wrong, and therefore now, with the help of God, we are resolved not to follow you one step further.'

At which the Bishop held down his head and bit his lip; and afterwards said: 'John, I think your beer is long acoming'.

The Chancellor and his colleagues would have found twenty-one graves there, among them that of Thomas Roberts, John's second eldest boy, tragically killed by a horse at the age of fourteen in 1666. He now lay beside his sister Lydia. They may have recognized the names of Roger Sparkes and Jacob Hewlings. Released from Gloucester gaol, both had been buried in Siddington in 1665.

At last the beer came, and with it something to eat. Lydia offered the cup to the bishop who found it very much to his taste. 'John, I commend you; you keep a cup of good beer in your house. I have not drunk any that pleased me better, since I came from home.'

Then John offered the cup round: to the chancellor next, and then to Thomas Master. This gave rise to another awkwardness, if not dangerous moment: deliberately the squire asked John to toast him, but he refused. They had been friends at the grammar school together, and the squire then passed it off with general conversation. He finished with: 'Honest John, give me thy hand! Here's to thee with all me heart; and according to thy own compliment, if thou wilt drink thou may'st; if not thou may'st let it alone.'

When John offered the cup to the rector of Siddington, George Bull point blank refused it: 'No John, your beer is so full of hops and heresies that I will have none of it.'

The whole tenor had now become openly antagonistic. This was not the way the bishop had planned the visit. As will be seen, this was no social visit. The seeming good humour and light-heartedness of the bishop's entourage were wearing thin in the face of John's grimly uncompromising stance. He was being too outspoken, even dangerously defiant. Before more damage could be done, the bishop lent out of his coach and whispered: 'John, I have some advice to give you, and that is that you have a care that you do not offend against the higher powers. I have heard great complaints against you, and that you are the ringleader of the Quakers in the country [region]; and if you are not suppressed, all will signify nothing. Therefore, pray, John, take care for the future that you do not offend more.'

But John did not lower *his* voice. He was not prepared to let the bishop's reference to 'higher powers' pass without comment. 'I like thy counsel very well and intend to take it. But thou knowest, God is the Higher Power, and you mortal men, however advanced to wealth and power, are still but the lower powers; and 'tis only because I endeavour to be obedient to the will of the Higher Power that you lower powers are angry with me. But I hope, with the assistance of God, to take thy counsel and be subject to the Higher Power, let the lower powers say or do by me as the Lord may suffer them.'

The bishop had not come to hear this and remarked tersely: 'I want some more discourse with you. Will you go with me to Mr. Bull's?' Had Bishop Nicholson lost all patience with John Roberts, and was this, in fact, the underlying reason for his visit? Had the bishop all along planned a formal hearing across at the rectory in the presence of his secretary, the chancellor, the local squire and justice of the peace, and the assembled group of clergy?

By now the earlier joviality had evaporated, and the tone of the conversation turned confrontational. John answered: 'Thou knowest he [George Bull] has no good will to me. I should rather attend on thee elsewhere.'

'Will you come tomorrow to Tetbury?'

'Yes, if thou dost desire it.'

The rector, George Bull, did not hide his feelings at this slight. Daniel saw that he was very angry. Not only had all his preparations to receive the bishop been wasted and an opportunity to create a favourable impression been lost, but, much more galling, this Quaker was still at large and as brazen in his defiance of authority as ever. These feelings of frustrated rage were not his alone. The 'Gentlemen' of the bishop's party were gentlemen indeed, from good families, well-connected, and moving in the circles of the

Gloucestershire gentry. This upstart, whose father had begun in trade and then come into some money, how dared he 'thee and thou' them, tell the chancellor to his face that he and his set of Quaker heretics would follow the Church no more, and then snub the bishop and the squire as 'lower powers' and scorn their wealth and standing!

As the cavalcade rode away, Daniel recalled the consternation of the Roberts family as they stood together in the drive-way. His father has been left in no doubt as to the mood of the clergy. Fearing the worst from his meeting with the bishop the next day, John arranged for the fourteen year old Nathaniel to accompany him to Tetbury and bring back the horse, should they arrest him. Older brother John was to keep out of trouble and stay at home to manage the farm.

In the event, the interview with the bishop in Tetbury took a different turn. The formal hearing was held in an inn with the assembled clergy present. John refused to give an undertaking to go to church and to keep no more seditious conventicles in his house 'to the terror of the country'; after which a mittimus was prepared to send him to Gloucester Castle. The bishop's party – secretary, chancellor, squire and twenty clergy – then departed, well satisfied with this result, confidently riding home to tell their friends that by this time the Quaker ringleader would be behind bars.

There was in Tetbury, however, a difficulty. The constable, bundled away into a room by the innkeeper's wife to hide him, could not be found to escort the prisoner to gaol, and John was given his liberty for the afternoon. When he returned to the inn that evening, the bishop held a lengthy informal discussion with him in private. Its outcome was the bishop's decision to overturn the findings of the morning's hearing and burn the mittimus. Against all earlier expectation, John was allowed to go home.

The evening's discussion did not turn on the charges of the morning's hearing, of not going to church or of harbouring conventicles. The bishop was keen to know more about certain matters that he had heard from George Bull, the rector of Siddington.

'I have heard Mr. Bull tell strange things of you, John. As, that if anything was lost you could tell, as well as any Cunning man of them all, where to find it. He would have Perswaded me to such things, as I could not believe of you; but I desire to hear it from your own mouth.'[85]

Was this the hidden agenda for the previous day's visit to Siddington? There would then have been particular reasons for holding a hearing in the Siddington rectory. Evidence could have been presented that John Roberts was a 'Cunning Man', a sorcerer. John observed, 'I find my Neighbour Bull has done his Endeavour to render me as odious to thee as Possible'.[86]

The bishop cited three separate instances of John apparently practising sorcery: finding a 'parcel' of cows, then a 'parcel' of sheep, and finally a gentleman's horse; and the bishop insisted on hearing John's explanation of all three. Finally he was reassured.

Referring to the owners of this lost livestock, John observed, 'Where is the cunning [witchcraft] of all this? This is no more than there [their] own reason might have directed them to, had they given themselves time to think.

'I wanted to hear Those three story's from your own mouth', replied the bishop, 'althô I could Not, nor should not, have Credited Them in the same sense that Mr. Bull Related them.'[87]

That cunning men and wise women existed in country areas and practised white witchcraft during this period is certain. Gough cites an inhabitant in Middle, Shropshire, who consults a wise woman to know what has become of his lost cow.[88] John Aubrey, writing of his native North Wiltshire (on which the parish of Siddington borders), associates the flora of the clay areas of the headwaters of the Thames and Avon with the spirit of the inhabitants: 'It is woodsere country, abounding much with sowre and austere plants as sorrel, etc., which makes their humours sowre and fixes their spirits. In Malmesbury hundred [where John located the missing cattle] there have even been reputed witches'.[89] And it was not unknown hitherto for the clergy to accuse Quakers of witchcraft.[90] Practising witchcraft was a serious charge, and, if proven, would have rid George Bull of John Roberts for ever. But, in the

event, neither this accusation nor the crime of failing to attend his
parish church succeeded in placing John Roberts in gaol.

*   *   *

The rage of the local clergy and the squire at John Roberts'
release has to be imagined. Not only had their own plans been frustrated and their efforts to have John Roberts jailed been to no avail,
but now they also had to live down the looks and comments of
friends and neighbours in Siddington or the market place in
Cirencester. Their standing was diminished, and their authority
had lost some of its credibility. They felt humiliated and betrayed.
It would have been strange if there had not followed a local council
of war, held, if anywhere, in Cirencester Abbey, the home of
Thomas Master. George Bull had an *entrée* there, and his patron
the Countess of Newburgh of Oakley Grove, would have taken an
interest in this unfortunate turn of events. Thomas Careles of
Cirencester and other justices of the peace would sure to have
received an invitation.

The clergy had felt so confident in their case – the incontro-
vertible issues of non-payment of tithes, holding conventicles and
non-attendance at national worship – that they had thought the use
of the consistory court the most appropriate and most effective
means of dealing with John Roberts. They had succeeded in con-
vincing Squire Master of this. He had been wanting to take to
himself the powers of the Second Conventicle Act since May, but
was prepared to accept some delay, leaving matters in the hands of
the bishop and letting him earn any opprobrium locally from
Quaker sympathisers. Now he was furious with himself. So much
for trusting to this bishop who, for all his public front of vigorous
prosecution of non-conformists, had been anything but impartial
to John Roberts. Firm and swift action was needed – and he had
the powers now to do it.

So the various parties at our imagined meeting at Cirencester
Abbey could have argued. They had had to swallow Roberts'
defiance and impudence at the abortive encounter in Siddington
Peter. They had had to suffer frustration and humiliation on discovering the bishop's improper behaviour in arbitrarily overturning

the consistory court's decision, and that behind their backs. They were now provoked to taking action on their own account.

They chose the last Sunday in July 1670. Did they utter a warning to the Cirencester Quakers of their intentions? It would have made very little difference: Friends would have continued to meet for worship, come what may. Strangely, Daniel Roberts makes no mention of this incident, but the full drama and horror were recorded by other Friends and preserved by Besse.[91]

The patience, gentleness, even politeness have gone: Justice Master intends to assert his authority. He arrives with a group of well-known thugs, among them John Cooke and Jenkins the hangman. The fifty or so Friends are meeting in an upstairs room of a house, possibly in Thomas Street.[92] Up the stairs charge Master's men and burst in on the silent meeting for worship, the justice at the head. The bellow of his first word is captured by Besse in capitals: 'HAYWARD!' No longer, 'John, old school fellow'; not even 'John Roberts, yeoman of Siddington Peter'; but plain 'Hayward' – Hayward, the chandler's son, Hayward from that shop at the end of Cricklade Street.

Daniel could well have recorded this episode, for his father's performance in the face of physical violence is without fear – more impressive and courageous than his handling the jibes of the bishop's entourage outside his house.

T.M.:	HAYWARD, what is the intent of your meeting here?
J.R.:	We meet for no evil end, the Lord knows.
T.M.:	What is the end?
J.R.:	We meet together in the fear of the Lord, to wait upon Him.
T.M.:	And worship Him, do you not?
J.R.:	Yes.
T.M.:	That's enough. We need no farther evidence. (calling his clerk) Take their names and fine them.
1st Friend:	By what law are we convicted?
T.M.:	Why, you have confessed that you meet to worship God.
2nd Friend:	Is that a crime?
T.M.:	Yes, that it is.

1st Friend: Show us that law.

T.M.:   Here is a law that you must not worship above five
                together, except at the Church. And as for your
                suffering, be it upon us.

3rd Friend: So said the Jews, His blood be upon us; but it proved
                a heavy burden upon them.

> With that the Justice trembled, and in a Rage laid Hands on
> several of them, and called his Company to help him: The
> Meeting being in an upper Room, they brought Friends to the
> Top of the Stairs, where one John Cooke, a wicked fellow,
> cried, 'Clear the Stairs', and Jenkins, said to be an Hangman,
> assisting, they threw the Friends down Stairs: An ancient
> Widow, named Hewlings, by the Violence of the Fall was
> lamentably bruised, and had her shoulder dislocated, of which
> she soon after died. She was an Useful Woman in the
> Neighbourhood, a skilful Midwife, and ready to do Good to
> all. The Coroner was sent for, a Jury called, and Jenkins appre-
> hended: But the Justice having an Influence over the Jury, who
> were most of them his Tenants, and the Coroner being willing
> to favour the Persecutors, smothered the Blood of the
> Innocent: And the Jury, notwithstanding the clearest Evidence
> of Eye Witnesses, and the Sight of the bruised Body, grievous
> to behold, gave in their Verdict, that she died of God's visita-
> tion. Thus the Murderer escaped, and was no more called in
> Question.[91]

Thus Elizabeth Hewlings, loved and cherished by Lady Dunch,
and freed by her from the Cirencester bridewell, met her death. A
fresh grave was dug in the orchard of John Robert's house. The
entry in the burial register reads:

> Elizabeth Hewlings widdow of Amny in the County of
> Gloucester was buryed at Siddenton on the (7th) day of the
> (6th) month [August] in the yeare (1670).

★   ★   ★

At this point William Nicholson, the Bishop of Gloucester, and
George Bull, rector of Siddington, drop out of our story. Nicholson
continued in office for another eighteen months, but failed to maintain the impetus of the archbishop's initiative. He died at the age
of 82 in February 1672 and is remembered by an elegant Latin

epitaph, composed by George Bull, mounted on the nave wall to the right of the south door to the cathedral.

George Bull also appears to have given up on the Quakers; at least there are few instances of his pursuing the Roberts family or the Fields through the consistory courts.[93] The issue of tithes remained, but the rector abandoned his earlier attempts at seeking legal redress and instead generously helped himself to John Roberts' produce each year.[94] He devoted his energies to his theological studies and eventually found international recognition for a series of learned works.[95] Over time he developed a practice of studying late into the night, which, in the end, began to tell on his health, and probably on his work in the two parishes as well.[96]

In 1685 he was taking the waters at Astrop Wells, Northants, at the same time as a Mr. Sheppard, patron of the living at Avening. During their stay news came that this living, worth £200 *per annum*, had fallen vacant, and the position was offered to George, which he gladly accepted. Once installed there he continued his practice of taking a curate to run the parish, while he occupied himself with his studies. In 1686 he was appointed Archdeacon of Llandaff by Archbishop Sancroft in recognition of 'the great and eminent services he had done the church of God by his learned and judicious works'. In 1705, at the age of 71, 'in an ill state of health and the evening of his life', he was appointed Bishop of St. David's, so as 'not to be allowed to decline in obscurity'.[97] He died in February 1710.

★　　　★　　　★

This chapter has attempted to trace the outworkings of a fluctuating, and often confused, policy of religious persecution during the first decade of the Restoration settlement. On the national stage we have seen the Earl of Clarendon toppled, reputed architect of that settlement and of the code of punitive measures introduced to secure universal conformity to Anglican beliefs and practices. A succession of initiatives, variously undertaken by the king's ministers, the church hierarchy or a rebellious parliament, has been identified and shown to be ineffective in quelling into submission a significant number of people, sufficiently distressed at high church dogma to stand resolute in resisting and rejecting it.

This changing national scene has ben used to illuminate extant local records and to provide a context for them. A particular opportunity has thus been created to view such repressive policies, not simply at the level of generality and principle, but also at the point of their implementation. Here the latent social conflict is expressed in terms of individuals who calculate and miscalculate, manipulate or are manipulated, support, subvert, inspire or provoke. Among them the conflict gathers momentum, a sense of proportion is sacrificed to matters of principle, and human tragedy ensues. We have examined also the point at which political power is expressed, and how the lesser agents of that power can work to their own agendas, often frustrating its purposes.

The question must be asked: to what extent did the authorities, church and civil, believe their own rhetoric that meetings of non-conformists to worship God were 'conventicles', clandestine gatherings, political in nature and seditious in purpose? Did the twice-weekly meetings of the 50 or so Cirencester Friends really strike terror in the neighbourhood? Was the neurosis of the establishment under the Restoration so severe that it still saw Quakers as 'reds under the bed', or was it from cynical political calculation that the king's secretaries encouraged such die-hards as Sir Philip Musgrave and Daniel Fleming to perpetuate the myth?

Among the country folk of Gloucestershire we have glimpses of an earlier uncertain, non-rational world, untouched by the modernism of trade and enterprise, not liberated by improved communication networks or increased literacy, but rather populated by evil and benign spirits which determine the fortunes of their livestock and crops. We see, too, thinking people living through it and discarding its superstitions. It is not by magic that John Roberts helps his neighbours: it is by patience, care and sensitivity. He undoubtedly did possess psychic gifts, and he cultivated them, but this is of a different order from necromancy. John Roberts may spurn the rector's insinuations of witchcraft and claim the skill of reason, but he retains a lively sense of the power of prayer and the importance of dreams and visions. For him, (and to convey this the *Memoir* has been written), God is an ever-present reality, a vital dimension to his experience, and a source of revelation, strength and guidance in times of crisis and distress.

NOTES

1 *CSPD* 1663-4, p.109, 13 April 1663.
2 *Ibid*, 1663-4, p.264. This was part of the king's attempt to reduce court expenditure.
3 *Ibid*, 1663-4, p.271.
4 *Ibid*, 1663-4, p.275.
5 *Ibid*, 1663-4, p.280.
6 W.R. Williams, *op. cit.*, p.162.
7 We met Thomas Careles earlier in religious debate with John Roberts at the instigation of Lady Dunch. Sir William Bourchier of Barnsley, where Thomas was minister, would have been influential as impropriator of the tithes of Cirencester in securing his preferment. According to the Cirencester Parish Book, 'the parishioners were desirous of having Mr. Bull [of Siddington] for their Minister but the largeness of the Parish and the great duty attending it deterred him from consenting to the endeavours they were making for that purpose'. (GRO P86 IN 6/3 f.108).
8 E. Calamy, *op. cit.*, Vol.1, p.504.
9 Cirencester Parish Book, GRO P86 IN 6/3.
10 *CSPD* 1663-4, p.12. Robert Johnston writing from the Tower to Secretary Bennet, January 1663.
11 *Ibid*, 1663-4, p.63, 2 March 1663.
12 *Ibid*, 1663-4, p.332, 8 November 1663.
13 *Ibid*, 1663-4, p.371, 11 December 1663. 'The people are making their returns on the supplementary Bill for hearth money, and have been walling up their chimneys, being informed that the returns they now make will stand for ever.' There were riots in Hereford in 1666.
14 Miller suggests that the court must have seemed like a cross between a brothel and a bear garden to the new queen. (J. Miller, *op. cit.*, p.97).
15 *CSPD* 1663-4, p.266, 4 September 1663.
16 *Ibid*, 1663-4, p.604, 2 June 1664.
17 *Ibid*, 1663-4, p.277, 22 September 1663.
18 *Ibid*, 1663-4, p.293, 10 October 1663.
19 *Ibid*, 1663-4, p.294, 10 October 1663.
20 *Ibid*, 1663-4, p.521, 18 March 1664; p.571, 28 April 1664.
21 *Ibid*, 1663-4, p.346, 23 November 1663.
22 *Ibid*, 1663-4, p.362, 2 December 1663. The writer instances the case of Mr. Wakerley, a sober Yorkshire Quaker who had been visited by Thomas Denham, a privileged government spy, who tried to persuade him to join the Northern design; he steadily refused, and even wrote to Sir Thomas Gower an account of what had passed, but his letter

was suppressed and he was summoned before the Duke of Buckingham as a plotter. He was only discharged after a search had been made for his letters and they were eventually located. The writer observes that others less discreet fall into the snares of such spies, and compares the present time with the reign of Tiberius.

23 *Ibid*, 1663-4 p.444, 16 January 1664. The Quaker Act of 1662 prohibited Quakers from assembling in groups of more than five persons. To do so incurred a fine of £5 for the first offence, a fine of £10 for a second offence, and transportation to one of his majesty's plantations beyond the seas for a third offence.

24 *Memoir*, p.162 (*OR* p.64).

25 *CSPD* 1664-5, p.35, 17 October 1664. Esther Biddle, now in jail, describes how Browne pinched her 'as black as a hat', kicked her son and struck her on the mouth, but she is content with the will of God and relies on him.

26 *Ibid*, 1664-5, p.513, 10 August 1665.

27 *Ibid*, 1664-5, p.35, 17 October 1664.

28 *Ibid*, 1664-5, p.47, 29 October 1664.

29 *Ibid*, 1664-5, p.120, 22 December 1664.

30 *Ibid*, 1664-5, p.80, 19 November 1664. See also W.C. Braithwaite: *Second Period of Quakerism*, p.41.

31 *Ibid*, 1664-5, p.164, 7 January 1665.

32 *Ibid*, 1664-5, p.244, 7 March 1665.

33 W.C. Braithwaite: *Second Period of Quakerism*, p.51.

34 *CSPD* 1663-4, p.560, 18 April 1664.

35 *Ibid*, 1664-5, p.39, 22 October 1664.

36 *Ibid*, 1664/5, p.15, 15 October 1665.

37 *Ibid*, 1663-4, p.457, 28 January 1664; p.523, 21 March 1664.

38 *Ibid*, 1664-5, p.20, 30 September 1664.

39 Refusal to take the Oath of Allegiance could incur the penalty of *praemunire*. Persons so sentenced were to be removed from the king's protection, their estates forfeited to the crown, and themselves imprisoned during life or at royal pleasure. (W.C. Braithwaite: *Second Period of Quakerism*, p.14).

40 *CSPD* 1664-5, p.207, 18 February 1665; p.218, 25 February 1665.

41 *Ibid*, 1664-5, p.353, 6 May 1665.

42 *Ibid*, 1666-7, p.xix, 16 September 1666.

43 *Ibid*, Addendum 1660-1670, 8 September 1666, p.712, a letter to Lord Conway. The correspondent observes: 'There has never been such a fire since the destruction of Jerusalem, nor will be till the last conflagration'.

44 'There was but little respite from persecution in twelve years time, from the year 1660 unto 1672, in which was the last war at sea between the English and the Dutch; so that one judgment and calamity followed another, plague, fire and war, unto great depopulation and devastation, shewing God's heavy displeasure against persecution and cruelty, and that spirit which hath been at work against innocent, conscientious and honest people.' George Whitehead: *Christian Progress*, p.346.

By royal proclamation 10 October 1666 was held as a fast day, with church collections being taken 'towards the releife of those Persons who were great Sufferers in the late Sadd Fire within the Citty of London'. £395 was sent from the Gloucester diocese, Cirencester parish raising £25. (Gloucester Reference Library, Hockaday Abstracts, General 1665-1666, 10 October).

45 G. Fox: *Journal*, p.487.

46 Letter to Margaret Fell, 2 October 1666, given in J. Barclay: *Letters of Early Friends*, p.157/8.

47 G. Fox: *Journal*, p.503.

48 *CSPD* 1666-7, 3 December 1666, p.313.

49 *Ibid*, 1668-9, 25 May 1669, p.342.

50 *Ibid*, 1667, 3 April 1667, p.9.

51 *Ibid*, 1667-8, 1 June 1668, p.418.

52 Most of the Gloucester diocesan records for our period have survived, arranged and abstracted by F.S. Hockaday. In particular, there is an almost complete run of the proceedings of the consistory court.

53 F.S. Hockaday (1924): 'The Consistory Court of the Diocese of Gloucester', *Transactions of the Bristol and Gloucester Archeological Society*, Vol.46, pp.195-287.

54 The preamble to the Act of 25 March 1733 requiring all writs and court proceedings to be in English, given in Hockaday, *op. cit.*, p.208.

55 GRO GDR 191, 8 December 1636.

56 GRO GDR 210.

57 GRO GDR 214.

58 See my *Quakers in Cirencester – the first Fifty Years*. The concept of formal membership of Friends did not develop until the 1730s, and then only over the issue of relieving poor Friends. No lists of members were, therefore, ever prepared, and reliance has to be placed on the registers of births, marriages and burials, or on accounts of Friends' sufferings.

59 F.S. Hockaday, *op. cit.*, p.239; A. Tarver, *op. cit.*, pp.27-29.

60 *Memoir*, pp.103-112 (*OR* p.26-32). The parameters for this dating are the death of John Robert's son Thomas on 2 October 1666 and the

death of John Ovenell on 11 September 1670. As will be shown, this
court hearing is likely to have taken place some twelve months before
a second summons served in March 1668.

Another example of a 'verbatim' account of a Quaker (Thomas Atkin
at Dursley) being interrogated by the Bishop of Gloucester is given in
J. Besse, *op.cit.*, Vol.1, pp.212-215.

61 William Nicholson was appointed Bishop of Gloucester at the
Restoration. Born in 1591, the son of a rich clothier in Stratford St.
Mary, Suffolk, he began his ecclesiastical career as chaplain to the Earl
of Northumberland and tutor to his son. In 1626 he was presented to
the rectory of Llandilo Vawr, Carmarthenshire, and in 1644 he became
archdeacon of Brecon. During the Commonwealth period he was
deprived of these preferments and kept a private school in
Carmarthenshire. In 1660 he resumed his appointments and became
residential canon of St. David's. Rumour had it that he owed his
elevation to the episcopacy to the Earl of Clarendon, whom he bribed
with £1,000; an alternative version was that it was due to the influence of the Bishop of London. Because the revenue of his see was
relatively small, he was allowed to hold his archdeaconry, canonry and
the living of Bishops Cleeve, Glos.

62 *Memoir*, p.105 (*OR* p.28).

63 *Ibid*, pp.107-8 (*OR* p.29).

64 G. Fox: *Journal*, p.517. Lawrence associates this second summons to
the consistory court with Fox's next visit to Gloucestershire in October
1669 and Fox's subsequent marriage to Margaret Fell in Bristol. I am
not convinced, since John Roberts' name does not appear among the
94 signatures on the marriage certificate.

65 *MSS Memoir*, p.19.

66 *Memoir*, p.114 adapted (*OR* p.33-34).

67 *Ibid*, p.103 (*OR* p.26/7).

68 *Ibid*, p.126 (*OR* p.40/1).

69 *CSPD* 1667-1668, p.318, HH reporting to Sir Robert Carr, March
1668, on 5 dissenters' meetings; and also p.385, May 1668, when HW
reports to Secretary Williamson on a Baptist meeting: 'They wished
their friends would not be so timorous but would be undaunted spirits,
for now the trying times grew apace, and there was no question but
the Lord would appear to his people, and a very short time would
manifest it.'

70 J. Banks, *op. cit.*, p.60.

71 *CSPD* 1667-1668, p.xxiii.

72 In the view of George Fox, this backlash was not unassociated with
his own visit to Nailsworth in 1669. His name had been confused at

the time with that of a Presbyterian preacher, John Fox. The confusion of names occurred again when John Fox subsequently drew a large crowd in Wiltshire from people thinking they were about to hear the famous Quaker. Disorder broke out between the Presbyterians and Episcopalians, and the Common Prayer Book, symbol of the restoration of both king and bishops, was publicly destroyed. There had also been cries of 'No king but Fox'. George Fox accused the Presbyterians of deliberately inserting his name in the account of the incident given to Parliament, which account was then repeated in a 'News Book that was sent over all the Nation'. (G. Fox: *Journal*, p.551ff).

73 Quoted in W.C. Braithwaite: *Second Period of Quakerism*, p.67.
74 G. Fox: *Journal*, p.559.
75 *CSPD* Addendum 1660-1670, p.231, 22 May 1670.
76 *Ibid*, Addendum 1660-1670, p.240, 29 May 1670.
77 *Ibid*, Addendum 1660-1670, p.243, 31 May 1670.
78 *Ibid*, Addendum 1660-1670, p.256, 6 June 1670, p.321, 6 July 1670.
79 *Ibid*, Addendum 1660-1670, p.273, 13 June 1670.
80 *Ibid*, Addendum 1660-1670, p.310, 3 July 1670, p.343, 24 July 1670.
81 GRO GDR 220, 'Apistola Archiepiscop.'
82 *Memoir*, pp.135-164 (*OR* p.46-50). I have preserved the sections of seventeenth dialogue but modernised the continuity between them. The interpolations are my own.
82 I place this episode before the one that is to follow because of John Roberts' amicable, if cautious, treatment of Thomas Master. If the chronology is reversed, then the discussion of the burial ground and the Quaker's reaction to the squire would have been quite other.
83 Thomas, the eldest son of Sir William Master, was baptised 30 June 1624. He sat as member of parliament for Cirencester April-December 1660.
84 Besse gives the following account of George Evan's behaviour when visiting Solomon Eccles in Gloucester, imprisoned for refusing to take the Oath of Allegiance in 1667:
> George Evans, the Bishop's Secretary, ... came to the Prison, and in a scoffing Manner, pulled off his Hat to Solomon, who thereupon advised him to be sober: This put the Man in a Chafe, and he struck Solomon a violent Blow on the Cheek, upon which Solomon turned to him the other Cheek, and he struck him again on that. Solomon turned again to him the other, and he smote him a third Time. All which Solomon bore patiently, thus literally performing the Precept of Christ, Matt. v. 39 and obtaining a Christian Conquest over his Opposer. (J. Besse, *op. cit.*, Vol.1, p.216).
85 *Memoir*, pp.150-1 (*OR* p.56).

86 *Ibid*, p.156 (*OR* p.60/1).
87 *Ibid*, p.159 (*OR* p.62).
88 R. Gough, *op. cit.*, p.106.
89 A. Powell, *op. cit.*, p.38.
90 Humphrey Smith, who introduced Quakerism to Nailsworth and Painswick, accuses the parish priest of Evesham: 'There is little persecution in England but that the Priests have a hand in it ... as thou, George Hopkins of Evesham, hadst in all the barbarous Persecution there. Thou didst liken that which is called Quaking unto Witchcraft'. ('The Sufferings, Tryals and Purgings of the Saints at Evesham' in *A Collection of the Several Writings and Faithful Testimonies of that Suffering Servant of God*)
91 J. Besse, *op. cit.*, Vol.1, p.217.
92 Local tradition, possibly apocryphal, locates this house on the site of the present meeting house in Thomas Street.
93 'The only dissenters he had in this parish were Quakers, who resisted all the endeavours he made to bring them into the Church, for they were as obstinate as they were ignorant: who, by their impertinent and extravagant manner, caused him no small uneasiness.' (R. Nelson, *op.cit.*, p.120).
94 *GBS* Vol.3, Part 1, p.503.
95 R. Nelson, *op.cit.*, p.154; J.B.T. Homfray: 'George Bull, D.D., 1634-1710', *Transactions of the Bristol and Gloucestershire Archaeological Society* 1973, pp.121-138. Bull was made Prebendary of Gloucester Cathedral on 9 October 1678 by the Earl of Nottingham on the strength of his *Harmonia Apostolica*.
96 R. Nelson, *op.cit.*, p.128. The churchwardens of the two Siddingtons were presented before the consistory court on 15 October 1677 to answer for the incumbent's neglect. In neither church was a terrier being maintained. At Siddington St. Mary the churchyard walls were out of repair. At Siddington St. Peter the paving and seats in the chancel were greatly out of repair, and almost all the utensils of the church, saving a Common Prayer Book, were missing. John Curtis was instructed to provide two copies of the Common Prayer Book, a pulpit cloth, a cushion and a bible (GRO GDR 231). When Joseph Stephens took over from George Bull, there was £10 missing from the Thomas Nicholas charity.
97 R. Nelson, *op. cit.*, p.348ff. Nelson's verbose account is condensed in *Gloucestershire Notes* and *Queries* Vol.3, pp.61-65.

CHAPTER 10

Declared Indulgence

'Keep out the Quakers from their meetings. Shut up their doors, deface their houses and lock them up.'

THE ABOVE QUOTATION IS taken from Secretary Williamson's memoranda, made in his own hand on 9 November 1671, and preserved among the State Papers.[1] Written eighteen months after the implementation of the Second Conventicle Act, it reveals the frustration of the King's Secretary at the failure of this new legislation to eradicate the sectaries and fanatics, and his determination to embark on his own course of forceful and decisive action. It is to be imagined that such jottings had been prepared to impart to assize judges going on circuit, and for them to pass on to the local justices of the peace.

Quakers continued to hold their meetings for worship, openly and regularly, usually in upper rooms or private houses,[2] and suffered the financial penalties: 5s. for a first offence, 10s. for a second, and a fine of £20 imposed on those hosting the meeting. It was a war of attrition waged by both sides, the justices bent on ruining the Quakers, and Friends determined to weary out the authorities. The incrementalism of such warfare gains little mention in the records of Gloucestershire Friends and is offered, if at all, only in summary form in the Quarter Session Order Books, a total of fines collected by a given justice for the quarter.

But, despite Secretary Williamson's impatience with the legislation, there was widespread and growing hardship among Friends. On 15 January 1672 Nottingham Friends protested to King and Parliament:

195

> We were once capable of doing good to others, and have
> relieved many of their wants, and paid our taxes to the King
> and our rents to whom they were due, and maintained con-
> siderable [a large number of] families in a comfortable manner,
> but are now incapable of doing such things through the
> violence of men who pretend they have your Act for what they
> do. ... O King and Parliament, remember the time of your own
> adversity, and be merciful as God has shown mercy unto you.
> But we continue to suffer. As informers clear one place, they
> go to another and some Justice appears ready to answer their
> minds.[3]

It was this open use of paid informers, unprincipled and increasingly vicious in their activities,[4] that most alarmed and outraged
Friends. In a book attributed to Ellis Hookes, Clerk to Friends in
London and compiler of the *Great Book of Sufferings*, informers
were described thus:

> The very Miscreants of the Nation, the Scum of the Country,
> the worst and basest sort of men (and both Drunkards and
> Swearers) without either credit or reputation among their
> Neighbours (who should be kept under by the Law) are let
> loose to do mischief, to make havock, rob and spoil without
> measure, and that under pretence of a Law, whereby they take
> encouragement thus to act against Law and Reason, and how
> many honest and industrious Tradesmen, Imployers and
> Maintainers of the Poor are deeply struck at, disabled and
> discouraged in their Vocations by these unchristian and
> inhuman proceedings. (p.3)

> How little are Informers and Witnesses so much as cautioned
> to take heed what they swear, nor closely examined. ...Goods
> [distrained in lieu of fines] are sold to some unconscionable
> persons (like the Distrainers) for not so much as a third part
> of their value. (p.5)

> [In Gloucestershire] they still continue very violent, making
> the Steeple houses [churches] the Den for their Prey, and after-
> wards bring the Goods unto the Market Street, and send the
> Bell-man to cry them, but few would buy them, though they
> could be had for little. (p.9)[5]

The sufferings caused by the Second Conventicle Act brought
Gloucestershire Friends to look again at the earlier attempt of
George Fox to establish an organizational network for the county.[6]

It would seem that only limited progress had been made in this direction following the general agreement in 1668 at Nathaniel Cripps' house at Upton, Tetbury, to establish monthly and quarterly meetings. But after the fatal injuries sustained by Elizabeth Hewlings at the hands of Thomas Masters' men and the increasing depredations of the informers an inaugural meeting of the Men's Quarterly Meeting was eventually held at John Roberts' farmhouse at Siddington on 28 February 1671.[7] 'It was the desire and agreement of the generality of friends then and there assembled that one or more friends out of every particular [local] meeting doe come to the quarterly meeting'. John Timbrell, mercer of Cirencester, whom we have already met among the arrests made in Cirencester ten years earlier, was appointed clerk, marking the first minute book 'John timberel His Book' and setting out the purposes of the quarterly meeting:

> This Booke belonginge to the freinds of the quarterly meeting within the County of Gloucester, wherein particular accounts are stated of monyes Collected for the Services of the poor and other Charitable Uses and also the Disposition thereof together with other memorials relatinge to the Service of truth.
>
> Friends fellowship must be in the Spirrit and all friends must know one another in the Spirrit and power of God.

At that first meeting £30 was collected from the constituent monthly meetings, and a bill [cheque] for £30 was delivered to John Roberts 'which monyes was ordered by friends of London to bee paid out unto the friends of the monthly meeting usually held at Naylsworth and to bee distributed to such friends as have been sufferers by the late act'. At the next meeting in May '£24 [was] given to Richard Smith and Robert Langley to redeem the loom and necessary goods [taken in lieu of fines] so that Walter Humphries of Painswick can maintain his family'. Later that year £5 was spent to apprentice Walter Simmons, the son of the widowed Sara Simmons of Harnhill, to John Cripps, woolcomber of Cirencester.

As the financial losses of Friends escalated under the new legislation it was agreed a year later, on 27 February 1671, to establish a system for reporting and relieving the suffering of Friends and their families:

> Every monthly meeting shall Apoynt some friends to Make
> Inquiry after the Sufering of friends in Every Meeting and to
> bring in an Account thereof to the next quarterly meeting and
> also what friends are not able to beare theire losses butt have
> need of Asistance from the body of friends.

The quarterly meeting also attended to general matters concerning deaths and marriages, deciding at its third meeting that all
headstones should be removed from Friends burial grounds,
agreeing in August 1672 the wording of the marriage certificate,
and in the November instructing that marriages were to be per-
formed in a public place at a meeting for worship called for that
purpose.

The Nailsworth Monthly Meeting, established after George
Fox's visit in 1668 and consisting of the particular [local] meetings
at Cirencester, Nailsworth, Painswick, Stinchcombe and Tetbury,
had held its first meeting at Robert Langley's house in Nailsworth
on 9 March 1669.[8] The monthly meeting was concerned with
ongoing detailed matters of organization, 'taking Care of the Poor,
and Exercising a true Gospel-Discipline, for a due dealing with any
that might walk disorderly under our Name, and to see that such
as should marry among us did act fairly and clearly in that respect'.[9]
At its first meeting it was agreed that Thomas Onion and Thomas
Bowly of Cirencester should be 'spoken with' by John Cripps, John
Roberts, John Timbrell and Richard Townsend; two months later
the matter had not been resolved and the decision was taken to
draw up a paper against them. Thomas Knight of Cirencester was
also to be 'spoken with', and in May 1669 'the said Thomas Knight
haveing been spoken with according to the agreement of Friends
his answer was brought in that he confessed his condition and that
he hoped he should be enabled to give A better Testimony'.

Procedures for those intending to marry required an application to be made to the monthly meeting for permission, each of the
pair bringing a certificate from their local meeting (usually the
Women's Meeting) confirming that they were eligible and had their
parents' consent. One of the bridal pair was then expected to attend
the subsequent monthly meeting before final permission was
granted. Thus, on 12 December 1671 it was agreed at monthly
meeting 'that William Bryan[t] and Ann Powell might go together

in the way of marriage, seeing that nothing could be objected against it, but to forbear untill after the next monthly meeting, one of them to be there'. At the meeting of 9 January 1672 it was agreed that 'William Bryan[t] and Ann Powell both of Cirencester might go together in the way of marriage after they are published in the meeting of Friends there'. They were married at John Roberts' house in Siddington on 11 January 1672.

On 8 October 1672 the procedure was developed further: at the request of the quarterly meeting three named Friends were appointed, one at least of whom was to be present at weddings: for Cirencester these were to be John Roberts, Richard Townsend and John Timbrell.

Incorporated in the monthly meeting minute book on 14 March 1671 is a copy of exhortations from George Fox. These include the sanction of disownment for any 'who go disorderly in marriage', i.e. those who marry 'one of the world' [a person who is not a Friend], or whose marriage is solemnized by a priest. On 10 June 1673 'it was agreed that Mary Wilkins should be spoke with upon information that shee intended to have one of the World and her answer brought into the next monthly meeting'. Mary May of Cirencester had been married by a priest and was advised on 14 May 1672 'to give a Testimony for the clearing of Truth in that she was married by a priest'; on 9 July 1672 'it was agreed that the Paper which was given forth by Mary May should be read in the meeting of Friends at Cirencester and afterwards that Coppies of it should be given into the World by John Timbrell and John Crips'.

The practice of disowning Friends for 'going disorderly in marriage' and the biblical use of the word 'world', marking Friends off from the rest of society, are indicative of a transition from the untidy, exuberant Quaker movement of the 1650s to a more ordered and disciplined organization by the early 1670s. The concept of a formal membership was still fifty years away, but already its leaders were beginning to define and protect the boundaries of each local group. All evil speakers, talebearers and railers, those gotten into the old rotten principle of Ranters, men that 'hunt after women', all such as goes up and down to cheat by borrowing, any being a scandal to the Truth, resorting to pleasures, drunkenness or gaming, getting into debt, not faithful in their callings, not honest

and just – all would come under the Gospel-discipline of the
monthly meeting, be 'spoken with', and if unwilling to reform, have
a paper drawn [up] against them. In contrast to the preoccupation
of the civil and church authorities with achieving a universal conformity in religious doctrine and church ceremonial, Friends were
placing a high priority on disciplined moral living.

★   ★   ★

The intensity of the persecution as a result of the Second
Conventicle Act also inspired some Friends to become travelling
ministers, i.e. unpaid laymen who abandoned their regular employment and devoted themselves to visiting local meetings to offer
support and encouragement. As we have seen, there had been such
travelling ministers ever since the beginnings of the Quaker movement, but now their help was urgently needed.

One such minister closely associated with the Cirencester
meeting was Charles Marshall of Bristol:

> In the Year 1670 and the Thirty Third Year of my Age, God
> Almighty raised me up by his Power ... to Preach the
> Everlasting Gospel of Life and Salvation. I received this
> Commission from God, 'Run through the Nation and visit my
> breathing, bruised Birth which I begat among my People in
> the Day of their first tender Visitation'. ... Then I cried unto
> the Lord, 'How shall I visit thy People in these times when the
> Rod of the Wicked is upon their Backs; and almost everywhere
> endeavoured, through Violence, to scatter the Assemblies of
> thy People?' ... And the Lord said, 'Go, I will prosper thy Way
> and this present Exercise, which is over my People, shall be as
> a Morning Cloud, and I will be as the tender Dew'.[10]

Marshall travelled from December 1670 until February 1673,
visiting in all some 400 local meetings. He visited Cirencester
Friends on 22 January 1671 on his way back from Wiltshire to
Bristol; was at Nailsworth for a General Meeting on 5 February
1671; visited Cirencester on 10 September 1671 and 4 January
1672, Siddington and Cirencester on 11 January 1672, and
Cirencester again on 18 January 1673 and 4 February 1673. He
continued his contact with Cirencester Friends over the years,
accompanying George Fox there in 1679, and becoming a close
friend of, among others, John Freame who wrote of him:

'he entertained a particular Kindness to me from a Child and continued his friendship steadfastly to the end ... And I can truly say That he was a Faithful and True Friend, having often observed, where he professed Friendship, it was so in Reality, not in Shew only.'[10]

Less clearly documented are the visits of Joan Vokins of Reading, who died in 1690. Theophila Townsend of Cirencester meeting wrote of her: 'I have known her about twenty years and have had a Correspondency with her by Letters, and have been at her House and she hath been often with me, whereby I had the knowledge of her Affairs relating to the precious Truth, and of her godly Care and Diligence in the work of the Lord.'[11] Another Cirencester Friend, Mary Drewett, recalled her visits: 'When it pleased the Lord to order her way to visit us, it was very Acceptable and Edifying to the Sincere Hearted that Loved the Truth: Her Innocent Life and Conversation lives in our Remembrance. ... Her care was great concerning the young Generation, Exhorting them to be inwardly staid in their Minds, that they might grow up in the Love and Life of Truth, so as to feel the work of it effected in their own Hearts that they might come up to serve the Lord.'[12]

A further visitor was Jane Whitehead, one of the original 70 Westmorland Seekers sent out in pairs across the country in 1655. In 1676 Theophila Townsend wrote an obituary for her, recalling how Jane, travelling in the ministry with Frances Raunce, had been known to her in Cirencester over the past 14 years, 'confirming many in the Truth, and to the strengthening of the Weak, and the comforting of the upright in heart who were refreshed by them through the blessed power and holy presence of the Lord'.[13]

★   ★   ★

An emerging pattern of Quaker organization elsewhere is confirmed in Lord Frescheville's correspondence with Secretary Williamson dated 2 August 1670.[14] Passing on a Quaker register book, he observed: 'I judge the discovery will be of service, as since there is order and regularity in their proceedings, more danger is to be apprehended.' He enclosed an explanatory letter from a Captain Herbert Jeffreys, where the linkage between persecution and resultant Quaker organization is unmistakable:

> I have got the register book of the Quakers which contains the
> names of 500 of the heads [leaders] and chief teachers
> throughout Yorkshire, and the towns and parishes of that
> county, divided into monthly and quarterly meetings, with a
> table for finding the names of either, as well as of those who
> have been imprisoned in York Castle and by whom, and also
> their mittimus, from 1652 to the present time.

No such register for Gloucestershire has come to hand, though
it is almost certain to have existed.

★   ★   ★

While the civil authorities were active in discouraging nonconformists from holding their religious meetings, the Gloucester
diocese made desultory attempts to urge the wayward back into
church by making examples of their leaders. At the consistory court
held before the Chancellor of the Diocese on 13 September 1671
John Roberts and Anne Bayden of Siddington, Thomas Eldridge
of Driffield, John Gabb and his wife of Ampney Peter, and Richard
Townsend, Richard Turner and John Roberts of Cirencester were
sentenced to excommunication for not attending their parish
church.[15]

Legal process against the sectaries was being frustrated,
however, by the activities of the Quaker Walter Clemens, as the
Bishop of Gloucester was to certify:

> He has given counsel and encouragement to the Anabaptists
> and Quakers in Gloucestershire ... and by his counsel some
> legally prosecuted have escaped the law after just imprison-
> ment ... He was seized at Gloucester, and because it was not
> easy otherwise to reach him, he was offered the oath of
> allegiance, and refusing to take it, was committed to prison.[16]

★   ★   ★

In March 1672 there was a surprising reversal of government
policy towards the nonconformists. In a Declaration of Indulgence
Charles II suspended all the penal laws against them and decreed
that a sufficient number of places would be licensed for holding
their religious services.

This move was taken without consulting parliament or
obtaining its consent, and appeared to be part of the king's

personal policy of alignment with Louis XIV of France as both monarchs secretly prepared for war against the United Provinces [Holland]. It would seem that Charles was hoping to conciliate dissenters at home, while giving the French king some earnest of his pretensions to relieving English Catholics and of his own promised conversion to Catholicism. The Declaration professed to abandon earlier policy because 'the sad experience of 12 years [is] that there is very little fruit of all those forcible courses'. It was not to be hoped that Quakers would recognize the king's authority in such matters and apply to be licensed: their position would be 'connived at'.[17]

On 18 April 1672 a licence was desired for James Greenwood to be a Presbyterian teacher in the Weavers' Hall in Thomas Street in Cirencester, the application being accompanied by 'a humble Adresse of your Majestys thankfull subjects In and about the Brough or Borrow of Cirencester' and signed by John Paine, Walter Herbert, Anthony Archer, Thomas Dickes, William Eisworth [Ebsworth], John Blissett, Giles Coates, Isaac Lawrence.[18] The same year a licence was desired for Thomas Greenwood to be a Presbyterian teacher at a place called the Recess in Cirencester, almost certainly the building that became the Unitarian chapel off Gosditch Street.[19] In Nailsworth, in April, the Presbyterians asked for a barn to be licensed as their meeting place.[20] On 9 December 1672 a licence was desired for the house of the Widow Joane Palteeres of Cirencester, with licences desired for Giles Watkins and John Oates to be Baptist teachers.[21]

These developments in the town among the Presbyterians and Baptists had their influence on Friends who began to consider how to acquire a meeting place of their own. One can imagine the series of discussions about costs, size and location of the building and the search for a suitable site or property. Eventually, on 27 December 1672, an initial lease for one year on three adjoining messuages in Thomas Street was negotiated with Mary Rutter by Richard Bowly the elder and his son Richard, which earmarked the site.[22] Mary Rutter was holding the lease of these properties from the Crown. On 1 May 1673 the final lease of two of the messuages was negotiated between the Bowlys and Mary Rutter on the one part and the eventual trustees of the meeting house on the other: John

Timbrell, Richard Townsend, Amariah Drewett, John Roberts the younger, Thomas Atkins of Stinchcombe, Thomas Daniel of Stinchcombe, William Rogers of Olveston, Glos., and Stephen Crisp of Colchester, Essex.[22]

Available to us are the final pages of a small notebook, kept by John Timbrell, giving details of the steady fund-raising that took place.[23] Substantial initial contributions were made by John Timbrell, Amariah Drewett, Richard Townsend, William Bowly and Richard Bowly the younger. There then follows a series of smaller amounts from poorer Friends, second and third donations from individuals as time passed, a number of contributions handed in by Richard Townsend, who seems to have acted as principal fund-raiser, even securing a donation from Francis Hareson, the stonemason engaged by Friends. The teenage children of the meeting – Daniel Roberts, the younger Theophila Townsend and the two Eldridges, for example – also contributed. £152 had been reached, with Richard Townsend's wife, Theophila, securing a contribution of £7 from Wiltshire Quarterly Meeting. Due mainly to the efforts of Richard Townsend, the figure was subsequently raised to £173.14s. There then seems to have been a point at which the project was about to founder for lack of financial support. It was eventually rescued by the redoubled efforts of Richard, who took up a collection of £50, supported by more modest individual contributions from John Roberts and William Worme, and with Theophila finding the last 11s. to meet the target of £234.15s. There must have been additional costs, for the Men's Quarterly Meeting was asking for financial support for the Cirencester meeting house on 24 February 1674 and again on 6 May 1674:[7] Nailsworth meeting sent £7.3s. and Stinchcombe meeting £2.[23]

Regrettably, the preceding 22 pages of the notebook, giving details of expenditure, have not been preserved. Only the final part of the account of the stonemason is available on page 23, itemizing the costs of hewing the window sills, the door-step, a window, and pitching the hearth.

The considerable cost to Friends of their meeting house suggests that a new building was erected on the site, its style in keeping with the new houses being built in adjacent Coxwell Street at this period, where timber-frame buildings were being replaced by stone.

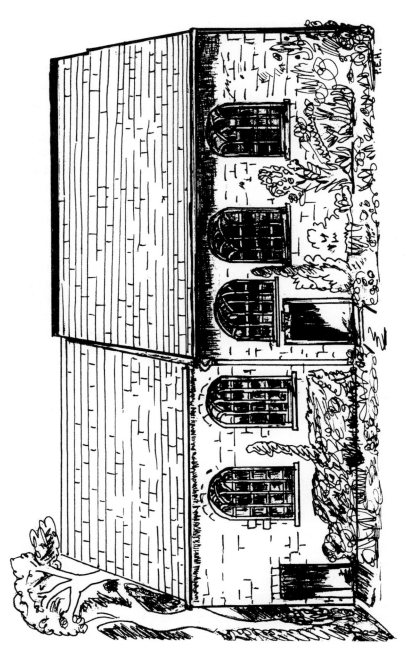

Cirencester Friends Meeting House.

It was set back some 30 feet (9m) from the building line of the street and had, at its front, a large central doorway, flanked by a stone mullion window on either side. The internal dimensions of the original building were 45 feet x 30 feet (13.5m x 9m), with walls 10 feet (3m) high supporting a steeply pitched roof of stone slates.

Behind lay the combined garden of the two messuages which became a Friends burial ground, the first interment being made on 27 November 1673. Some significant modification, as yet not identified, was made to this building in 1726, indicated by the date inscribed on the south-east cornerstone; followed by a substantial extension in 1810 and further Victorian additions.

★   ★   ★

Nationally, Friends used the opportunity of the Declaration of Indulgence to secure the pardon and release of 480 prisoners in May 1672,[24] and in June the release of a further 114 Friends under sentence of *praemunire*, most of whom had been in prison from 7 to 10 years for not going to church or refusing to take an oath.[25] In their submission to the king Friends estimated that besides these

> there remain prisoners
>> under the sentence of banishment about 60 persons
>> upon Excommunications about 30 persons
>> for fines and meetings above 100 persons
>
> Alsoe of late time very many more are deep sufferers upon the late Act by the great loss and spoile of their goods for their innocent meetings; many whereof being poor labouring men, who have not had soe much as their working tooles left them but their poor children and familyes ruined by the Spoylers (and severall more of late imprisoned on their tender Consciences), who are soe numerous that at present we have not a particular account of them.[25]

On 12 June there was issued 'a general warrant of pardon to Quakers in gaols of several counties of England for all offences, contempts, misdemeanours in not coming to church'.[26] This was followed in August 1672 by a further grant of pardon to several Quakers for contempts and misdemeanours against several statutes in not coming to church and hearing Divine Service.[27]

Among those who were in prison on a writ of *excommunicato capiendo* for not attending their parish church was John Roberts.

The Bishop of Gloucester, William Nicholson, who had sympa-
thized with John and acted as his protector after the consistory
court hearing in Tetbury in 1670, had died on 5 February 1672.
Shortly after that time, but concurrently with the Declaration of
Indulgence and the series of royal pardons which flowed from it,
application was made to a justice of the peace by the episcopal
authorities to secure John's imprisonment in Gloucester Castle on
the grounds of his excommunication by the consistory court in the
previous September; perhaps Richard Parsons, who was both
Chancellor of the Diocese and justice of the peace, arranged it by
himself.[28] It was not until the Epiphany Quarter Sessions of 1674,
almost two years later, that John Roberts succeeded in securing his
release on the basis of the royal pardons of 1672.[29]

★   ★   ★

As sudden and surprising as the Declaration of Indulgence in
March 1672 was the reversal of government policy in March 1673.
Need of money for promoting his Dutch war had forced Charles
II to call together parliament in February 1673, which provoked a
month-long constitutional crisis over his arbitrary decision to
suspend the penal laws against nonconformists. In the end the crisis
could only be resolved by the king agreeing to revoke his Declaration
and breaking its seal with his own hands.

The hostility of parliament and the unpopularity of his Dutch
war, with its damage to trade, placed a curb on the king's French
adventures. He had to abandon his pretensions to absolutism and
his dallying with Catholicism and was forced to revert to the
traditional alliance with the Church of England. On 3 February
1675 an Order in Council urged that the penal laws of the Second
Conventicle Act be more actively enforced and revoked the licences
granted for nonconformist meeting places. Persecution was
resumed.[30]

In Cirencester the newly established nonconformist meeting
places were closed down. While the Presbyterians and Baptists met
surreptitiously, Friends continued their Sunday and Thursday
meetings, this time not in private houses but outside their new
meeting house in the yard or street until the local justices reversed
their policy in April 1675 and the constables allowed them back

into the building. However, on 9 May Sir John Guise of Rencombe broke up the meeting and fined 16 Friends 5s. each. The following week Sir John and Justice William Bourchier of Barnsley fined 8 Friends 10s. each, and on the information of Sam Allen, an informer, they fined John Roberts, John Timbrell, John Cripps, William Bowly, William Drewett and Jacob Hewlings (who were *not* present) £40 for two strangers [travelling ministers] speaking in meeting.[31]

These bare facts are vividly amplified in the *Memoir* by Daniel Roberts who provides a dramatic eye-witness account of, presumably, the meeting on 9 May.[32]

At the point at which Theophila Townsend knelt down to offer prayer, the meeting house door burst open and in came John Prichett, the new Bishop of Gloucester, the two justices, Sir John Guise and William Bourchier, together with a large following. The bishop went up to Theophila, laid his hand on her head and said sternly, 'Enough, good woman! Enough! Desist, good woman, desist!' Then Richard Bowly knelt and prayed, upon which Sir John asked for his name and fined him £20 for preaching. After this Sir John moved on to fine the owner of the house: 'Whose house is this?'

'This house has many owners', replied John Roberts.

'But who is the landlord of it?'

'One who is able to give us a quiet possession of our bargain.'

'I demand of you, who is landlord of it?' ordered Sir John.

'The King is our landlord.'

'How is the King your landlord?'

'It is King's land', answered John Roberts, 'and we pay the King's auditors. And we are not only his peaceable subjects, but we are his good tenants and pay his rent duly, and therefore we have reason to hope our landlord will give us a peaceable possession of our bargain.'

'Who pays the King's auditors?', insisted Sir John.

Richard Bowly replied, 'I do.'

Sir John thereupon instructed, 'Set down Richard Bowly £20 for the house.'

The narrative proceeds to describe the heated exchange between the young justice and the ageing John Roberts, John telling him to learn from his father's mistakes, the justice threatening John with the stocks. The constable displays a distinct reluctance to arrest the Quaker, and it is Sir John who has to take one arm, the constable the other, to propel John Roberts out of the meeting house. Once outside John follows them back in again and the arguments continue. Eventually the meeting house is cleared of Friends and furniture, whereupon John Roberts has Friends arrange the wooden forms in the street and resume their meeting for worship – which has to be broken up all over again.

The matter does not rest there. John Timbrell writes to William Bourchier, expressing his disappointment that the justice should allow himself to become involved in such an affair. Learning of the letter, Sir John issues a warrant for John Timbrell's arrest, which, because it is market-day, the constable intends to deliver when the market is over, though he informs John Timbrell straight away. John Roberts' support is enlisted and the two Johns go straightway to Rencombe to confront the justice, where John Roberts reminds Sir John that after violently breaking up a Quaker meeting at Stoke Orchard, near Tewkesbury, his father took to his bed and died.

Nevertheless, the warrants of distress for recovering the fines are prepared and given to the constables. 'But the officers, being civil, were unwilling to make spoil of their neighbours' goods, and would send one or another, before they came, to let down our windows, or lock up our doors; and then they would come with their staves and knock at our doors, and finding them fast would go their ways.'[33]

Dissatisfied with their lack of progress, on 3 June Sir John interviews the constables at the *Ram Inn* and offers some of his own men to assist them. But before the warrants can be served, Sir John is involved in a drunken argument over cards with Sir Robert Atkins at the fashionable gaming house for the gentry at Perrots Brook. The argument becomes a question of honour, a duel ensues and

Sir John is run through with a rapier. Surgeons from Cirencester and Oxford are fetched.

Shut up in a darkened room, Sir John experiences remorse:

'If God will be pleased to spare me and try me again, I will never have a hand against them [Quakers] any more; For Hayward [Roberts] told me, If I went on Persecuting, the same hand that overtook my Father would overtake me, before I was aware; and said I was set on by some envious Priest; and I might have time to repent it, and so I do with all my heart. But I could never come in company with Mr. Freame and Mr. Careless [Careles], but they would be stirring me up to put the Penal Laws in Execution against Dissenters.'

But the sword missing his Entrails, he lived Through it, and stood Candidate for the County after it, But did not any more Disturb our Meetings.[34]

Sir John's reference to Mr. Thomas Careles, vicar of Cirencester, and Mr. William Freame, surgeon of Cirencester,[35] demonstrates the invisibility of the social processes behind the terse historical records usually available to us.

It would seem that, in general, the Anglican clergy had lost faith in the effectiveness of their consistory court to bring the recalcitrant to heel, and that the spasmodic causes brought for not attending the parish church are indicative of stubbornness on the part of the incumbent or of personality clashes. Over the next five years no dissenter had to answer for not attending Cirencester parish church, despite the return of 155 nonconformists for the town in 1676 (Fig. 10.1). It is only from the smaller, closer village communities that causes appear: the Gabbs of Ampney Peter, the Hewlings of Harnhill, Sara Simmons and Elinor Hay in Ampney Mary or Mary May of Ampney Crucis seem to have regularly provoked the incumbents or churchwardens into taking action against them.[36]

In September 1676 an unusual situation arose in Coln Aldwyns when Richard Hunt, appointed three years before under the patronage of Giles Fettiplace, was driven, most probably by outside pressure, to cite his own patron, the lord of the manor, as a Quaker who did not come to hear divine service. Giles and his wife Mary were admonished by the judge of the consistory court, Chancellor

Figure 10.1: *Compton Census 1676**

Deanery of Cirencester: Conformists   6,500
                            Papists   18
                            Nonconformists   236

Parish	Conformists	Papists	Nonconformists
Ampney Crucis	243	1	2
Ampney Mary	66	–	3
Ampney Peter	76	–	2
Barnsley	107	–	2
Bibury	285	–	9
Cirencester	1,745	–	155
Coln Aldwyns	110	2	4
Daglingworth	84	–	3
Driffield	60	–	8
Harnhill	59	–	6
Siddington Mary	37	–	3
Siddington Peter	58	–	9
South Cerney	294	–	11

No nonconformists were returned for the following parishes (number of conformists in brackets):

Bagendon (56), Baunton (56), Coats (60), Coln Rogers (48), Down Ampney (141), North Cerney (123), Preston (73), Rencomb (69), Stratton (86)

* GRO Photocopy 377, Compton Census SMS, pp.429-440.

Richard Parsons, to frequent their parish church and to certify the same by Michaelmas. They failed to do so and were excommunicated on 11 October. Probably also pressured from outside, George Bull for Siddington cited John Roberts at the same hearing: John's sentence was '*simil* [the same as] Fettiplace'.[37]

Apart from the brutal treatment of Cirencester Friends which began the decade, the breaking up the meeting for worship by Sir John Guise in 1675 was the only incident during the 1670s that so outraged them as to prepare an account for transmission to London. We must conclude, therefore, that the Friends had become resigned to the effects of the penal laws and had developed some *modus vivendi*, accepting the intermittent closure of their meeting house and the frequent depredations on their property to pay tithes, church rate, militia tax and the fines for meeting.[38]

A principal reason for the inclusion of such a lengthy and lively treatment of the incidents involving the young Sir John Guise in the *Memoir* would have been that the seventeen year old Daniel Roberts was party to the events.[39] He would have shared with other Friends their relief at being spared the warrants of distress, their sense of God's continuing protection, and the belief that the justice of the peace, having been so clearly warned, had suffered a just retribution. But in the *Memoir* there is no malice nor gleeful satisfaction; instead we find a concern for the well-being of the justice. The events are linked to another of John Roberts' vivid warning dreams; he woke in a cold sweat, having dreamt that 'Sir John Guise was going to throw himself headlong into a Deep pitt to destroy himself and I would feign have held him back, but he would run into it'.[40]

★   ★   ★

The outworkings of the penal laws had the effect of confirming the identity of the local Friends meeting in Cirencester, widening the gulf between it and 'the world', and at the same time strengthening its ties with other local meetings within the monthly meeting. In April 1676 the monthly meeting was helping Mary Edwards of Cirencester meet her late husband's debts, while in September 1677 it was resolving a quarrel that John Roberts and Richard Townsend had had with Robert Sylvester of Nailsworth meeting: 'it was the sense of the meeting that what had happened between them, as concerning words that had formerly passed, should also be passed by, and for the future never to be mentioned any more, unto which they gave their consent'.

Children were being born, and young people were growing up and marrying within the meeting. John Stephens and Ann Hewlings were married on 12 May 1674, Richard Bowly and Mary Drewett on 8 August 1676, Thomas Loveday of Painswick meeting and Martha Drewett on 13 November 1677, Thomas Estington and Alice Smith on 8 January 1678, and Thomas Eldridge and Ann Sparkes on 11 January 1679. Each couple would have had to appear before the women's meeting in Cirencester, and then at the monthly meeting, before being granted permission to marry.

There were still those in the meeting who entered into 'disorderly' marriages and either confessed their fault or were disowned. The women's meeting was arranging to visit Joan Rundle in January 1679, and Richard Bowly and Amariah Drewett were deputed to interview John Stone and Rebecca Hewlings to ascertain who had married them.[41]

At the end of February 1679 there would have been great excitement among Friends locally over a visit from George Fox. On 26 February he attended the Gloucestershire quarterly meeting held at Stinchcombe; on 27 February he was in Nailsworth and was present at a large meeting held there the next day. On Friday, 1 March, he came on to Cirencester, visiting Richard Townsend, and then made his way to Coln Aldwyns, where he stayed with Giles Fettiplace at the manor house. On the Saturday he fitted in a visit to Charles Marshall, who was living with his son at Poulton, near Swindon. 'The 3: day being the first day of the week George Fox and Samuel Smith was at Friends meeting [at Cirencester] which was exceeding Large and peaceable, and at night there A large meeting at Gyles Fetteples home.' On the Tuesday George Fox and Charles Marshall travelled with Giles in his coach to Cheltenham, where there was another large meeting. There Charles Marshall and Giles left him and afterwards brought Richard Townsend back in the coach to Cirencester.[42]

★   ★   ★

The quarterly meeting, still preoccupied with the persecution of Gloucestershire Friends, was widening the scope of its activities.[7] In addition to providing financial relief for individuals and families, it found itself becoming a crucial link for local and monthly meetings with the emerging central work of Friends in London. In August 1675 William Rogers was asked to travel to London 'and Cary with him A list of the Suffering of friends in this County And it is desired that the friends of Every particular [local] meeting be Careful to Collect the Sufferings of friends of their respective Meeting and to bring Copys thereof to the Monthly Meetings who are desired to send them with Speed to Hezekiah Cole of Winterbourne'. A general letter was brought back by Anthony Roberts from London in November 1675 'and sent to John Timbrell who is desired to send Coppys thereof to Every Monthly Meeting'.

The accurate reporting of persecution was of paramount importance in this process, so that in May 1676 the quarterly meeting was asking that for each account local Friends should 'examine it and correct it and amend it and sign it'. Possibly outraged by the death of Ralph Langley in Gloucester Castle and the imprisonment of Matthew Andrews for refusing to pay a church rate of 16 pence, the quarterly meeting started to maintain its own record of sufferings and deaths under persecution on 14 January 1678.[43]

It was after the excesses of the Justice John Meredith in Gloucester and Justice Gabriel Low in Frenchay, and of the informers at Little Badminton,[44] that quarterly meeting began serious campaigning for redress. On 26 February 1678 it lobbied the assize judges and the moderate justices and high sheriff of the county. On 24 April 1679 an address was sent to the members of parliament for the county, together with an account of Friends' sufferings,[45] and on 25 March 1680 it decided to lobby them individually: 'severall meetings that have a knowledge or acquaintance with the Knights and Burgesses of the County [members of parliament] should write to them to stirre them up to be mindfull of the suffering of our friends and brothers and that Care be taken from Gloucester by ... Tewxberry by ... and Cirencester by Richard Bowly and Edward Jefferis'.

In February 1679 it resolved to send two Friends 'to attend every Sessions and Assizes to see to the Sufferings of friends and to take care in that businesse and that theire Charges and expense should be payd them by this meeting'. Support for prisoners in Gloucester, in the Castle and the City Gaol, was being organized in February 1680, the quarterly meeting undertaking to meet any costs.

While these developments were taking place in the Gloucestershire quarterly meeting, centrally in London a Meeting for Sufferings was established. This body sought not only to arrange the work of maintaining the records of persecution nationally and organizing whatever financial relief it could for the victims, but also, where possible, to find legal remedies for prisoners and to conduct deputation work, enlisting the support of national figures or, if necessary, confronting them. Thus, on 23 August 1677, Meeting for Sufferings was assuring the Gloucestershire quarterly meeting that it had sent a copy of its account of the outrageous behaviour of the informers at Little Badminton to the Marquis of Worcester, whose servants they were. On 24 April 1679 it agreed to forward a copy of the quarterly meeting's address to the Gloucestershire parliament men to the Earl of Shaftesbury 'or to any other where they may be of service'.[46]

On 6 November 1679 Meeting for Sufferings took up the cause of Friends who were prisoners in Gloucester.[47] Its clerk, Ellis Hookes, had collected the relevant legal papers and was asked to make a fair copy of the cases to present to the Bishop of Gloucester. Further imprisonments delayed matters, but by 20 May 1680 a full account had been prepared and the prisoners' consent obtained. On 29 May Job Bolton attempted to deliver the documents to the bishop in London, but he had already left town for his country seat at Harvell, two miles from Rickmansworth, Herts.. Accompanied by William Clarke, Job followed him there and reported his visit to Meeting for Sufferings on 15 July:

> And haveing after some tyme Admittance to the Bishop – they comeing before him with their hatts upon their heads – the Bishop was greatly Inraged thereatt, and with fury and violence pulled of Job Boltons hatt flinging itt on the other side of the Roome Saying he was Bishop of the Diocese and

Commanded William Clarke with fury to pull of his hatt againe and againe Upon which Job Bolton haveing delivered the Friends Letter to the Bishop and he readinge 2 or 3 Lynes and finding the word thee or thou therein the Bishop fell into a greater Rage and flung downe the Letter upon the ground and notwithstanding all moderate discourse used to him in Rage he left the Roome and Left them so they could not have further Admittance to him.

Waiting some tyme the Bishop came out againe and Job Bolton discouraging him expressing the word thee or thou to him he againe fell into Rage and left the Roome claping the door after him. Upon which after considerable Attendance and waiting in vaine Job Bolton made up the said Letter againe and delivered itt to one of the Bishops servants who promised them to deliver the same to his Master as he had a Convenient opportunity.[48]

★   ★   ★

The preceding sections of the chapter have discussed the continuing persecution of the Quakers in Cirencester during the 1670s and the processes by which their earlier movement, based on exuberance and enthusiasm, was steadily modified and transformed into a structured and increasingly exclusive society. Clearly Cirencester Friends were more inward-looking by the end of the decade. It would be a mistake, however, to assume that as a result they withdrew from public life. In fact there were few years between 1663 and the Toleration Act of 1689 when at least one Quaker was not serving the town in public office.

In 1671, when the church authorities were making determined attempts to have John Roberts arrested, he was nevertheless chosen constable in Siddington, and on his way into Cirencester over Kings Mead he took into custody an escaped prisoner, still in chains, and had him returned to Gloucester Castle.[49] In 1672 he was to serve as supervisor of the highways, and together with Thomas Pollard was ordered by the Easter Quarter Sessions to collect a rate of £20 from the Siddington parishes to repair the roads. But such is the inefficiency of bureaucracy, the justices had already consigned him to Gloucester Castle on a writ of *excommunicato capiendo*.[50]

Local administration under the Stuarts relied on the work of unpaid officials, chosen to serve for a year at a time. In Cirencester, town affairs were overseen by a vestry meeting, held in the town hall adjoining the parish church on Easter Monday of each year. The vestry, despite its name, was a secular body, composed of self-selected notables of the town.[51] Among its regular tasks was the appointment of two overseers of the poor, who were to levy and collect a poor rate and make weekly payments to the needy (the overseers of the poor were increased to four from 1675). It also regularly appointed two supervisors of the highways until 1670, from which point the constables and churchwardens jointly made the appointment. Fig. 10.2 shows a list of Quakers serving in either capacity.

In 1668 Giles Watkins, the Baptist minister, was appointed supervisor of the highways, and in 1686 he served with another Baptist, Thomas Sowdley, and the two Quakers as overseer of the poor. In 1669 Amariah Drewett was one of the two overseers of the poor charged by the vestry meeting with the task of issuing 'publick farthings for the benefit of the poore of this Towne ... with the name of Cirencester on both sides, with the yeare of our Lord god when they be stamped'; the face of this coin bore a phoenix and the rays of the sun.[52] In 1665 Robert Morse, the Attorney who had so brutally arrested the Quaker stallholders in the market place in 1662, was appointed to serve as supervisor of the highways with Amariah Drewett, and as overseer of the poor with the Baptist William Chance in 1668; was this an unfortunate choice, or had feelings subsided by then?

★   ★   ★

This chapter has traced the fortunes of Cirencester noncon-formists during the 1670s, now in favour, now not, according to the changing policies of what must have seemed a capricious government. Raised from despair at their powerlessness to prevent the destructive activities of paid informers, they established their meeting places and enjoyed at least twelve months of freedom to worship God after their own manner; only to be thrust down again by a resurgence of persecution at the hands of the Established Church.

Figure 10.2: *Quakers serving in a public capacity*[50]

1663 William Drewett – supervisor of the highways

1665 Amariah Drewett – supervisor of the highways

1667 Richard Bowly the younger – overseer of the poor; attends vestry
       meeting

1669 Amariah Drewett – overseer of the poor
       Robert Freame – supervisor of the highways

1670 John Cripps – overseer of the poor

1671 John Timbrell – overseer of the poor
       John Roberts – constable

1672 Richard Townsend – supervisor of the highways
       John Stephens – overseer of the poor
       John Roberts – supervisor of the highways

1673 John Cripps – attends vestry meeting

1674 Robert Freame – overseer of the poor
       William Drewett – overseer of the poor

1675 William Burge – overseer of the poor
       Richard Townsend – overseer of the poor

1680 Amariah Drewett – overseer of the poor
       William Bowly – supervisor of the highways

1684 John Stephens – overseer of the poor
       John Cripps – overseer of the poor

1686 Richard Townsend – overseer of the poor
       John Stone – overseer of the poor

1687 William Hinton – overseer of the poor

1689 William Drewett – overseer of the poor

We have been able to penetrate the opaqueness of the historical record and catch glimpses of the main characters involved: the local gentry frequenting the fashionable hostelry out at Perrots Brook, strolling by its bowling green or quarrelling at cards; local tradespeople turning their organizing skills to having their meeting house built, struggling with their fund-raising, establishing the procedures for their religious group and keeping its records; constables caught up in the religious squabbles and pleading for common-sense and humanity; and an increasingly beleaguered Anglican clergy, no longer certain of its own authority nor its vision of universal conformity to its ways, maintaining a low profile and jealous of its privileged status.

Social processes have become visible: groups learning to use the political tools of canvassing, lobbying and shaming; communication networks being established; systems being developed for mobilising action. Of particular significance for our study has been the steady erosion under persecution of the original exuberance and vitality of the Quaker movement, and its search for respite under a protective covering of structure and internal discipline.

John Roberts, now in his mid-fifties, still occupies a leading role in the Quaker group, boldly confronting its persecutors, fearless in the face of physical threat. But his temporary removal by imprisonment at a critical point in its history – the building of its meeting house – has given space for new leaders to emerge, in particular Richard Bowly and Richard and Theophila Townsend, whom we shall now see courageously defend the Quaker group against the redoubled onslaught of the 1680s.

NOTES

[1] *CSPD* 1671, p.561.
[2] Richard Farnsworth: *A Toleration sent down from Heaven to Preach*, written in Gloucestershire December 1665. Farnsworth draws parallels between the practices of Friends and those of the Apostles as to their place and manner of meeting for worship.
[3] *CSPD* 1671, p.594.

4 See the account of the physical abuse of Friends at Gloucester in 1670 and at Little Badminton by informers in 1677, given in J. Besse, *op. cit.*, Vol.1, p.217 and p.219.

5 *A Short Relation of some part of the Sad Sufferings and Cruel Havock and Spoil Inflicted on the Persons and Estates of the People of God, in scorn called Quakers, for meeting together to Worship God in Spirit and Truth Since the late Act against Conventicles.* The persecution of Friends in Gloucestershire is given prominence in this work, opening with a fuller account of Thomas Master breaking up the meeting in Cirencester and the death of Elizabeth Hewlings (see Chapter 9) than is contained in the *Great Book of Sufferings*.

6 George Fox: *Journal*, p.517.

7 GRO D1340 A1/M1.

8 GRO D1340 B1/M1.

9 T. Ellwood, *op. cit.*, p.209. Ellwood accompanied George Fox on his tour of the West Country, setting up monthly and quarterly meetings.

10 Charles Marshall: *Sion's Travellers Comforted and the Disobedient Warned*, London 1704.

11 Oliver Sanson: *God's Mighty Power Magnified: as Manifested and Revealed in his Faithful Handmaid Joan Vokins*, London 1691, p.a1.

12 *Ibid*, p.a7.

13 T. Townsend: *A Testimony concerning the Life and Death of Jane Whitehead*, London 1676.

14 *CSPD* Addenda 1660-1670, p.361.

15 GRO GDR 224. William Field of Siddington, Ann Bayden's future husband, was also brought before the court but not excommunicated. As we shall see (note 29), the accuracy of the diocesan records at this period is less than perfect. The duplication of the name of John Roberts suggests a misreading for John Cripps or John Timbrell. Richard Turner is unknown among Cirencester Friends; perhaps Richard Bowly?

16 *CSPD* 1671, p.193.

17 *Ibid*, 1671-2, p.217, 19 March 1672. 'That so far as with safety may be, a connivance be had to those whose wild principles suffer them not to accept this act of so great grace.'

18 G. Lyon Turner, *op. cit.*, Vol.1, p.240 and 245. Turner quotes the full text of the humble address as an example of the height of obsequiousness.

19 *Ibid*, Vol.1, p.404. This building suggests that it was a large cottage, or pair of cottages, converted into a meeting house by removing the internal walls and the floor of the upstairs rooms, and replacing them with stairs and a gallery. The lintel over the entrance door bears the

date 1672. (See G.H. Clennell: 'Memorials of an Ancient Presbyterian Meeting House in Cirencester', *Transactions of the Unitarian Historical Society* 1933, p.262ff).

20 *CSPD* 1671-2, p.314, 12 April 1672 and p.432, 1 May 1672.

21 G. Lyon Turner, *op. cit.*, Vol.1, p.581.

22 GRO D6518/1.

23 GRO D1340 B3/Z2.

24 *CSPD* May-September 1672, p.489, 8 May 1672.

25 *Ibid*, May-September 1672, p. 214, June 1672.

26 *Ibid*, May-September 1672, p.214, 12 June 1672.

27 *Ibid*, May-September 1672, p.551, August 1672.

28 According to the *Memoir*, p.164 (*OR* p.66) John Roberts was imprisoned again in Gloucester Castle shortly after the death of William Farmer, the keeper of the gaol and bridewell. This had occurred by the Easter Quarter Sessions of 1672 when payment of 'the last quarter's pay to the late keeper' was suspended (GRO Q/SO1 p.4). Farmer was still alive on 5 October 1671, when he was instructed to release a prisoner (GRO GDR 222).

29 GRO Q/SO1, p.49. 'It is ordered by the Courte that John Hayward [Roberts], William Millett and Josiah Carrier who have been for severall years past prisoners in the Castle of Gloucester upon severall writts de Ex. Capiendo for contempt by them severally committed before 25 day of March last past, be forthwith discharged out of prison, they having severally pleaded the Act of pardon.' It was during this period of imprisonment, on 6 June 1673, that John Roberts is recorded as being sworn in as a churchwarden at Siddington Peter (GRO GDR 223).

30 W.C. Braithwaite: *The Second Period of Quakerism*, p.86.

31 *GSPD* Vol.1, p.417. Sir John Guise, born in 1654, was the only son of Sir Christopher Guise of Elmore. He matriculated at Christ Church, Oxford, on 3 December 1669, and would have been aged 21 at the time of this incident.

32 *Memoir*, pp.164-168 (*OR* p.70-72).

33 *Ibid*, pp.172-3 (*OR* p.75).

34 *Ibid*, p.177 (*OR* p.77).

35 Surgeons had to apply to their bishop for a licence to practice and had often been trained for the Anglican ministry themselves. On 14 June 1689 Edmund Wilkins of Cirencester, applying to be admitted to practice surgery in the diocese of Gloucester, had to swear that he subscribed to the Articles of Religion contained in the 36th Canon made in the year 1562 and would conform to the liturgy of the Church of England (GRO GDR 226a, p.113).

36 GRO GDR 231, 27 November 1677; GRO GDR 233, 4 December
    1678; GRO GDR 235, 8 October 1679; GRO GDR 230, 11 March
    1680.
37 GRO GDR 227.
38 An example of this process is the letter written by John Roberts to
    George Bull in 1671. 'Now, friend, it having been much upon me to
    clear my conscience thus to thee in the sight of God, I shall, I hope,
    rest satisfied in his will, if it please Him to permit thee to try me further.'
    (given in E. Lawrence, *op. cit.*, pp.324-7).
39 Daniel Roberts' account suggests that he has left the farm in
    Siddington and is now living in Cirencester, most probably learning
    the trade of mercer apprenticed to another Quaker, such as John
    Timbrell.
40 *Memoir*, p.176 (omitted in *OR*).
41 GRO D1340 B1/M1.
42 N. Penny (ed.): *The Short Journal and Itinerary Journals of George Fox*,
    p.265.
43 GRO D1340 A1/A2.
44 J. Besse, *op. cit.*, Vol.1, p.219.
45 *MMfS* Vol.1, p.80.
46 *Ibid*, Vol.1, p.32 and p.95.
47 We do not have available to us details of the prisoners in Gloucester
    and their indictments. John Whiting, imprisoned in Ivelchester in
    1679, found 33 Quakers there, 13 at the suit of impropriators and
    tithe-farmers, 15 at the suit of priests, 2 for not receiving the Eucharist,
    and 1 for refusing the oath of allegiance. Three quarters of them had
    been imprisoned for more than two years, one quarter more than five
    years. (John Whiting, *op. cit.*, p.18).
48 See W. Penn: *No Cross, No Crown*: 'True honour does not consist in
    hats and titles, performed according to the mode or fashion of the
    times (p.129) ... We cannot esteem bows, titles and pulling off hats to
    be real honour because such customs have been prohibited by God,
    His Son and servants in days past (p.133) ... We consider that self-love
    and desire of honour from men is inconsistent with the love and
    humility of Christ (p.140).
49 *Memoir*, p.163 (*OR* p.65).
50 GRO Q/SO1 folio 2a.
51 GRO P86 VE 2/1.
52 *Gloucestershire Notes and Queries*, Vol.1, p.347. In the period 1650-
    1670 at least 16 Cirencester tradesmen issued tokens of this type; a
    quarter of them were Quakers and Baptists.

CHAPTER 11

The Cirencester Contest

'They [Quakers in Cirencester] are a pack of Rogues, and gave
their Voices against me: And I will be even with them.'

James Georges

IN AUGUST 1679 CIRENCESTER was caught up in a parliamentary election for the second time that year. The 'Cavalier'
Parliament, elected in 1661, had run until the end of 1678, when
the king had dissolved it in an attempt to rid himself of its Whig
majority. In February 1679, however, the Whigs had been returned
in force, and now the king was making a further attempt to out-
manoeuvre his political opponents. The principal issue of contention was the succession to the throne. Charles II's queen was
barren and as next-in-line stood the king's brother, James, Duke
of York, an unpopular figure with many because of his open espousal
of Catholicism. Discredited and despatched to the continent
following the bogus revelations of Titus Oates in 1678, James had
become the subject of an Exclusion Bill, which would have debarred
him from ascending the throne. To kill off this legislation Charles
had dissolved parliament in May 1679.

It was only the previous year that a new face had appeared
among the county gentry and the polite circles of Cirencester. His
name was James Georges,[1] the new lord of the manor of Baunton,
two miles from the town. His uncle, John Georges, who, as member
of parliament in 1643, had led a spirited defence of the town
against Prince Rupert, found himself in his later years in financial
difficulties. With no son to succeed him, John had allowed his

Georges coat of arms.

prosperous nephew James to rescue him and in October 1678, as consideration for a handsome annuity, had bequeathed him the lordship of the manor together with the treasured family heirloom, the Great Bowl Sare.[2] Apart from a period of disqualification under the Commonwealth, John Georges had held one of the parliamentary seats from January 1626 until his death in January 1679. Now in the summer of 1679, as one of the squirearchy and a little more known locally, James felt the moment opportune to imitate the example of his uncle, enter the political lists and unseat Sir Robert Atkyns, who had been burgess of the town for less than six months.[3]

Atkyns, himself, later records in his *The Ancient and Present State of Glostershire* that the town 'sends two Parliament Men. Every Housekeeper, not receiving Alms, has a Voice. The number of electors is betwixt six and seven hundred.'[4] Among these were a significant number of Quakers.[5]

It had become the practice of Friends to make the choice of candidate a matter of prayerful concern for the whole local meeting, and they were enjoined by Meeting for Sufferings to give their voices at this election for 'sober, discreet and moderate men, such as live in love with their neighbours, that are against persecution and Popery, and that deport themselves tenderly towards our Friends'.[6] Aware of this, James George prepared an appropriate canvassing letter, addressing them:

> Dear Friends, I am sorry that ill Persons should appear to Asperse you and charge me with any Unkindness to any Honest and Godly People. I do assure you all, I ever had a great respect to the Godly People of this Nation and ever shall; and I am sure my Family ever had a great Respect and Kindness for all my Neighbours of this Town of Cirencester: And by the Grace of God I will continue in the same Opinion as long as I shall live, and I will be very plain with you, for Complements I do abhor: I am resolved by the Grace of God to oppose the Interest of that abominable Antichrist the Pope, and all his private and subtle Adherents and Incendiaries, and remain your True Friend to serve you.[7]

On the 19 August Cirencester Friends gave their considered reply:

Loving Friend, these lines are to acquaint thee that we have
tenderly considered the lines; whereunto we have this much
to say, and that in good Conscience in the sight of God, who
knows our hearts: that as for Aspersions, we have learned to
go through good Reports and evil, and for unkindness we
charge thee not; but do assure thee that we have no prejudice
or ill will towards thee, nor on any such account have we
appeared to give our Voices in this Election for the other
Persons, but as pre-engaged in our minds for such Reasons,
as intended no Reflection upon thy Honesty, Reputation or
Person, but as free-born English subjects, have taken the
liberty to act according to our perswasions without Reflection,
not knowing at present which side may carry it, but shall be
content which soever it be: Thy respect to the Godly People
of this Nation, and Abhorrence of Popery and Popish Interest
we desire thou mayest retain in Sincerity, and then we doubt
not but to have a share of thy Respects; and thou wilt so far
be of the same mind with us against Persecution, which is the
principal part and support of popery, so we

Remain thy well-wishers[8]

The Whig Sir Robert Atkyns was again successful in what must
have been a closely fought contest. James Georges identified the
Quakers as being a deciding factor in his defeat and was heard to
exclaim in his disappoint and anger: 'They are a pack of Rogues,
and gave their Voices against me: And I will be even with them'.[7]

*   *   *

Parliamentary politics had polarized into those who *petitioned*
the king to secure a protestant succession to the throne, and those
who *abhorred* any curtailment of royal prerogative. The Petitioners,
nicknamed *Whigs*, tended to be Puritan in outlook and represented
commercial wealth, while the Abhorrers, known as *Tories*, reflected
the interests of the landed gentry and church establishment. As the
issue of the succession, or rather the exclusion of the Catholic Duke
of York, intensified during 1680 and early 1681, the Tories found
themselves thrust into offering almost unqualified support to the
king and a likely Catholic succession.

Successful in further secret negotiation with Louis XIV for a
substantial annual subsidy, Charles II brought matters to a head
by holding a parliament in Oxford, and then summarily dissolving

it – the last parliament he would have to endure during the remainder of his reign. One of the casualties of abandoned legislation was a bill ensuring toleration for protestant dissenters, which had already passed through the Commons and Lords and needed only the royal assent.

Charles' last four years of absolutist rule rested, then, on Tory support and French gold. The Earl of Shaftesbury, leader of the Whigs was imprisoned in the Tower on a charge of treason but was acquitted by a Middlesex jury in the November. Stephen College, a prominent Whig propagandist, was tried in Oxford and executed in the August. The judiciary and lists of justices of the peace were steadily cleared of Whig supporters, and powers were acquired to control the appointment of aldermen and officials in the towns. Among those to be purged in Gloucestershire was Sir John Guise, who had been elected in both February and August 1679 to represent the shire: the lieutenant of the county, the Marquess of Worcester, confirmed to Secretary Jenkins the deletion of Sir John's name from the revised list of deputy lieutenants and justices, whom 'I told you at Hampton Court I had then immediate order from his Majesty to put out from being deputy lieutenant'.[9]

As the newly vetted judges went on circuit, the king's repressive policy towards dissent was made known. In October 1681 Sir William Smythe of Stepney reported to Secretary Jenkins:

> I waited on you yesterday to have given you an account of our proceedings for suppressing the Conventicles. The orders of the Quarter Sessions have been read in our churches, and the parish officers have readily obeyed in making their returns. ... We intend to send to the landlords of the meeting houses to let them know their danger and likewise to the teachers to wish them to desist.[10]

The Bishop of London requested the king's secretary 'to order Stephens to seize 'a most pernicious book', the *Everlasting Gospel*, published by Quakers'.[11] In Middlesex, after the vexing acquittal of the Earl of Shaftesbury, the king assembled all the justices to impart 'a strict charge to put the laws in execution against Papists, and more especially against Dissenters or frequenters of unlawful conventicles and meeting houses, such as they call Quakers,

Presbyterians, Baptists, and other such like vermin, which swarm in the land'.[12]

During the first half of 1681 in Gloucestershire there had been three Quakers imprisoned for refusing to take the oath of allegiance, and another three imprisoned on writs of *excommunicato capiendo* issued by the bishop.[13] But in the autumn there was a hardening of policy, with eight Quakers presented at the Michaelmas Quarter Sessions as Popish recusants, indicted for not going to their parish church nor taking the sacrament;[14] and in November 1681 Meeting for Sufferings in London received a letter from Little Badminton, 'intimating the severe persecution of Friends there on the Act of Conventicles: severall being convicted by the Information of the Parish Priest there, and Samuel Pell the Marquess of Worcester's servant. And of 4 Friends who by the Justices of a Petty Sessions were committed to Glocester Goal'.[15] Two further letters from Little Badminton were sent in December 1681, reporting physical abuse by the Marquess' son, Lord Herbert, and his servants, and further arrests.[16]

The village of Little Badminton adjoined the country seat of Henry Somerset, Marquess of Worcester, and later Duke of Beaufort. Charles, his son, was born in December 1660, and became Lord Herbert of Raglan in 1667.[17] Meeting for Sufferings decided to confront the Marquess with an account of the behaviour of his son and servants, and two experienced Friends were deputed to visit him at his London house. Refused an interview, they were followed two weeks later by two Quaker gentlewomen, Griselda Tolverly and Mirabella Farnborough.[16] By the end of December 'Marrabella Farmborow and Martha Fisher had been with the Marquess of Worcester with the state of the Case of Friends sufferings in that County and delivered the same to the Marques who did answer That he would search into the Business when he went into the Country'.[18]

The father's advice to the son, however, in the matter of the Quakers seems to have been quite other from that which Friends were anticipating. The twenty-one year old Lord Herbert proudly reported to Secretary Jenkins:

My father having told me how acceptable it was to his Majesty to have the laws against Dissenters, both Papists and Sectaries, put in execution, I thought it my duty to propose it to the Bench, where the enclosed order was agreed to by all those present, and I do not doubt it will be signed by all the rest of the Justices of this county, for we have ordered the Clerk of the Peace to send it to be signed by every Justice in this county, that we may be unanimous in our proceedings. The Grand Jury ... without being in the least prompted, gave us their thanks, as you will find in the enclosed. It was made up of persons scarce known to us, but substantial men from all parts of the county. By them and all other circumstances in this county I find, if we keep steady in our proceedings against the Dissenters and more care be taken that they be not excused in the Crown Office (which is a general complaint in all these countries), we shall have no more trouble with them, and in a short time I believe a Dissenter will scarce be heard of, for in my own precincts within five miles of a town called Marshfield, where conventicles have been continually kept, we did but send out warrants on the Monday to all constables, etc., to bring in their presentments against all Dissenters, conventicles, etc., to us at our petty sessions intended to be held the following week there, and they pulled down their pulpits and seats themselves before we came the next Sunday; of the great numbers who used to absent themselves from church, there was scarce anyone who did not come into church before Common Prayer began. ... We have ordered two copies to be delivered to the Bishop and Chancellor of the diocese with our desire of their doing the like with the spiritual power as we have done with the civil.

The king sent his personal thanks to Lord Herbert and the justices.[19]

The order of the Quarter Sessions referred to was entered in the Order Book at the Easter Sessions 1682. It required the constables and churchwardens of every town to present a monthly account of all recusants in their towns and parishes absenting themselves from church, and to give to some justice of the peace information of all unlawful conventicles and meetings. The clerk of the peace was to prosecute every such officer on any neglect of his duty.

As evidence of their intentions, the bench fined the three arrested Badminton Friends £4 each in January 1682; a fourth, John Pierce, had already died in jail. Lord Herbert was also party to the jailing of three more Badminton Friends, come to offer support to those originally arrested, who were themselves apprehended as they were walking in the Sessions hall.[20]

One of the first results of Lord Herbert's initiative was the wholesale arrest of adult Quakers in their meeting house in Gloucester on 5 February 1682, the men and their wives, some pregnant, some with babies in arms, and their imprisonment in the city jail in Northgate. Meeting for Sufferings in London agreed to make application to the Marquess of Worcester or others on their behalf.[21] No progress having been made, it was decided on 12 May to approach Lord Herbert's father-in-law, the wealthy Sir Josiah Child, with the pitiable case of the Gloucestershire Friends.[22] On 19 May John Vaughan reported that 'he spoke to the Marques of Worcester who treated them kindly, directing them to advice where there would be a Sessions, desiring not to mention what he does for friends, or any good effect of his assistance by print or otherwise'.[23] But by 7 July the Marquess had abandoned his double game, George Whitehead reporting 'that the Marques of Worcester will not Endeavour their Reliefe because their meeting is so near unto his house'.[24]

★   ★   ★

In Cirencester Lord Herbert's initiative provided James Georges with his opportunity for crossing off old scores with the Quakers. He seems to have begun in February 1682 with fines and intimidation, which culminated on 3 March in the arrest of Richard and William Bowly and Amariah Drewett, who were jailed in Gloucester Castle. They were brought before the Assizes on 22 July, charged with having 'lately departed from places of theire severall habitacions and assembled themselves the nineteenth February last past at Cirencester aforesaid in a certaine place there called the Quakers burying place ... under the pretence of ioyning in a Religious worshipp not authorised by the laws of this realme'. They were given the choice of a £5 fine or three months in jail. They refused to pay the fine and spent a total of 22 weeks in Gloucester Castle.[25]

These proceedings so outraged Theophila Townsend, the wife of Richard, that the same day as their arrest she sent to Meeting for Sufferings an account of the 'severe persecution which is inflicted on severall Friends there by One James George a Justice so called and others'.[26] The response of Meeting for Sufferings was to send two Friends to Henry Powell and Sir Robert Atkins junior, 'the last Representatives in Parliament for that Towne to endeavour to gain what relief they can'. George Whitehead and Charles Marshall were received sympathetically:

> George Whitehead did propose to them [Henry Powell and Sir Robert Atkins] to write into the County to intimate to Justice James George the Account and Observation that is here made by severall of his severe Proceedings against Friends, And the Occasion he Takes against them for their giving their Voices in the Elleccion of them for Burgesses [members of parliament] of Cirencester, and because they did not give their voices for him, He Threatened to be even with them. And they [Powell and Atkins] promised to write accordingly. And Henry Powell had spoken to the Marques of Worcester about their sufferings, which the Marques promised to Enquire into when he came into the County.[27]

On 13 March Sarah Wadden reported to Charles Marshall how the meeting for worship had again been broken up by the constables the previous Sunday, and Friends pulled out of the meeting house and dispersed, but with no fines or arrests.[28]

Pressure from the two Cirencester burgesses and the attentions of the lord lieutenant of the county may have deterred James Georges a little. A pamphlet appeared in London, detailing his behaviour but not mentioning him by name 'in some Hopes that he may better bethink himself'.[29] An incident from the *Memoir*, taking place in spring weather, warm enough for the windows to be open, also suggests restraint and circumspection of the justice's part.[30]

On market day he had sent a message to Daniel Roberts and his elder brother, Nathaniel, who had set up as mercers in the centre of the town, to appear before him at the *Ram Inn* at the top of the market place. It so happened that their father, John, was in the shop

Cirencester market place.

at the time, and the three went together, to be warned that it was 'his majestye's Pleasure to have the Laws put in Execution'.

Through the open window 'we had a Prospect of Cirencester [church] tower; and the Justice, pointing to it, said, 'What do you call that, John?'

'Thou mayst call it a Daw-house if thou Please. Dost not see the Jack Daws flock about it?'

Justice George retorted, 'Well, notwithstanding your Jesting, I warn you in the King's name, that you meet no more, as you will answer it with your Perrill.'[31]

Shortly afterwards Theophila Townsend herself was arrested in the street on a warrant signed by James Georges and Sir Thomas Cutler and taken before Georges. 'She asked her crime. Hee said the day before she had directed the people to turn from ungodliness, which was enough. He turned to severall Acts which did not concern her. At last required surety for good Behaviour, And after well clearing her conscience to the Justice, she was committed to Gloucester County Jaile' for 11 weeks.'[32]

James Georges was correct in identifying her as one of the most formidable characters among the Cirencester Quakers, one that he wanted put behind bars. Almost certainly self-taught, Theophila was used to speaking in public: John Gratton, attending Yearly Meeting in 1674, had been moved by her oratory, despite the heckling, at a large, crowded meeting in London.[33] We have already noted her close association with women Friends travelling in the ministry, Joan Vokins and Jane Whitehead at the least. The justice would not have enjoyed listening to her 'well clearing her conscience'.

Consequent to his warning to the Roberts family at the *Ram Inn*, in early May the justice instructed the constables to break up the Friends' meeting for worship the following Sunday and take names.[34] Very unwilling to carry the instructions out, the constables warned Daniel Roberts and begged him to have either the time or place of the meeting changed, but Friends met as usual. The constables came, names were taken and James Georges issued warrants distraining Friends' property. In particular, all of John Roberts' corn was seized and his barn doors locked, a fine of

£20.10s. was placed on Daniel Roberts, and the two brothers were expected to pay a total of £70, covering the fines of those no longer able to pay them.

★ ★ ★

But there were problems on the justice's estate at Baunton, where, in spite of attempts to cure them, half his cattle had already died of murrain. Eventually, when the bull became sick, he acquiesced with great reluctance in his steward's suggestion of approaching John Roberts, who had a reputation of being able to cure animals. The Quaker saw it his duty to return good for evil and was successful in saving the remainder of the justice's beasts.

James George had hoped to avoid all personal contact with John and keep the matter a strictly financial transaction, but, as it happened, they met face to face in the outbuildings.

'Well,' said the Justice to the steward, 'pay John.'

'No,' said my Father, 'I will have none of thy money.'

'None of my money!' said the Justice, 'Why so?'

'To what Purpose is it,' said my Father, 'for me to come and take a little of thy money by retail, and thou come and take my goods by wholesale.'[35]

From this unpromising start, the tone of the conversation softened, with the Quaker accepting the justice's invitation to stay to dinner, and the justice accepting a tract by Thomas Ellwood on persecution.[35] The justice relented, and none of John's corn was distrained.

★ ★ ★

His treatment of Daniel and Nathaniel Roberts, however, was quite different. On a market-day in the middle of May 1682 there assembled at the *King's Head* on the market place the sheriff of the county and his men, the jailor of Gloucester Castle, the chancellor of the diocese Justice Richard Parsons, Sir Thomas Cutler, James Georges and other justices, and the town constables. When news got round that they had come to seize the Roberts brothers' goods, some of the young men's neighbours arrived to lock up the mercer's shop and take away the key. The butcher's wife from Cricklade, who always had her stall in front of the shop, pulled down the shop windows and threw her butcher's cleaver down the cellar grating to prevent it being used to break open the door. While hundreds of people were looking on, constables were posted back and front of the shop, with the two Quakers and a woman customer locked inside, and a justice peering through the keyhole, claiming he could see a conventicle taking place and commanding them in the king's name to open the doors.

Daniel answered that he had not locked the doors, nor could he open them, if he would. Sir Thomas threatened to blow up the house and sent for gunpowder but no shopkeeper was willing to sell it to the officers. The woman living next door to the mercer's began screaming, 'Lord, have mercy upon us! What, are you come to kill us all and blow up our houses about our ears?' The justices then sent for a sledge hammer and crowbar, but the first black-smith refused to part with them. At another blacksmith's, the master being absent, the officers managed to secure a sledge hammer from the assistant. The constables at the back of the building pleaded with the young brothers to open the door: if the constables themselves did not break down the door, then the sheriff's men would. Then, in full view of the crowd, the front door was hammered off its hinges and Sir Thomas Cutler, with his hand on his sword, rushed into the shop, shouting that there were five hundred escaping from the conventicle at the back, the officers following him.

Daniel wryly observed to him that ''tis not reasonable to think that tradesmen should keep a conventicle in their shop on a market day in the middle of market time'.[37] Both brothers were tendered the oath of allegiance and, refusing it, were committed to the county jail.

While Nathaniel stayed in the shop to list the goods being seized, Daniel recalled:

> I, in the meantime, went down into the Cellar, and, Kneeling on a Drink stand, besought the Lord in Prayer, that he should be pleased to strengthen us in this day of tryal, that we might stand faithful in our testimony for his truth. And he was pleased to fill with his goodness and carry us far above the fear of man and to give us assurance.[38]

As they were escorted across the market place to the *Kings Head*, several of their neighbours shook their hands, and at the entrance to the inn James Georges, who has not been at all prominent in the affair, also took their hands: 'You know, young men, that some time agoe I sent for you to the Ram, and told you what would follow, if you continued to meet as usual; and now it is come upon you, and I can't help it.'[38] Inside, Sir Thomas Cutler again tendered them the oath of allegiance, and warned them that they ran the risk of transportation to the West Indies, but they still refused. Finally, horses were brought and, on the young men's insistence, they were publicly led off across the market place, along Dollar Street and Gloucester Street, with many of their neighbours coming to say goodbye to them. Stopping outside Amariah Drewett's house, they went into the packed meeting for worship, where their parents and brother were, joined in prayer with them and then set off for Gloucester Castle to join the other four Cirencester Friends.

★   ★   ★

The prison, in which they were to spend the next two and a half years, was housed in the remains of a mediaeval royal fortress, located to the west of the city, near the docks. Its site has continued to be used as a jail to the present day, the mediaeval stone fortifications since replaced by a less romantic high brick wall. In the seventeenth century it was in a ruinous state, and repairs were a constant preoccupation of justices at the quarter sessions.[39]

Being a royal castle, proprietorship of the jail was never a clear cut issue, and the justices devoted considerable expense to remove the ambiguity, basing their claim on the fact that 'the said Castle neither within time of living memory not since the Reigne of Richard the third or at any time since hath beene a fortresse or Castle of Defence but as a Common Goale only for the keepinge of prisoners'.[40] Final victory came in January 1677 with a judgment confirming the sheriff in possession 'of that Range of buildings called the Stonebuildinge or Common Goale and the Gatehouse leadinge to the same and of all that ground conteyned in the Inner Wall of the said Castle together with the Bridewell or new Brickbuildinge thereupon lately built and erected'.[41] In addition, there was 'a small house for the keeper or deputie of the sheriff to dwell in'.[40]

County gaol in Gloucester Castle.

Thus there were two sections to the prison, the jail and the bridewell or workhouse.

The Common Jail, consisting of 'some few Roomes for the keepinge of Prisoners', was intended as a kind of transit camp for felons awaiting trial at the assize court, which was held twice yearly in the city. At a time when the barbarism of the penal system condemned even petty thieves to the gallows, most of the prisoners – murderers, highwaymen, housebreakers, coin clippers, thieves – would be without hope, awaiting certain execution, or, if clemency was shown, transportation for 14 years of servitude on the plantations of the West Indies. There were also a very large number of debtors, imprisoned at the will of their creditors until they or their friends should pay what they owed. Prisoners of all types appear to have been kept herded together until January 1685, when the justices of the peace ordered 'that a partition be made in the maine goale dividing off the felons from the debtors pursuant to the statute'.[42]

Workhouses or houses of correction had been established in 1576 under the supervision of the quarter-sessions. They were originally intended as a remedy for vagrancy and 'to set to work such as be already grown up in idleness'. Known later popularly as bridewells, taking this name from the Bridewell Jail in London, they were also used to carry out custodial sentencing and became a place of forced labour for prisoners. In 1674 it was directed that the master 'doe receive from time to time such prisoners as shall be sent from any parte of the County ... and sett them to hard labour and give them due Correction'.[43]

Both sections of the prison were in the charge of John Langbourne in 1682, who received a salary of £15 per annum as master of the bridewell. Letters patent from the king for running the common jail were held by a consortium of investors, led by Captain Thomas Price, which farmed out the business to Langbourne.[44] Profits were to be made by charging the prisoners fees, and by supplying food and ale or bedding. The size of the jailor's income would, therefore, depend on his ingenuity and ruthlessness.[45] Every incident in prison life was made the occasion of a fee, from paying the 'garnish' on admission to 'turning the key' on discharge.

Gloucester Castle made a favourable impression on Thomas Baskerville, who visited it in January 1683 in the course of his travels:

> These civil gentlemen showed us the town and its rarities, amongst which the prison or gaol must not be forgotten, being esteemed for a house of that use the best in England, so that if I were forced to go to prison and make any choice I would come hither. Mr. Langbourne, the keeper or chief master of the prison, entertained us kindly and gave us good ale, and while we were there one Mr. Powell, a minister, read prayers to the prisoners, for which he and another have a yearly allowance to read prayers to them twice a week. Here is within the walls of this gaol a fair bowling green, and hither the townsmen come to divert themselves; the jailor's wife also deserves to be commended for adding to the beauty of the place a neat garden.[46]

One wonders how far Baskerville ventured inside. His optimistic view contrasts sharply with that of John Howard, who inspected the same buildings and arrangements a century later.[47] There were still the congested, airless rooms, one sewer, no bath, and a well that became contaminated whenever the Severn flooded. The chaplain mentioned, James Powell, was dead by September 1683, having lasted some two years in that office, an average for most of the chaplains in Gloucester Castle for that period. Eight Quakers died there between 1677 and 1686, and Theophila Townsend, imprisoned for four years, was near to dying on several occasions with jail fever. She also recalled seeing how 'severall other of our Friends have been Beaten and Bruised, by knocking and throwing hither and thither till they Died'.[48]

★   ★   ★

In this renewed wave of persecution Gloucester Castle became once again the destination of those whom the authorities wanted to see out of the way. As Sir Thomas Cutler had warned, refusing to take the oath of allegiance was a most serious offence, risking the sentence of *praemunire*, i.e. the forfeiture of one's goods, the removal of the king's protection and indefinite imprisonment or even banishment. Equally, to be sentenced on a writ of *excommunicato capiendo*, at the urging of the church authorities, meant continuous imprisonment until the individual was willing to submit to the requirements of the Church of England.

But now, for our story, the Castle takes on a particular significance: whereas, until now, the locus of our eye-witness reports has been Cirencester, with individuals consigned to the remoteness of the county jail, from now onwards our two main correspondents, Daniel Roberts and Theophila Townsend, spend most of their time imprisoned within its walls, and events are observed and recorded from inside the prison. Daniel Roberts, the calmer of the two, with greater literary gifts and a more obvious sense for the absurd, has the leisure to reflect and compose an extended and often humorous account.[49] Untutored, and with a voice that is more strident and urgent, Theophila Townsend uses her pen to engage the attention of both the civil authorities and Friends in London and reports flagrant acts of injustice and the viciousness of the persecutors.[50]

Quite soon after his admission to Gloucester Castle Daniel encountered his first bizarre experience. The jailor was required to attend the assizes in Oxford, and because he had no confidence in the drunken turnkey, he handed Daniel the keys and placed him in charge of the county jail. Among his fellow prisoners were two notorious highwaymen, awaiting trial and execution, who decided to use the jailor's absence to make a break-out. Daniel learned of the plan and was able to foil the attempt. On his return the jailor was so overjoyed and grateful that Daniel was able to exercise some influence - preventing the use of thumb-screws on the highwaymen, entering a plea for a Welshman (which led to his death sentence being commuted to transportation), and obtaining some privileges for the Quakers, including leave for individuals to visit their families on compassionate grounds.[51]

$$\star \qquad \star \qquad \star$$

At the beginning of June 1682 the royal mail brought to the town a letter from Secretary Jenkins, addressed to the mayor. As Cirencester was not an incorporated borough with its own council and mayor, this caused some difficulty, which was finally resolved by passing the letter to Justice James Georges. The king had been taken ill, but to allay all rumours (and deter any precipitate action by the followers of the Duke of Monmouth), the king's secretary had written to all mayors, ministers and consuls abroad, assuring them that his majesty was suffering from no more than a chill, caught travelling in his barge. James Georges proudly replied: 'Yours of 30th came to Cirencester directed to the Mayor. It being an ancient borough and no mayor town, the letter came to me, I being the nearest Justice to the place, signifying his Majesty's sudden indisposition and recovery. I immediately made it known to the people to our great joy by ringing of bells.'[52]

★   ★   ★

If the proposed use of gunpowder on a shop belonging to Quakers had surprised or alarmed Cirencester inhabitants in May 1682, then more directly disconcerting for a large number were events later that summer. On 17 July 361 parishioners of Cirencester were cited to appear before the bishop's court.

Thomas Careles, the vicar, had died on 7 October 1675, to be replaced by the 24 year old Jeremiah Gregory, son of the earlier vicar, Alexander Gregory, who had been ejected from his living in 1662. As we have seen, since 1666 virtually no use had been made of the consistory court by the vicar and churchwardens of the town to enforce church attendance. Jeremiah Gregory had been content to continue this policy for six years, but now it would seem that pressure had been put on him from outside, most probably by Richard Parsons, Chancellor of the Diocese.

The 361 names, occupying 44 pages in the consistory court's register, are grouped into: 'the poorer sort who seldom go to church and neglect the sacrament'; 'a loose sort of carelesse persons that goe not to the sacrament and seldom to the church'; then the sectaries by denomination, including the 57 'Quakers that disown the sacrament'.[53] The defendants appear to have been admonished and fined. Of the presentments from the surrounding villages on 13 July six persons were excommunicated, among whom were Giles and Mary Fettiplace of Coln Aldwyns.[53]

As an attempt to re-establish the authority of the Church of England in Cirencester, the exercise was a failure. The large number of presentments were not followed up at subsequent sessions of the consistory court, in contrast to the presentments from the villages, and only spasmodic efforts were made to pursue selected individuals.

But in the villages absence from church was steadily punished. Fined 16s. at the court hearing, Thomas Eldridge and his wife of Driffield had a coverlet, a blanket, a pewter plate and a pewter tankard, value 30s., taken.

From Harnhill the 65 year old Sarah Simmons was fined 4s. Sarah was a poor widow, who managed to maintain herself by carding and spinning. When the constable and churchwarden took her two pewter plates, she said, 'Prayse the Lord that he hath counted me worthy to suffer the loss of any thing for his names sake. The warden [John Howse] being smiten said: It is the worst pece of work I ever did in my life: so now people may see what a worke the persecuting justices are seting men about by their sessions order: by which they fright men that have no better under- standing then to obey it to act against thier contiences and bring trouble on their felows'.[54]

Thomas and Catherine Eldridge and Sarah Simmons, together with 49 others from the villages, were presented again at the consistory court three months later.[55]

★   ★   ★

During this period Meeting for Sufferings was preparing to publish an account of the areas where there was harsh persecu- tion of Quakers: Gloucestershire, Leicestershire and Northamptonshire. Theophila Townsend was consulted as to whether she, Daniel and Nathaniel Roberts were willing to have their names mentioned. A printer's proof was sent to them in Gloucester Castle, and finally Theophila decided that she wished her name excluded.[56]

On 28 July she wrote to Meeting for Sufferings, 'intimating the severe proceedings at the Assizes against her and several other Friends, who tho cleared by Law, yet they are detained (as is said) for their Fees'.[57] (Quakers maintained their innocence of any crime in worshipping God: if they were unjustly arrested, and subse- quently found innocent in court, why should any fees be demanded of them? In fact, to pay fees would be to acknowledge their guilt.)

Meeting for Sufferings asked for the name of the assize judge so that an approach could be made on their behalf.

At some point in the autumn, most probably at the Michaelmas Quarter Sessions, Richard and William Bowly, Amariah Drewett and Theophila were released from the county jail. (How the issue of the fees was resolved is not clear.) For on 14 November they were present at the Friends meeting for worship in Thomas Street. There was a re-run of seven years earlier, with the justice, the bishop and their retinue of subordinates bursting into the meeting house; and again Theophila was praying aloud – perhaps they had chosen that moment for their entry. The actors had changed: James Georges had replaced Sir John Guise, and Bishop Robert Frampton had succeeded Bishop John Pritchett.

> James George, after I was discharged, came to our peaceable Meeting with several Officers, and the Bishop of Gloucester with him; and when they came in, I was making Supplication to the Lord; and the Bishop said, 'Is this the Woman you were speaking of', he said, 'Yes, my lord'. then he [the bishop] laid hands upon me, and shook me and pulled me by an Arm so hard, that he almost pulled me backward, saying, 'Woman, you should give over, and obey the King's Officers.' But I chose rather to obey God than Man, and the Lord was with us, blessed be his Name, and his Power was over all. And the Bishop said to the Justice, 'Take their Names.' ... And the Justice set fines upon Friends, and Twenty Pounds on Richard Bowly for Praying in the said Meeting.[58]

Richard's brother William asked a question and was fined £20 for preaching. He, like Richard, was a malster. His doors were broken open at night, 200 bushels of malt were taken, 'even grains, to 2d., James George informed his fellows', and £4 in cash.[59]

In late November 1682 James Georges developed another ploy to rid the town of the Quakers. Together with the vicar, Jeremiah Gregory, and other citizens, he petitioned the king for permission to take over the Friends meeting house 'under pretence to make a Work House for the Poor'.[60] Theophila sent two urgent letters to Meeting for Sufferings 'with a Query touching the title of their meeting house, etc. Their title being from the crown. And some apprehension of seizing the said house into the hands of the king'.[61]

★   ★   ★

It was about this period that another score was being settled in Cirencester.

One evening, the previous February, Thomas Mole, the rector of Stratton, had been walking past the *Half Moon* in Cirencester and had heard the raised voice of the young attorney, Miles Sandys. Going in, he found the assembled company in full political debate about the Whigs and Tories, and the right of succession to the throne. Miles Sandys 'was fierce against the Duke of York and said that, if he [the Duke of York] was a Papist, it was lawful to take up arms against him. I [Thomas Mole] said, 'Dare you say so?' He answered, 'I dare according to the statute in *primo Elizabethae*'; on which I called for the reckoning and said I scorned to keep such rebellious company.' Oliver Dowle of Duntisbourne was able to confirm this, and insisted that the attorney was quite sober at the time.[62]

Although the alleged incident took place in February 1682, it was not until the following October that Sir Thomas Cutler began an investigation: Thomas Mole made his deposition at the end of November, and Oliver Dowle in the following March, more than a year after the event. Was the justice looking for material to quell the local Whigs, or was there a personal motive, now hidden to us? Sir Thomas reported to the Earl of Craven:

> Having information that Miles Sandys [was] endeavouring to seduce the ignorant into notions of rebellion under a pretence of law, being an attorney and therefore sooner credited amongst the misguided multitude, being a ring-leader of all the young factious party there, who are not an inconsiderable number, I immediately issued my warrant to have him brought before me and found him guilty of uttering those words ... I have other informations against him endeavouring to encourage Dissenters against authority.[63]

Miles Sandys appeared before the Assizes in Gloucester at the end of March 1683. Such was the way of seventeenth century justice that Sir Thomas, the prosecuting magistrate, was also foreman of the Grand Jury for the case. Earlier in March Sir Thomas was urgently writing to Secretary Jenkins for instructions and wanted an answer by Thursday's post to the *Old Bear*, Gloucester, before the Assize hearing on the Saturday. After the trial, on 7 April, he wrote an apology to Secretary Jenkins for his lack of success: 'I used my utmost endeavours to bring Mr. Sandys to a condign punishment ... but he was acquitted by the petty jury.'[64]

Sandys may have won his legal battle, but his career was in ruins. Secretary Jenkins had passed the papers to the Lord Chief Justice, 'desiring him to consider what is fit to be done with such an attorney'.[65]

★   ★   ★

Whether it was that Theophila Townsend had succeeded in thwarting James Georges' plans to appropriate the Quaker meeting house, or whether she had provoked in some other way, the justice had her arrested in January 1683:

> In the Tenth month 1682 [January 1683] James George sent a Warrant to the Constable of Cirencester who saw me going to a Neighbours House, they run after me and took me into Custody and had me to the petty Sessions at Barnsley [William Bourchier's mansion], three miles from Cirencester, in the Cold Winter Season, not considering my Age and Weakness, but hurried me up and down at their pleasure, tho they knew me a weakly Woman, and it was Frost and Snow, yet they had no Regard or Pity – sent to Gloucester Goal where I lay three Years and four Months, and James Georges gave the Goaler a charge not to let me out of the Gate, so great was their Fury and Rage against me.[66]

She was sentenced by James Georges, Sir Thomas Cutler and William Bourchier, 'they using very defaming language before they made her mittimus'.[67]

★   ★   ★

In the same month James Georges appears to have taken the unprecedented step of fining one of his own sort, his Quaker neighbour, the lord of the manor of Coln Aldwyns, Giles Fettiplace, and paying the king's share of the fine ($£3.11s.8d.$) into the Epiphany 1683 Quarter Sessions, so having it recorded in the Order Book. Sir Thomas Cutler supported him by fining Giles Fettiplace $£20$ and paying in the king's third.[68] Giles had been excommunicated at least twice before by the bishop, but had never been challenged by his fellow squires. Two other propertied Quakers were also fined,

Jacob Hewlings of Harnhill and the clothier Thomas Loveday of Painswick.

According to their own records, Quakers in Gloucestershire were fined £718.3s.6d. in the year ending with the June 1682 Yearly Meeting, and £340.5s. for the following year.[69] How the justices dealt with these fines, and where they recorded them, is not clear. But following the initiative taken by James Georges at the Epiphany 1683 Quarter Sessions there are from then on regular entries in the Order Book of the king's third, paid in by individual justices. Fig. 11.1 summarizes these.

Total fines levied by the Cirencester justices James Georges, his brother William, Sir Thomas Cutler and William Bourchier amount to £259.10s.0d. or 26% of the total fines for the county. Payments by the county justices to the under-sheriff cease at Epiphany 1685/6, with the Chancellor of the Diocese, Richard Parsons, maintaining the campaign for another six months. The Cirencester justice, William Georges, makes the last payment in September 1686.

★   ★   ★

Fines and imprisonments continued through the early months of 1683. In March Quakers in York sent £20 for the relief of the prisoners in Gloucester.[70] In April several Quakers were convicted at the Quarter Sessions, and on 14 April Charles Marshall reported that in Cirencester the constables had broken into Amariah Drewett's house and taken all his possessions, even the beds, except the maid's. Other Friends in the town had had their houses broken into.[71] On 2 May Theophila Townsend reported to Charles Marshall that all Jacob Hewlings' goods and chattels had been seized; that again goods had been taken from poor widows; that the constables, themselves, had been fined for not carrying out their duties thoroughly enough, and the fines laid on Friends; and that for all of these James Georges had granted the warrants.[72]

At the Assizes four Quakers had been fined, two of them not even present at the meeting in question. Meeting for Sufferings had made application to the judge for the release of two prisoners in Gloucester Castle, and three had been set at liberty, but the rest had been placed under 'a more strait confinement'. The prisoners,

Figure 11.1: *Fines imposed on dissenters*

Gloucester Quarter Sessions Order Book

Date	For his majesty's use	Total fine
1682 Epiphany	11.18.4	35.15.0
1683 Easter	71.12.5	214.17.3
Trinity	29.13.4	89. 0.0
Michaelmas	18.5	2.15.3
Epiphany	19.12.4	58.17.0
1684 Easter	46.12.4	139.17.0
Trinity	2. 1.8	6. 5.0
Michaelmas	–	–
Epiphany	–	–
1685 Easter	52. 6.6	156.19.6
Trinity	18. 4.0	54.12.0
Michaelmas	23.12.2	70.16.6
Epiphany	24.11.5	73.14.3
1686 Easter	3. 6.6	9.19.6
Trinity	27. 6.0	51.18.0
Michaelmas	6.16.8	20.10.0
		975.16.3

themselves, had presented a paper to the judge, detailing their long imprisonment, some for four years, some five, some eighteen months.[71]

On 14 May Daniel Roberts reported to Meeting for Sufferings on 'the proceedings against friends for a meeting [for worship] in prison, severall being fined and levies made on severall allready'. At this time there were between 40 and 50 Quakers in the county jail, who saw themselves as a large family of Friends, holding a meeting for worship each Sunday in the prison, which was also attended by other prisoners and a number of the inhabitants of Gloucester. On the Sunday in question John Roberts was there, visiting his sons, and had been warned by the mayor's wife at the inn where he was staying, that the Chancellor of the Diocese, Justice Richard Parsons, intended to break up the meeting. But Friends met as usual.

First the Chancellor sent his page-boy, dressed in livery, to ascertain whether a meeting for worship was being held. Then he came in person, with others, and attempted to silence Henry Ponton, who was standing to speak, by seizing his grey hair to pull him down. Henry, a tall man and a former fencing master, stood his ground and continued to speak. The Chancellor attempted to push his glove into his mouth, but Henry turned his head aside. When he had finished, Theophila Townsend stood up and declared, 'It is a Sign the Devil is hard put to it to have his Drudgery done, that Priests must leave their Pulpits and Parrishoners to come and turn Informers against Poor Prisoners in Prisons.'

The Chancellor commented to his companions, 'That is Theophila. She *will* speak.' Turning to an Irishman, he asked, 'Who are you? Are you a Quaker?'

O'Neale replied, 'No, sir. I hope you don't take me for so good a Christian.'

Chancellor addressed a woman visiting her husband in prison, 'Are you a Quaker?'

The woman answered, 'No, sir, I am not, but would to God I was.'

Chancellor then instructed John Tiffin, the former turnkey, 'Come and tell me your prisoners' names.'

Theophila Townsend intervened, 'I have read many law books, but have never read in any of them that any man was obliged by Law to turn Informer.'

John Tiffin exclaimed, 'I scorn the name of Informer' and turned away, not telling the justice the names of the prisoners.

'I see now how matters go', commented the Chancellor. 'It is no wonder here are such meetings.'

Returning home, the Chancellor found a list of a number of Quakers imprisoned for refusing to pay tithes, assumed that they were at the meeting and sent out warrants to distrain their goods for attending a conventicle, albeit in prison. This caused him further embarrassment since several of them had been granted leave to go home, either by the jailor or by Daniel Roberts. One of them, Francis Boy, a physician, was treating one of his patients among the gentry at the time. The patient was quite outraged at the chancellor's conduct and saw to it that his physician's cattle, distrained by the bailiffs, were returned to him. Another was a widow, Lettice Gush, who had a warrant served on her to distrain her goods to the value of £20, which incensed her landlord, the local squire.

Squire (to the Officer): What a Rascal is this Parsons! Here he says he will take his oath that my Tennant was convicted by him at a Conventicle at Gloucester Castle, such a day of the month; and I will take my oath that she was at her own home, which is 20 miles distant. If you touch her goods, by vertue of this Warrant, be it at your Perril. I will assure you, if you do, I will stick Close to your Skirts.

Officer: But, sir, what can we do in this Case? How can we make a legal return of the warrant without Executing it?

Squire: Do! Carry it back to Mr. Parsons, and bid him ... and I will bear you out in it.[73]

★   ★   ★

In June 1683 there was the uncovering of yet another plot against the life of the king. As with earlier 'revelations', it is uncertain to what extent the plot existed in reality but rather represented a tactical manoeuvre to reduce political opponents, this time the Whigs. Known as the Rye House plot after the farm in

Hertfordshire from which the conspirators were to ambush the king on his way to Newmarket, the plot led to the flight of the Duke of Monmouth, the execution of Lord Russell and Algernon Sydney and the supposed suicide of the Earl of Essex in the Tower. It also became an occasion for creating a climate of hysteria, conducting house searches and interrogations and unleashing a new wave of persecution against the sectaries.

Against this political background four Cirencester Quakers, Richard and William Bowly, John Drewett and Philip Gray, were arrested and conveyed to Gloucester Castle on a Sessions process on 26 June.[74] Inside the prison Theophila Townsend and Daniel Roberts were now being kept as 'very close prisoners', which would have meant segregation from the others, in more harsh and unhygienic conditions, most probably in chains. In spite of this, Theophila was managing to send letters almost fortnightly to Meeting for Sufferings. In the warmer weather smallpox had broken out, and Thomas May had died, leaving a widow and seven children. '6 prisoners more left in the same Jaile, in like danger, 4 having never had them [smallpox]'. A poor old blind Friend, Thomas Holborrow, had been arrested on the highway near Little Badminton and was brought to the prison in June; by August he was dead of jail fever. As the summer wore on, so the smallpox spread, claiming another victim among the Quakers, Ralph Langley. In the Northgate prison in Gloucester the Quaker prisoners were also being closely confined.[75]

Among the mayors who diplomatically sent messages of congratulation to the king on his escape from the plot was William Jordan of Gloucester:

> On the good news received today of the preservation of his Majesty and his Royal Highness the Mayor and Aldermen unanimously resolved on some demonstration of our joy and met at our Tolsey, and by bonfires and ringing of all the bells in the city we have endeavoured to show that we are no less loyal than we are reported to be.[76]

In Cirencester house searches for arms and ammunition had been taking place, when a chest containing 1 cwt [50kg] of lead musket bullets was discovered, hidden not on the premises of one of the sectaries but under old bell ropes in the tower of the parish church. The chest had been there, according to the sexton, for about four years, left by a workman, but the two churchwardens at the time, William Cletheroe and Ralph Willett, who held the key to the chest, had kept the contents concealed from him, and so had succeeding churchwardens; and none of them had ever mentioned the chest during the searches.

William Cletheroe was now dead,[77] so that James Georges, who had taken charge of the enquiry, decided to interrogate Thomas Perry, churchwarden in 1680, as well as Ralph Willett, and to send his report to the lieutenant of the county, the Duke of Beaufort:

> I have examined Willett and Perry, the former churchwardens, and all I can get from them is that they were prepared in the time of the Isle of Purbeck business for the defence of the King and kingdom. When demanded why they did not discover [disclose] them [the bullets], when their houses were searched, Willett answered that he did not know, and declaring to Perry that all loyal subjects were bound to give thanks for the discovery of the plot, he answered, they were so, if it were a plot, though the proclamation was proclaimed from the market cross but the Monday before, on which answers I bound them to their good behaviour till further directions, being satisfied of their disaffection to the government, they often having declared their good liking of the Duke of Monmouth and Lord Shaftesbury, as I have been credibly informed, and having ever refused to sign any address to his Majesty. I beg your Grace's commands for the disposing of the said bullets.[78]

Using the excuse that the Duke of Beaufort was visiting Bath and may not have seen his report, James Georges ensured that his name came to the attention of the Stuart government by despatching a copy to Secretary Jenkins five days later.

Such attention-seeking activities on the part of the gentry were not wasted. Lord Herbert, now elevated to the rank of Marquess, and Sir Thomas Cutler, both engaged in hounding another utterer of treasonable words, were assured of the king's favour by Secretary Jenkins: 'The King has already experience of Sir Thomas Cutler's care and zeal, therefore he is desired to send up this information in form that it may be laid before his Majesty and his directions had on it. We are infinitely beholden to the Duke of Beaufort and yourself [Lord Herbert] for your care and speed in sending up this information.'[79]

* * *

On 19 November 1683 James Georges had the meeting for worship in Cirencester broken up, fining Richard Bowly and young Thomas Loveday of Painswick, who had come to visit Sarah Wathen, £10 each.[80] But towards the end of 1683 social pressures were beginning to tell on the justice. He confided to the jailor of Gloucester Castle that he was suffering conscience pangs over sending Daniel and Nathaniel Roberts to prison: 'I can go into no company but one or another complains to me of their hard usage.' He suggested that he would overlook it if the jailor allowed them to go home from time to time to see to their shop. So it was that towards Christmas the two young men came back to Cirencester, opened up the mercer's shop on market day and were overwhelmed with customers from among their neighbours and the Quakers.[81]

That evening they met with Friends at Amariah Drewett's house for worship. As James Georges and his brother William were passing the house on their way home, they heard a Quaker praying. They stopped and went in to break up the meeting. At first Daniel had his back to the justices, but then made a point of turning round to face James Georges and, without a word, left the meeting, others following him. William Georges grew agitated, concerned that the Quakers were slipping away, but James said, 'Let them go if they will. I have got the preacher here, and that's enough.' Later that evening he sent round the officers to seize Amariah's brass, pewter and bedding to a considerable value, but took no steps against the two young Roberts.

Daniel and Nathaniel soon returned to Gloucester Castle, but it was not long afterwards that their father John became seriously ill, and they were given leave to visit him during his last days.

> And the Lord was pleased to accompany him with his Living Presence in his Last moments. Having faithfully finished his Day's work, he departed this Life In the year 1683; and was Intered in the Piece of Ground he had long before given to friends for a burying place at the Lower End of his orchard at Siddington.

John Roberts was buried on 19 January 1684.

While still at home Daniel learnt that that he and Nathaniel and the other four Quakers from Cirencester, Richard and William Bowly, John Drewett and Philip Gray, had been discharged at the Assizes,[82] but that the four had been detained in the county jail for fees. Hoping to use his influence with the jailor to have the jailor's fees remitted, Daniel visited the prison, where he discovered that all six of them were required to pay fees to the under-sheriff. The four were kept in the Castle until the Easter Quarter Sessions, when James Georges met the fees from his own pocket and had all six discharged.

★   ★   ★

James Georges' pity did not extend to Theophila Townsend, or, if it did, then she had made too many enemies among the justices for him to act. She was detained in Gloucester Castle for a further two years, sending her reports to Meeting for Sufferings and giving encouragement to Cirencester Friends. In September 1684 her case was heard at the assizes and she was acquitted, only to be remanded in custody for being unwilling to find sureties for good behaviour. In January 1685 she was brought before the Quarter Sessions, where she made a spirited defence:

> Justice Powell said I broke the Kings Law by preaching. I said I had been a prisoner for two years and was never convicted of the breach of any Law. Powell being Chairman said, the Court was not willing to discharge me without sureties, I said I was discharged of that twelve months since. Cutler said I was a dangerous person, and the Court is afraid to trust me without sureties. I said it is a poor Business for a Court of Justices to say they are afraid of such a poor weak Woman, as I, that have been like to Dy severall times since I came into prison, so I was within these 4 days. But the Lord hath raised me, and made me able to appear before you, to see whether you will do me Justice or no. How do you look upon me as a dangerous Person? Do you suppose me like to Raise an Army to subvert the Government? The Law saith no person shall be deprived of their Liberty unconvicted, and that I never was, for you have no proof. They made me be Taken away from speaking. ... Powell spoke of discharging me, But Cutler said if they did, I would be in again in a month.

In March 1685 she appeared again at the assizes and made a plea before the judge for her liberty, but in vain.[83]

James Georges died at the end of June 1684, but the impetus of the persecution of sectaries was maintained by other justices, in particular Sir Thomas Cutler and Chancellor of the Diocese, Richard Parsons. The Quaker John Stephens, appointed overseer of the poor in Cirencester on 31 March 1684, was imprisoned on the orders of Sir Thomas in June.[84]

The practice of fining for attending or hosting 'subversive conventicles' was extended by reviving defunct legislation from the reign of Elizabeth I, in particular *Eliz. Cap. 6* whereby a fine of £20 could be imposed for every month's absence from the parish church. Under this legislation further depredations were made on Amariah Drewett, the Bowlys, Jacob Hewlings and Philip Gray. Richard Bowly had his doors smashed in at night while he and his family were in bed, his house occupied by the bailiffs for three days, and the whole of his stock of malt carried off. The contents of Nathaniel Cripps' house were cleared by the bailiffs, and both Amariah Drewett and Thomas Loveday of Painswick faced fines of £220 for absence from church; Thomas had goods worth £60.19s. removed and sold for £10. A host of other fines and distraints from this period must have gone unrecorded.[85]

In the Gloucester civil courts, with the judges and justices of the peace screened for their compliance to the royal will, and high church Tories in the ascendant, the principle was introduced that defendants were deemed guilty until they could prove their innocence, as Theophila reported:

> The persecutors wax worse and worse and would make Friends their own accusers, because they cannot Clear themselves of what they charge them. They make them Transgressors. Severall are Indicted for not going to the parish Church (so called) and asking for their answers, The Clerk Benjamin Hyet said, I accuse you for the King, and papers do accuse you (holding some presentments up) and the Justices said, 'tis not possible for the King to prove you guilty, but you must prove yourselves not Guilty, so the Jury found Friends Guilty, when no Evidence came in against them, and one part or half of Friends were absent, and not in the sight or hearing of the jury,

and one sick and not at all in Court, yet they proceeded to
Fine about 22 Friends £20 apiece. They take no notice of the
Law, But their wills.[86]

At the same time the Chancellor of the Diocese maintained
pressure in the consistory court, continuing to make examples of
selected individuals in Cirencester and the surrounding villages.
The Bowlys, Drewetts, Hewlings, Hintons, Roberts, Stephens,
Townsends and the old widow, Sarah Simmons, were regularly
fined or excommunicated for not going to church.[87]

On 6 February 1685 Charles II died, and his Catholic brother
James ascended the throne. In the summer of that year the Duke
of Monmouth attempted his anticipated rebellion, which was
crushed at the Battle of Sedgemoor on 6 July. James II continued
the absolutist stance of the Stuarts, this time to the benefit of the
long persecuted dissenters, with the Quaker William Penn
becoming an influential adviser to the king. In February 1686
Meeting for Sufferings was able to secure the king's grant to relieve
sufferers from the penal laws and submitted lists to halt the
processes in the Court of the Exchequer against the 628 Quakers
who were being prosecuted under the £20 a month Act.[88] The king
issued a Declaration of Indulgence on 10 March 1686, and as a
result, at the Easter Quarter Sessions, 56 Quaker prisoners were
set free from Gloucester Castle and 15 from the Northgate prison.
Theophila Townsend's name headed the list.[89]

On 2 September 1686 there was a wedding at the Friends
meeting house in Cirencester. Frances Fettiplace, one of Giles'
daughters, married John Bellers, the future social reformer. John
had been a member of Meeting for Sufferings through the dark
years of the last persecution, and was able to meet up with the
Friends he had only known by name from Theophila's letters.
William Penn was one of the guests. Cirencester Friends would
have celebrated much more than just a wedding.

★   ★   ★

The climax of our story has been reached in the showdown
between a small section of the town's inhabitants and a local
justice of the peace. Ostensibly the issue centred on church attendance, but in the view of these townsfolk the springs of the justice's

animosity lay rather in his thwarted political ambitions. The local clergy, in fact, remained in the background, undoubtedly partisan, but content to let other major players make the running.

Circumstances had driven individuals to action and to print, so that in this later stage much fuller documentation, from a variety of standpoints, is available to us, and a more defined picture of individual motivation and social division emerges. In particular, light is shed on the vested interests of the gentry and the reactions of a number of lesser citizens to them.

Vetted for current political orthodoxy, members of the squirearchy can be seen striving to make show of their unflagging zeal and unswerving loyalty to the crown. Functioning as local watchdogs, they rush to suppress all signs of political comment and individual opinion. Their claim is to champion the Church of England, but in its name, aided by an energetic and determined chancellor of the diocese, they find themselves driven to extreme and quite unchristian measures to coerce the unwilling to enter the door of their parish church. Ruining the recalcitrant financially, consigning the outspoken to rot, and even die, in stinking disease-ridden prisons, and quite the most bizarre of all, calling for gun-powder to blow in the doors of hard-working tradesmen, the gentry reveal that the matter in question is not religion but a struggle to preserve their own status and power. In this they are bolstered by punitive legislation, misleadingly termed 'to suppress seditious conventicles', and a network of paid snoops, but for all the charade of legal process, as Theophila Townsend observed, 'the law is their will'.

We have seen clear indications that at differing social levels the townsfolk are far from convinced. Thomas Perry was not alone in questioning whether there ever was a Rye House plot, nor Miles Sandys in thinking that as a Catholic the Duke of York should never ascend the English throne. Intimidation of the churchwardens and constables leads only to subterfuge and deliberate attempts to sabotage the justices' purposes. There are those bold enough to distance themselves publicly from the frequent orchestrations of civic joy and affection towards the monarch, and less courageous souls who will warn, secretly encourage or relieve the justices' victims.

Clearly, the steady, peaceful resistance of the Quakers in particular, and less visibly of the Baptists, to the values and practices of the political and church establishments unnerves the squires, even winning over some of their own sort to a vision of a more egalitarian, more just and more loving society. Stripped of their possessions, physically abused and manhandled, and unjustly imprisoned, Friends stand firm in their belief that there is that of God in everyone, and eventually find it, by patience and love, in James Georges.

Such are some of the general social trends this conflict has revealed. But there is a personal, human side. The subject of our story, John Roberts, has reached the last stage of his earthly life, though still with energy and vitality. We find him in his sixties supporting his two sons with his old humour and courage in their confrontation with the justice; present at the meeting for worship to pray for them; visiting them in prison and enduring the excesses of the bishop's chancellor; and using his skills to heal James Georges' cattle and deflect him from his vengeful intentions. Slowly John slips out of the leadership of the local Friends meeting, his place taken by a group of names as resolute and fearless as he. He is finally laid to rest at the end of the orchard he has known since childhood, alongside his only daughter Lydia and his son Thomas.

John Robarts

NOTES

1 Although the spelling 'George' appears throughout the *Memoir*, indicating local popular usage, and also frequently in local records, I shall use 'Georges' which appears in legal documents and seems to have been consciously adopted by the family in the latter half of the seventeenth century.
2 GRO P86/CH1/4, 13 June 1677 and 10 October 1678. James Georges had been successful in London as an alnager, a sworn official appointed to attest the measurement and quality of woollen goods.

[3] We encountered Sir Robert duelling with Sir John Guise at Perrotts Brook in 1675. Born in 1647, he matriculated at St. Edmund Hall Oxford at the age of 15 and was called to the Bar at Lincoln's Inn in 1668. He was knighted by the king on his visit to Bristol in September 1663. He had unsuccessfully petitioned for the parliamentary seat at Cirencester made vacant by the death of the Earl of Newburgh in 1670, but was returned with Henry Powle of Williamstropp as burgess for the town on 11 February 1679.

[4] Sir R. Atkyns, *op. cit.*, p.347.

[5] In 1695 Henry Ireton, who was standing for Parliament for Cirencester, received a report from his agent: 'The Quakers are twenty Voyces, but they are resolved not to poll at all. Yet we have found from one who is a considerable shopkeeper that if they polled at all it should be for Mr. Ireton. We were informed that there was one Mr. Fettiplace, who has a very considerable estate, who lives twelve miles from hence at Coln Allens, who could very much influence the Quakers.' (Ruth G. Burtt: 'Records from Cirencester', *Journal of the Friends' Historical Society* Vol.35, pp.82-86).

[6] Quoted in W.C. Braithwaite: *The Second Period of Quakerism*, p.98.

[7] *An Account of the late Hardships and Violence Inflicted upon certain Persons called Quakers for their Peaceable Religious Meetings in the City and County of Gloucester*. London, 1682, p.5 (Gloucester Reference Library, 7888(6)). After his lack of success at the hustings, James Georges petitioned the king and obtained the Mastership of St. Lawrence's Hospital for his life-time. This, as we saw in Chapter 1, was one of the local charitable foundations, and provided for two poor women. Did this position carry status in the town, or was there a particular financial advantage? (*CSPD* 1679-80, p.263, 23 October 1679).

[8] *Ibid*, p.6.

[9] *CSPD* 1680-1681, p.319, 18 June 1681. On the death of Charles II Sir John Guise fled to Holland to escape the wrath of James II, whose accession to the throne he had vigorously opposed. (J. Johnson, *op. cit.*, p.125).

[10] *CSPD* 1680-1681, p.503, 9 October 1681.

[11] *Ibid*, 1680-1681, p.634, 27 August 1681.

[12] *Ibid*, 1680-1681, p.610, 10 December 1681.

[13] *MMfS* Vol.2, pp.34-35, 18 March 1681.

[14] *Ibid*, Vol.2, p.63, 14 October 1681.

[15] *Ibid*, Vol.2, pp.71, 11 November 1681.

[16] *Ibid*, Vol.2, p.77, 9 December 1681, and p.79, 23 December 1681.

[17] Lord Herbert did not become the Marquess of Worcester until 2 December 1682 (W.R. Williams, *op. cit.*, p.60).

18 *MMfS* Vol.2, p.80, 30 December 1681.
19 *CSPD* 1682, pp.24-25, 14 January 1682; p.33, 19 January 1682. 'His Majesty was very well pleased with your account of putting the laws in execution in that county. His Majesty gives you his hearty thanks, of which he desires the rest of the Justices may partake that have shown themselves so active and unanimous.'
20 *Ibid*, Vol.2, pp.86-87, 20 January 1682.
21 *MMfS* Vol.2, pp.95-96, 17 February 1682.
22 *Ibid*, Vol.2, pp.118-119.
23 *Ibid*, Vol.2, p.122.
24 *Ibid*, Vol.2, p.132.
25 GRO D 1340 AI/A2; PRO ASSI 2/2, 22 July, 34 Car II.
26 *MMfS* Vol.2, p.99, 10 March 1682.
27 *Ibid*, Vol.2, p.101, 17 March 1682, and p.103, 24 March 1682.
28 *Ibid*, Vol.2, p.102, 17 March 1682.
29 *An Account of the late Hardships and Violence Inflicted upon certain Persons called Quakers for their Peaceable Religious Meetings in the City and County of Gloucester*. London, 1682.
30 *Memoir*, pp.178-183 (*OR* p.77-80).
31 *Ibid*, pp.179-180 (*OR* p.78-79).
32 *MMfS* Vol.2, p.122, 19 May 1682, and GRO D1340 A1/A2.
33 J. Gratton: *A Journal of that Ancient Servant of Christ, John Gratton*, pp.98-99.
34 *Memoir*, pp.180-182 (*OR* p.80-82). See also *MMfS* Vol.2, p.120, 12 May 1682, where reference is made to Daniel Roberts' letter of 7 May.
35 *Memoir*, p.183ff (*OR* p.82ff).
36 This could well have been *A Caution to Constables and other Inferior Officers concerned with the Execution of the Conventicle Act. With some Observations thereupon, humbly offered by way of Advice to such Well-meaning and Moderate Justices of the Peace as would not willingly Ruin their Peaceable Neighbours*, although it is not listed as being published until the following year.
37 *Memoir*, p.192 (omitted in *OR*).
38 *Ibid*, p.195 (*OR* p.85).
39 For example, at the Easter sessions of 1673: 'Whereas it appeares to this Courte that the Castle of Gloucester is out of repair, this Courte doth desire that Henry Norwood [*et al.*] doe survey the decay thereof and do procure the same to be amended and the Charge thereof to be borne by the County.' (GRO Q/SO1 f.27).
40 GRO Q/SO1 f.133.
41 *Ibid*, f.135v.
42 GRO Q/S02 f.73.

43 GRO Q/SO1 f.143v.

44 *CSPD* 1677-8, pp.275 and 276, 30 July 1677. See also *ibid*, 1660-1, p.509, 12 February 1661, where Alice Beck held the letters patent and farmed the custody of the jail.

45 *Ibid*, 1666-7, p.xvii, 18 November 1666. Henry Jackson petitioned the king from Warwick jail where prisoners were 'thronged up in stinking rooms and sometimes in one room above 20 of us, where we could not all lie down at once, and no straw allowed us to lie upon, except we pay 2s.6d. for one bolting, which was sold to felons for 2d. and no manner of victuals allowed to be brought to us, except we would pay 6d. for one penny loaf of bread and as much for one quart of milk, and 3d. for a quart of water'.

46 Historical Manuscripts Commission 13th Report, Appendix Part II, MSS of his Grace the Duke of Portland Vol.2, pp.294-5. HMSO 1893.

47 J. Howard, *op. cit.*, p.216ff.

48 GRO D1340 A1/A2; T. Townsend: *A Word of Counsel in the Love of God to the persecuting Magistrates and Clergy of the City and County of Gloucester*, p.7.

49 The vitality and detail of the *Memoir* from p.177 (*OR* p.77) onwards suggest that the accounts were written down very shortly after the events had taken place. The piece on Sir John Guise, pp.164-177 (*OR* p.70-77), also gives the impression that it was worked up by Daniel Roberts at his leisure. Other Friends, such as Thomas Ellwood or John Whiting, and George Fox himself, occupied their long hours of imprisonment in literary activities.

50 *MMfS* Vol.2, 19 and 28 May 1682, 4 August 1682. On 2 August 1682 she wrote to the judge of the Assizes concerning her imprisonment and that of the other Cirencester Friends. (Friends House Library, MS Portfolio 17.56).

51 *Memoir*, pp.202-210 (omitted in *OR*).

52 *CSPD* 1682, p.228, 3 June 1682.

53 GRO GDR 243.

54 From a list of sufferings compiled by Theophila Townsend, dated 7 August 1682 (Friends House Library, MS Portfolio 17.56). In Siddington John Roberts had a sack of malt, valued at 12s., taken for a 4s. fine.

55 GRO GDR 244, 28 September 1682.

56 *MMfS* Vol.2, p.137, 14 July 1682; p.143, 4 August 1682; p.147, 18 August 1682; p.168, 24 November 1682.

57 *Ibid*, Vol.2, p.143, 4 August 1682.

58 *Ibid*, Vol.2, p.167, 24 November 1682; T. Townsend: *A Word of Counsel in the Love of God to the persecuting Magistrates and Clergy of the City and County of Gloucester*, p.4.

59 *MMfS* Vol.2, p.167, 24 November 1682.

60 T. Townsend: *A Word of Counsel in the Love of God to the persecuting Magistrates and Clergy of the City and County of Gloucester*, p.8. Jeremiah Gregory 'did this not because he loved the Poor, but because he had the mind of a Thief and coveted his Neighbours House'.

61 *MMfS* Vol.2, p.170, 15 December 1682.

62 *CSPD* 1682, p.552, 25 November 1682; 1683 January-June, p.118, 20 March 1683. Miles Sandys came from an influential family which held the manor of Brimsfield. His father was High Sheriff of Gloucestershire in 1678 (Sir R. Atkyns, *op. cit.*, p.300).

63 *CSPD* 1682, p.492, 24 October 1682.

64 *Ibid*, 1683 January-June, p.131, 24 March 1683; p.162, 7 April 1683.

65 *Ibid*, 1683 January-June, p.142, 29 March 1683.

66 T. Townsend: *A Word of Counsel in the Love of God to the persecuting Magistrates and Clergy of the City and County of Gloucester*, p.5.

67 *MMfS* Vol.2, p.179, 12 January 1683.

68 GRO Q/SO2 f.20v. There is an earlier entry at the Michaelmas Sessions 1682, ordering that 'Sir Thomas Cutler Kt and James George Esq., have liberty to bringe in the Records of the Conventicles till the next Sessions' (f16). It would appear that these two justices were preparing their ground and gaining support for what would have been a very contentious step among members of their own social group – making an example of one of their own sort.

69 *GBS* Vol.3, Part 1, pp.506 and 515. These totals refer, of course, to reports of fines sent up to London. They are only a proportion of the actual fines imposed.

70 *MMfS* Vol.2, p.193, 16 March 1683. In an appeal made by Quakers to the king before 25 March 1683 an account is given of the prisoners in the Gloucester Northgate jail: '24 continued prisoners above a year, the greater part women, some with suckling children, several poor tradesmen in a strait prison, first committed for their religious meetings, then the oath of allegiance put to them and to the women also'. (*CSPD* 1683 January-June, p.133).

71 *MMfS* Vol.2, p.210, 11 May 1683, p.201, 20 May 1683.

72 *Ibid*, Vol.2, p.210, 11 May 1683.

73 *Ibid*, Vol.2, p.215, 25 May 1683. A very full and amusing account of the incident is given in the *Memoir*, pp.212-219. The omission of the vulgarity is made in Victorian editions of the text. The original read: 'Carry it back to Mr. Parsons and bid him wipe his Breach with it; and I'll bear you out.'

74 GRO D1340 AI/A2.
75 *MMfS* Vol.2, p.217, 8 June 1683; p.221, 22 June 1683; Vol.3, p.9, 14 August 1683; p.19, 30 August 1683.
76 *CSPD* 1683 January-June, p.337, 23 June 1683.
77 William Cletheroe was buried in the porch to the church. His epitaph read:

> Under your Feet lyeth the Body of
> William Cletheroe, Gent.,
> an humble Penitent, who thought himselfe
> unworthy of the lowest Place
> in the House of God
> He departed this Life the 18th Day of November 1680

(R. Bigland, *op.cit.*, Part 1, p.384; BGAS Gloucestershire Record Series Vol.2).
78 *CSPD* 1683 July-September, pp.64-5, 7 July 1683; p.95, 11 July 1683.
79 *Ibid*, 1683 July-September, p.244, 2 August 1683.
80 *GBS* Vol.3, Part 1, p.508. The presence at this meeting of Richard Bowly, imprisoned in the county jail the previous June, is puzzling; perhaps he had leave to visit Cirencester. Thomas Loveday and Sarah Wathen were married in the following February (GRO D1340 B1/M1).
81 *Memoir*, pp.219-222 (abridged *OR* p.95). James Georges was intending to re-marry at this time and perhaps wished to impress Mrs. Ann Shadwell, whom he married at Westminster Abbey on 5 January 1684. (*Gloucestershire Notes and Queries* Vol.6, p.84).
82 Theophila Townsend sent Charles Marshall a report on the proceedings at the last Assizes, commenting on the kindness of the judge to them. (*MMfS* Vol.3, 11 March 1684).
83 *MMfS* Vol.3, p.255, 3 October 1684; Vol.4, p.19, 3 April 1685; *GBS* Vol.3, Part 1, p.529, 29 January 1685.
84 GRO P86 VE 2/1, 31 March 1684; GRO D1340 A1/A2, June 1684.
85 *GBS* Vol.3, Part 1, pp.527-8, 27 May 1685; p.533, June/September 1685. GRO D1340 A1/A2, 1 February, 12 June, 25 June, 31 August 1685. *MMfS* Vol.4, p.168, 16 October 1685.
86 *GBS* Vol.3, Part 1, p.529, 29 January 1685.
87 GRO GDR 247, February 1684; GDR 252, Easter and Michaelmas 1684, 1685, Michaelmas 1686; GDR 259, July 1686.
88 *MMfS* Vol.4, p.289, 26 February 1686; Vol.5, p.15, 19 March 1686.
89 J. Besse, *op. cit.*, Vol.1, p.227. Quakers had to wait for another three years and a revolution before they were assured of freedom of worship, originally promised in the Declaration of Breda in 1660, but not made law until the Act of Toleration of 1689.

End-Piece

WITH THE RELEASE OF the Quakers from prison and the suspension of the penal laws against the sectaries, the main props for the policy of repression had been removed. Its main protagonist in Cirencester, James Georges, was dead, and though his brother William shared his views and had lent close support, the new royal will forced him to abandon such activities.

We can imagine, then, a new pattern of public behaviour emerging at the hour of Sunday worship in the autumn of 1686. No longer would constables, justices or churchwardens be patrolling the streets; and the services of the paid informers would have been dispensed with. The Anglicans would be gathered in their magnificent parish church, following the Book of Common Prayer, and listening to the new organ, built three years before and played by the new organist, Charles Badham.[1] The service would be led by the vicar, Jeremiah Gregory, or his curate, who, robed in white surplices, would celebrate the sacrament before the Laudian altar, positioned at the east of the choir, and marked off by suitable communion rails.

The previous year a new seat book had been written,[2] following the established principle that on no account would any parishioners be expected to have next to them their social inferiors. Almost all the men appearing in our story, or their widows, can be located: the Master family sitting at the front of the nave on the right side of the central aisle, their servants in the pew behind them; prominently at the front of the choir, on the right, would be the Georges; on the left of the choir, in the sixth pew, was the vicar's family; the bell-ringers and the sexton, Henry Belcher, in the ninth pew. Under the pulpit would be sitting Richard Morse's widow; Ralph Willett, seated behind her until 1667, had had to make way for the influential lawyer, Robert Brereton. Along the north aisle, and less prominent, were the Breaches and Rutters. The scholars of the grammar school had been moved from the organ loft and were now occupying four pews along the south aisle, opposite to the pews of the Company of Weavers.

A stone's throw away from the parish church, up one of the side lanes off Gosditch Street, the Presbyterians would have re-opened their chapel, with perhaps a second Presbyterian service taking place in the Weavers' Hall in Thomas Street. A little further away, at Widow Pelteare's, most probably in Coxwell Street, Giles Watkins would have been ministering to the Baptists.

Also in Thomas Street, the Quakers would have gathered in their meeting house. In the yard and street outside would be tethered a number of horses, including the six which drew the Fettiplace coach. Inside the meeting house those assembled, many of whom we now know by name, would be seated informally on plain forms or benches arranged in rows at right angles, and facing inwards to a small central open space. They would be worshipping in silence, until one of them felt called to minister; praising God that there was no longer any fear that the door would burst open and their meeting be rudely disturbed. At the end of the morning meeting those that had come in from the villages, small farmers and tradesmen and some labourers, would stay on to eat the food they had brought with them until a second meeting began in the afternoon.[3]

A social accommodation between the religious groups had been reached. The issue of tithes continued unreformed until this century, and without doubt there were still many among the Anglican clergy and laity who would have had all dissenters firmly dealt with. But, by and large, from 1686 by custom, and from 1689 by statute, episcopalianism and protestant non-conformity learned to live together as neighbours, hostile certainly, but not belligerent. There had, however, been a price to pay. The Anglicans were driven to relinquish their aspirations to a universal conformity to the Book of Common Prayer, while the Friends of Truth grew more used to the name of Quaker and learned to curb their passion. The social process of their transition from an exuberant movement of the spirit to an organised religious sect has been part of our study.

We have attempted to see the events associated with the religious upheavals of the seventeenth century through the eyes of a Gloucestershire yeoman, John Roberts of Siddington. He was old enough to respond to the call to arms in 1642, and we have traced his ensuing disillusionment and sense of betrayal. His search for an alternative society, which he and his friends would have seen as re-discovering primitive Christianity, led to the growth of a Quaker meeting in the town and hinged on the discovery that there is that of God in each of us.

This was his spiritual journey, and it is this which can, above all things, link us with him over the centuries. Thanks to his son's *Memoir*, we catch his sense of God's continuing guidance and over-riding power, and his acceptance that in the end all will be well.

It had already become the practice of Quakers to write a testimony to the grace of God in the lives of leading Friends, and a testimony was published after the death of Amariah Drewett in 1687, with contributions made by his family, Theophila Townsend and Charles Marshall.[4] But no testimony was ever written for John Roberts. The *Memoir* must therefore stand in its place.

There is a wealth of historical data available to us for this period in Gloucestershire, but what breathes life into otherwise dull, impersonal records is Daniel Roberts' lively and often humorous account, prepared for private circulation among his family and Friends, and taking us into that close community of local tradesfolk, small farmers and agricultural labourers, joined in their spiritual search and impatient to bring in social and religious reforms.

Central to this study, then, has been the *Memoir*, and I suppose that my ultimate aim in this enterprise has been to make the *Memoir* more widely known, encouraging the reader to pick it up and open it; and consequent on that, I have aspired to render it more meaningful by holding up the events it describes against their historical background. If I have succeeded, to whatever degree, in either of these respects, I shall be satisfied.

I conclude, where we began with John Roberts' Quakerism, with the advice Richard Farnsworth once gave him:

Some in our Day are Climbing up into the tree of Knowledge
thinking to find Christ there. But the Word now is, 'Zacheus,
come down! come down!' for that which is to be known of God
is manifest within.

NOTES

[1] Shortly afterwards Jeremiah Gregory and Charles Badham had a
serious disagreement, which led to litigation. To compound his difficulties, the vicar had his legal expenses of £24 paid from the poor fund,
which sparked a row in the Vestry Meeting of 1690, with Richard
Morse insisting that the money be re-paid. (GRO P86 VE 2/1).

[2] GRO P86 CW/4/1.

[3] This is part of local oral tradition, written down by William Crotch
Bowly in a letter to the *Friend*, New Series Vol.1, pp.176-177, 29 June
1861.

[4] *Some Testimonies of the Life, Death and Sufferings of Amariah Drewet of
Cirencester in Gloucestershire, lately Deceased; To the way of Life wherein
he walked*, London 1687.

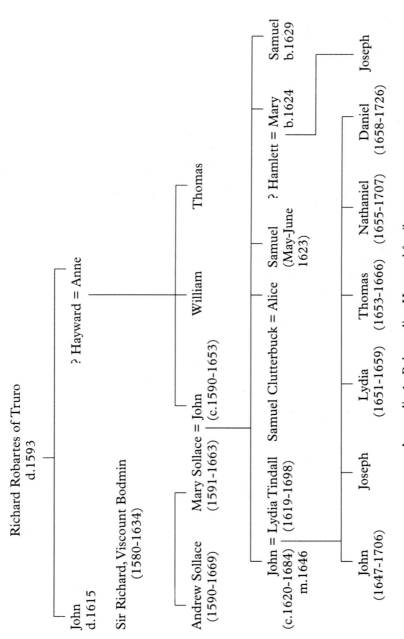

Appendix 1: *Roberts alias Hayward family tree.*

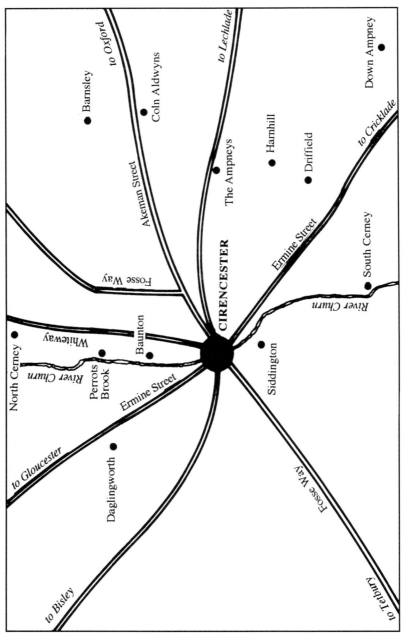

Appendix 2: *Map of Cirencester and the surrounding parishes.*

Bibliography

ATKYNS, Sir Robert (1712): *The Ancient and Present State of Glostershire*, reprinted 1974, EP Publishing, Wakefield.

BANKS, J.: *A Journal of the Life, Labours, Travels and Sufferings* (2nd ed,) James Phillips and Son, London 1798.

BARCLAY, J.; *Letters of Early Friends*, Harvey and Darton, London, 1841.

BASKERVILLE, T. (1682/3): 'Travels in Gloucestershire' in *Historical Manuscripts Commission 13th Report*, Appendix Part II, MSS of his Grace the Duke of Portland Vol.2, published 1893, H.M.S.O., London.

BAUMAN, R. (1983): *Let Your Words be Few*, Cambridge University Press.

BEECHAM, K.J. (1887): *History of Cirencester*, reprinted 1978, Sutton, Gloucester.

BESSE, J. (1754): *Collection of the Sufferings of the People called Quakers*, London.

BIGLAND, R. (179?): *Historical, Monumental and Genelogical Collections*, reprinted 1992 in the Gloucestershire Record Series, Vols. 2-5, Bristol and Gloucestershire Archaeological Society.

BRAITHWAITE, A.C.: 'Early Tithe Persecutions – Friends as Outlaws'. *Journal of the Friends Historical Society*, Vol.49, No.3, pp.148-156.

BRAITHWAITE, W.C. (1912): *Beginnings of Quakerism*, reprinted 1981 by Sessions, York.

BRAITHWAITE, W.C. (1912): *Second Period of Quakerism*, reprinted 1981 by Sessions, York.

BROCKLEHURST, G. (1911): *A Textbook of Tithes*, Bede, Newchurch, Kent.

CALAMY, E. (1727): *A Continuation Account of the Ministers, Lecturers, Masters and Fellows of Colleges and Schoolmasters who were Ejected or Silenc'd after the Restoration in 1660.* 2 vols., London.

CARLTON, C. (1992): *Going to the Wars*, Routledge, London.

COCKBURN, J.S. (ed.) (1977): *Crime in England 1550-1800*, Methuen, London.

CORBET, J. (1645): *A Historicall Relation of the Military Government of Gloucester*, reprinted in Washbourn, J. (1825): *Bibliotheca Gloucestrensis*.

DEFOE, D. (1753): *A Tour through England and Wales*, reprinted 1928, Dent, London.

ELLWOOD, T. (1714): *The History of the Life of Thomas Ellwood*, reprinted 1908, Headley Brothers, London.

EMMOTT, E.B. (1923): *A Short History of Quakerism*, Swarthmoor Press, London.

EVANS, E.J. (1976): *The Contentious Tithe*, Routledge, London.

FIENNES, C.: *Through England on a Side Saddle in the Time of William and Mary*, printed 1888, Leadenhall Press, London.

FOSBROOKE, T.D. (1807): *Abstracts of Records and Manuscripts respecting the County of Gloucester*, Gloucester.

FOX, George: *Journal of George Fox*, a revised edition by J.L. Nickalls 1952, Cambridge University Press.

GOUGH, Richard (1701): *The History of Myddle*, Penguin, Harmondsworth, 1981.

GRATTON, J. (1720): *A Journal of that Ancient Servant of Christ, John Gratton*, printed and sold by James Phillips, London, 1779.

GRATTON, J. (1720): 'The Clergy-Man's Pretence of Divine Right to Tithes, Examined and Refuted' in *A Journal of the Life of that Ancient Servant of Christ, John Gratton*, London.

HARDING, A. (1966): *A Social History of English Law*, Penguin, Harmondsworth.

HILL, C. (1971): *The World Turned Upside Down*, Penguin, Harmondsworth.

HILL, C. (1990): *A Nation of Change and Novelty*, London, Routledge.

HOCKADAY, F.S. (1924): 'The Consistory Court of the Diocese of Gloucester', *Transactions of the Bristol and Gloucester Archeological Society*, Vol.46, pp.195-287.

HOMFRAY, J.B.T.: 'George Bull, D.D., 1634-1710', *Transactions of the Bristol and Gloucestershire Archaeological Society* 1973, pp.121-138.

HOWARD, J. (1777): *The State of the Prisons*, reprinted Dent, London, 1922.

INGRAM, M.J.: 'Communities and the Courts: Law and Disorder in Early Seventeenth Century Wiltshire' in J.S.Cockburn (ed.) (1977) *Crime in England*, Methuen, London.

IRELAND, J. (1994): *History of Cirencester Grammar School*, Old Grammarians Reunion Comittee, Cirencester.

JOHNSON, J. (1989): *The Gloucestershire Gentry*, Sutton, Gloucester.

JONES, A.E. (1983): Protestant Dissent in Gloucestershire: a Comparison between 1676 and 1735. *Transactions of the Bristol and Gloucestershire Archaeological Society* Vol.101, pp.131-146.

KAIN, R.J.P. & PRICE, H.C. (1985): *The Tithe Surveys of England and Wales*, Cambridge University Press.

LAWRENCE, E.T. (1898): *A Quaker of Olden Time*, Headley, London.

LESLEY, C. (1700): *An Essay concerning the Divine Right of Tythes by the Author of 'The Snake in the Grass'*, London.

MARSHALL, W. (1796): *Rural Economy of Gloucestershire*, reprinted 1979, Sutton, Gloucester.

MILLER, J. (1991): *Charles II*, Weidenfeld and Nicholson, London.

MURRAY, J.A.H. (ed.) (1908): *A New English Dictionary on Historical Principles*, Clarendon Press, Oxford.

NELSON, R. (1713): *The Life of George Bull*, published John Henry Parker, Oxford, 1840.

O'MALLEY, T.P. (1979): 'The Press and Quakerism 1653-1659', *Journal of the Friends Historical Society* Vol.54, No.4, pp.169-184.

PEARSON, A. (1754): *The Great Case of Tithes, Truly Stated, Clearly Open'd and Fully Resolv'd*, London (first published 1657).

PENN, W. (1682): *No Cross, No Crown*, reprinted William Sessions Book Trust, York, 1981.

PENNY, N. (1907): *First Publishers of Truth*, Headley, London.

PENNY, N. (ed.) (1925): *The Short Journal and Itinerary Journals of George Fox*, Cambridge University Press.

PERCIVAL, A.C. & SHEILS, W.J. (1976): A Survey of the Diocese of Gloucester 1603 in *Ecclesiastical Miscellany*, Bristol and Gloucestershire Archaeological Society.

POWELL, A. (1988): *John Aubrey and His Friends*, Hogarth Press, London.

PUNSHON, J. (1984): *Portrait in Grey*, Quaker Home Service, London.

REECE, R. and CATLING, C. (1975): Cirencester, the Development of Buildings of a Cotswold Town, *British Archaeological Report* No. 12.

ROBERTS, O. (1859) (ed.): *Some Memoirs of the Life of John Roberts, one of the early Friends, written by his son, Daniel Roberts*, facsimile reproduction 1973, Friends Home Service Committee, London.

ROLLISON, D. (1994): *The Local Origins of Modern Society: Gloucester 1500-1800*, Routledge, London.

RUDDER, S. (1779): *A New History of Gloucestershire*, reprinted 1977, Sutton, Gloucester.

SHARPE, J.A.: 'Crime and Deliquency in an Essex parish 1600-1640' in J.S.Cockburn (ed.) (1977) *Crime in England*, Methuen, London.

SMITH, H. (1683): *A Collection of the Several Writings and Faithful Testimonies of that Suffering Servant of God*, London.

SMITH, J. (1608): *Men and Armour for Gloucestershire in 1608*, reprinted 1980, Sutton, Gloucester.

STEEL, D.J. (ed.) (1968): *The National Index of Parish Registers*, Society of Genealogists.

STRATFORD, J.(1867): *Good and Great Men of Gloucestershire*, Savory, Cirencester.

TANNER, J.R. (1922): *Tudor Constitutional Documents 1485-1603*, Cambridge University Press, Cambridge.

TARVER, A. (1995): *Church Court Records*, Phillimore, Chichester.

TOMKINS, R. (1987): *Street Names of Cirencester*, Red Brick, Swindon.

TOWNSEND, T. (1688): *A Word of Counsel in the Love of God to the persecuting Magistrates and Clergy of the City and County of Gloucester.*

TURNER, G. Lyon (1911): *Original Records of Early Nonconformity under Persecution and Indulgence*, Fisher Unwin, London.

UNDERDOWN, D. (1993): *Fire from Heaven: Life in an English Town in the Seventeenth Century*, Fontana, London.

VANN, R.T. (1969): *The Social Development of Early Quakerism 1655-1755*, Harvard University Press, Cambridge, Mass.

WASHBOURN, J. (ed.) (1825): *Bibliotheca Gloucestrensis*, Gloucester.

WELSFORD, J. (1987): *Cirencester: a history and guide*, Alan Sutton, Gloucester.

WHITEHEAD, G. (1725): *Christian Progress of that Ancient Servant and Minister of Jesus Christ, George Whitehead*, London.

WHITING, John (1715): *Persecution Exposed*, London.

WICKS, H.J. (1899): *Chronicles of the Baptist Church in Coxwell Street, Cirencester 1639-1899*, Harmer, Cirencester.

WILLIAMS, W.R. (1898): *The Parliamentary History of the County of Gloucester*, Hereford.

Index